FLYING IN THE FACE OF CRIMINALIZATION

Flying in the Face of Criminalization

The Safety Implications of Prosecuting Aviation
Professionals for Accidents

SOFIA MICHAELIDES-MATEOU

&

ANDREAS MATEOU

ASHGATE

Published by
Ashgate Publishing Limited
Wey Court East
Union Road
Farnham
Surrey, GU9 7PT
England
www.ashgate.com

Ashgate Publishing Company
Suite 420
101 Cherry Street
Burlington
VT 05401-4405
USA

British Library Cataloguing in Publication Data
Michaelides-Mateou, Sofia.
Flying in the face of criminalization : the safety implications of prosecuting aviation professionals for accidents.
1. Aircraft accidents--Investigation--Law and legislation. 2. Malpractice. 3. Prosecution. 4. Evidence (Law) 5. Aircraft accidents--Prevention.   I. Title II. Mateou, Andreas.
346'.0322-dc22

ISBN: 978-1-4094-0767-6 (hbk)
       978-1-4094-0768-3 (ebk)

Library of Congress Cataloging-in-Publication Data
Michaelides-Mateou, Sofia, 1965-
Flying in the face of criminalization : the safety implications of prosecuting aviation professionals for accidents / by Sofia Michaelides-Mateou and Andreas Mateou.
    p. cm.
Includes index.
ISBN 978-1-4094-0767-6 (hardback) -- ISBN 978-1-4094-0768-3 (ebook)
1. Aircraft accidents--United States. 2. Aircraft accidents--United States--Prevention. 3. Air pilots--United States. I. Mateou, Andreas. II. Title.
TL553.5.M43 2010
363.12'460973--dc22

2010022183

Reprinted in 2011.

Printed and bound in Great Britain by the MPG Books Group, UK

Contents

List of Figures

List of Abbreviations

AAIB   Air Accident Investigation Branch

AAIASB   Air Accident Investigation and Aviation Safety Board of the Hellenic Ministry of Transport and Communications

AIB   Accident Investigation Branch

ANO   Air navigation order

ATC   Air traffic control

ATCO   Air traffic controller

ATSB   Australian Transport Safety Bureau

BASI   The Bureau of Air Safety Investigation was the agency of the Australian government responsible for the investigation of accidents and incidents occurring to civil aircraft in Australia and its territories.

CAB   Civil Aeronautics Board

CVR   The cockpit voice recorder records communication between the flight crew and between the flight crew and air traffic control, the automated radio weather briefings, any conversation between the pilots and ground or cabin staff as well as any other sounds inside the cockpit. It consists of a cockpit area microphone, usually located on the overhead instrument panel between the two pilots, a data storage module and an underwater locator beacon (ULB). The microphone records all sounds in the cockpit, including engine noise, radio transmissions, explosions and voices.

DFDR   Digital flight data recorder – records all aspects of pitch, yaw and roll and all other flying, engine and aerodynamic parameters.

DME   Distance measuring equipment

FAA   Federal Aviation Authority

FL   Flight Level

FOM   Flight operation manuals

GPWS   Ground Proximity Warning System

IAS   Indicated Airspeed

ICAO   International Civil Aviation Organization

IFATCA   International Federation of Air Traffic Controllers' Associations

ILS   Instrument Landing System

ISASI   International Society of Air Safety Investigators

LDSM   Legal Defensive Safety Management

MEL   Minimum Equipment List

NTSB   National Transportation Safety Board

PIC   Pilot in command

RPT   Regular public transport

RVSM   Reduced vertical separation minimum

Rwy   Runway – A defined rectangular area on a land aerodrome prepared for the landing and take-off of aircraft.

SIDs   Standard Instrument Departures

TCAS   Traffic Alert and Collision Avoidance System

TSB   Transport Safety Board of Canada

UTC   Coordinated Universal Time

VOR   Very High Frequency Omnidirectional Range

List of Cases

Adomako [1995] 1 A.C. 171.
AG's Reference (No. 3 of 1994) [1997] 3 WLR 421.
Australian National Airlines Commission v The Commonwealth of Australia & Canadian Pacific Airlines [1975] High Court of Australia, reported at (1974-5) 132CLR 582 on other issues.

Blyth v Birmingham Waterworks Co [1856]11 Ex 781.
Bolam v Friern Hospital Management Committee [1957] 1 WLR 583.
Brooks v United States [5th Circ. 1983] 695 F. 2d 984, 987.
The Bywell Castle [1879] 4 PD 219.

Capital and Counties plc v Hampshire County Council (1997) 2 All ER 865.
Caparo Industries Plc v Dickman [1990] 2 A.C. 605.
City of New Orleans, Etc. v American Commercial, Etc. [5th Cir. 1981] 662 F 2d 1121, 1123.
Coatney v Berkshire [1974] 500F 2d 290 (8th Circ).

David R.Hinson, Administrator, FAA, v Hulbert G. Ferger. [1994] NTSB Order No. EA-4228.
Delta Airlines Inc. v US [1977] 561 F2d 381 (1st Circ).
Donoghue v Stevenson [1932] AC 562 page12.
DPP v Newbury [1977] AC 500.

FAA v NTSB [1991] (Columbia Circuit) argued 8 April, 1999; decided 21 September, 1999; No. 98-1365.

Glasgow Corp. v Muir [1943] AC 448.
Goldman v Thai Airwys International Ltd [1983] 1 WLR 118.

Hartz v United States [1965] 249 F.Supp.119.
Hayes v United States [5th Cir. 1990] 899 F.2d 438.
Hedley Byrne & Co v Heller & Partners Ltd [1964] 2 QB 412.
Hill v Chief Constable of West Yorkshire [1988] 2 All ER 238.

Joseph M. Del Balzo Acting Administrator, FAA v Ray Edward Delgmant, Jr.[1993]. NTSB Order No. EA-3954.

Kack v United States [D.Minn. 1977] 432, F.Supp. 633,624-35.

About the Authors

Dr. Sofia Michaelides-Mateou   Sofia holds a Doctorate from the University of Middlesex, UK, a BA and a law degree (LLB) from the University of Witwatersrand, South Africa. She practised law in South Africa before returning to Cyprus to start her academic career and is currently an Associate Professor in the Law Department, University of Nicosia and is a guest lecturer, at Cranfield University, UK.

Sofia is a member of the Just Culture Task Force of Eurocontrol, an Associate Member of ISASI and a Member of the Executive Board of the Flight Safety Foundation – SE Europe-Cyprus (FSF-SEC). Sofia was an advisor to the Cyprus Air Accident and Incident Investigation Board (AAIIB). She attended a number of CRM, Safety and Quality Management System and Accident Investigation courses. Sofia has published articles on numerous aviation areas, has presented many papers in international aviation conferences and is the author of the book, 'Air Law: A Practical Perspective'. She is an aviation-legal consultant who has participated in a number of aviation litigation cases and currently a director of MM Aviation Consultancy Ltd, now renamed Alstco Aviation Ltd.

Captain Dr. Andreas Mateou   Captain Andreas Mateou holds a Doctorate from the University of Middlesex, UK, a MSc in Aviation Management from the University of New South Wales, Australia and a law degree (LLB) from the University of London. He was Head of Flight Safety, the Head of the Flight Data Monitoring Program and the Head of the Emergency Response Programme of Cyprus Airways for a number of years. He has 25 years flying experience with more than 16000 flying hours and is a Type Rating Instructor and Examiner on the Airbus A320. He is also a part-time lecturer in Law at the University of Nicosia and is a guest lecturer at Cranfield University, UK.

Andreas has written extensively on aviation topics and participated in a number of aviation conferences. He is an Associate Member of ISASI and has been an aviation safety and legal consultant in a number of aviation litigation cases and is a director of MM Aviation Consultancy Ltd, now re-named Alstco Aviation Ltd.

Acknowledgements

Achieving a success and attaining goals are never possible without the support and assistance of a diverse group of persons. We would like to express our deepest gratitude to all those who were instrumental and without whom the book would not have been feasible.

This book would not have been possible without the assistance of the respondents and interviewees who participated in our doctoral dissertation, whom we dearly thank.

Our thanks also goes to Dr Paul Gibbs for his never-ending motivation and guidance and Dr Graham Braithwaite for his invaluable assistance. A special thanks goes to our research assistant Chrystel Erotokritou for all her help.

Last but not least we would like to express a special acknowledgement to our parents for all their support and encouragement; our children, Evyania and Stephanos for their patience and above all to each other for the continuous thought-provoking discussions and hard work that went into the book.

Foreword

Accidents happen. They form part of our daily life and we accept their possible occurrence because we hope and expect that we can avoid some of them by our actions and by abiding by established rules and practices. Aviation is consistently one of the safest means of transport. But as passengers in an aircraft we have no control at all and when things go wrong the consequences are sometimes terrible.

In such a safety critical domain as aviation, the legal consequences of (contributory) actions or behaviour that could result in serious personal harm, death or other damages are plentiful and very significant, both in the private law and, increasingly, in the criminal law domain. Criminal law forms an essential element for a sovereign State in the exercise of its responsibility for enforcing specific domain-related norms as well as for the prevention and sanctioning of unacceptable behaviour.

Recent years have shown a growing concern on the part of aviation professionals and the aviation industry about the interpretation by the general public, as well as the criminal judiciary, of flight safety and aviation accidents. These concerns are associated with what is seen as the increasing emphasis on legal issues in aviation safety occurrences. This has led to growing fear of litigation and the threat of criminal sanctions against individuals and organizations that are seen as partly or fully responsible for an accident or incident in which they were involved.

Flying in the Face of Criminalization is an impressive and, in my view, highly instructive and sometimes revealing book for those wishing to understand the complicated relationship between the administration of justice and the safety investigation. As in a classical drama, two antagonists are involved: one with the aim of preserving justice by investigating and prosecuting possible perpetrators and the other with the aim of enhancing aviation safety through independent investigation and reporting.

The book raises the consequences of criminal liability and demonstrates how the involvement of judicial authorities may impact the collection of information that is vital to aviation safety. The fear of legal proceedings and involvement of judicial authorities can have an impact on the level of reporting of safety incidents. With respect to aviation, failure to gather all available safety data may have potentially serious consequences. The ability to learn from mistakes and prevent new ones is one of the most valuable tools for the improvement of aviation safety.

There is an evident need for those involved in the administration of justice and aviation safety to exchange views and to establish balanced processes, which must ultimately support and improve aviation safety. That realisation has lead to the concept of 'Just Culture', which is based on the support and understanding of both groups of professionals.

Efforts to introduce a safety culture are not new. In other specialised professional domains with potential risks of death or serious injuries, such as the medical sector, similar initiatives are entertained and introduced. In aviation, ICAO, the European Union and EUROCONTROL have already put legislation in place and are reviewing further measures. The problem is that effective measures need to reconcile both the needs of judicial authorities and of aviation safety.

With this objective in sight, a EUROCONTROL Just Culture Task Force has been established for the creation of a pan-European Just Culture network open to all professionals concerned. The Task Force seeks to facilitate and promote exchanges, experiences and best practice. A number of States have taken initiatives involving their criminal investigation procedures. Policies, rules and guidelines as well as specialised aviation prosecutors are being implemented or are under consideration to ensure the participation of the judiciary in the concept of Just Culture.

This study by Dr. Sofia Michaelis-Mateou and Capt. Dr. Andreas Mateou represents a very comprehensive and meticulously researched study into the Criminalisation of Aviation Accidents. It is also a work of love and dedication, although that may sound a bit strange in view of the grim subject. I have had the privilege of regularly working together with Sofia and Andreas at conferences, meetings and workshops and have come to appreciate and admire their professional approach to this complex subject that often seems to evoke strong opinions and sometimes even prejudices among the different parties involved.

This book will provide the reader with a unique and elaborate insight into the interaction of the many parties and regimes that are involved in the enhancement of aviation safety and the administration of justice. The writers provide interesting remedies for addressing some of the issues at stake, but decisive solutions may still be elusive in the coming years in view of the very nature of the issue at stake.

An indispensible book for anyone seriously interested or involved in safety of aviation and the role of the judiciary.

Roderick D Van Dam
Head of Legal Service EUROCONTROL
Chairman of the EUROCONTROL Just Culture Task Force

Preface

Our basic aim is to place in the hands of pilots, ATCOs and other aviation professionals a text that will provide knowledge and insight into the law of negligence and how this is applied to their profession. We also aim to provide an overview of the technical and judicial investigations that are conducted subsequent to an aviation accident as well as a discussion on how the data and evidence obtained and the technical report is used in a court of law to apportion blameworthiness and liability.

The book provides a comprehensive collection of cases which cannot be accessed from one single resource or text dealing with the criminalization in aviation accidents. The key purpose of this initiative is to highlight and draw attention to the profound effect that the criminalization of aviation professionals has on aviation safety and is directed to a wide cross-section of stakeholders in the aviation industry, namely but not exclusively, international safety organizations, air traffic control service providers, unions, safety experts, pilots, air traffic controllers, engineers and other aviation personnel, safety officers, airline managers and post-holders, airport and ground handling managers, air accident investigators, judges, prosecutors, lawyers, scholars and aviation consultants. Such a wide audience means that the book can be used in a number of ways, as a full read or as a reference text to be dipped into and out of as required.

Our hope for the book is that it will:

- assist aviation professionals to minimize the fear of prosecution
- alert aviation authorities and experts of the increasing trend of criminalizing aviation professionals and the consequential safety implications thereof, and
- provide the judicial authorities with food for thought as to the broader perspective of the complex wide-ranging issues involved and the possible negative impact thereon in their endeavour to implement the 'letter of the law' at all costs.

The book is largely based on our doctorate, which gathered data to determine the perception of pilots and ATCOs in the EU regarding the investigation of aviation accidents and the intermingling between the technical and judicial investigation. Further, it considered the effect that the criminalization of pilots and air traffic controllers has on aviation safety. The research was conducted on three key stakeholder groups. The first was air traffic controllers, the second safety pilots and the third airline pilots. The findings are indicative of a trend that exists amongst ATCOs and pilots of the EU Member States. Case studies, questionnaires, interviewing and the use of documents and records constituted the methods of collecting data.

Sofia Michaelides-Mateou and Andreas Mateou

Chapter 1
Introduction

Following an aviation accident or serious incident, many complex legal issues may arise for the organization, the members of its board of directors, the accountable manager, post-holders, safety, quality and other managers, the airline pilots and engineers involved, the managers of air traffic control service providers and the air traffic controllers on duty at the time of the accident, the managers and inspectors at civil aviation authorities as well as the aircraft manufacturers and designers. Aviation professionals are being held accountable for any of their actions or omissions that contributed to or played a role in an aviation accident and are being criminally prosecuted for unintentional death.

Prosecuting air traffic controllers (ATCOs) in Greece following the Yakovelev-42 accident of 17 December 1997, Judge Peristeridou stated:

> In order to be found guilty of manslaughter, in the case where the negligence of the accused is not intentional, in terms of Art. 302, para 1 of the Criminal Code the following elements must be present:
> - the accused must not have exercised the required objective judgment and attention that the average reasonable man in the same circumstances would have exercised
> - a person having the personal skill, knowledge and capabilities of the accused will have to have foreseen and to have taken appropriate steps to avoid the punishable result and
> - there was a causal connection between the acts and/or omissions of the accused and the result.[1]

It is clear that, based on the well-established legal principles of the duty of care and the standard of care required by the law of such professionals, aviation professionals who breach their legal responsibilities and duty of care face serious legal consequences. In cases where an aviation accident or serious incident involves loss of life, aviation professionals may face criminal charges in accordance with domestic law and be charged with, inter alia. involuntary homicide, manslaughter and interruption of air traffic. Professional pilots, ATCOs, engineers, post-holders, managers and other aviation professionals are thus being held accountable for their actions or omissions and are being criminally prosecuted for their contribution to or role in an aviation accident or serious incident.

---

1   Multi-member first instance court, Thessaloniki, no. 20200, p. 631 (translated by the authors).

Subsequent to an aviation accident or serious incident two parallel, but separate, investigations are conducted, namely the technical and legal investigation, each having a clear, specific but different purpose. In the legal sphere, redress normally takes the form of damages (compensation) or punishment (accountability) whereas in the aviation community and in the interest of safety, emphasis is given to causation and prevention.

The technical investigation is conducted in accordance with ICAO[2] Annex 13, which contains international standards and recommended practices for the investigation of aviation accidents and incidents. It is clearly stated that the sole purpose of investigating an aviation accident is to prevent future accidents and not to apportion liability. The cornerstone of such technical investigations is a 'no blame' approach. The sole objective of the investigation of any accident or incident shall be the prevention of accidents and incidents. It is not the purpose of this activity to apportion blame or liability (ICAO 1994). This approach is entrenched by both Annex 13 and EU Directive 94/56,[3] which lays down principles governing the investigation of civil aviation accidents and incidents within the European Union. Both these legal instruments stipulate that the main objective of investigating an aviation accident is to undertake an investigation for the sole purpose of identifying all the circumstances that led to the accident, in order to facilitate safety recommendations to prevent similar accidents in the future. This technical investigation is non-punitive in nature, and the accident scenario and sequence of events leading up to the accident are derived from the facts collected. Conclusions are reached on the probable cause or causes of an accident, for the purpose of enhancing aviation safety.

The lack of specific rules from international conventions or other instruments on the actual process of conducting the investigation, specifically in relation to the extent and scope of the investigation, results in a lacuna. It is therefore up to each contracting State and its relevant investigating body, particularly the chief accident investigator, to determine the process of investigating aviation accidents as well as the depth of the investigation that will be carried out.

In addition to the technical investigation, a judicial investigation subsequent to an aviation accident is carried out in order to determine who was at fault or responsible for the accident, and to assign blame and apportion liability to the guilty party or parties. This is a punitive approach, normally focusing on a conclusion supported by the facts and evidence gathered during the investigation. This approach aims to satisfy the many different interested groups after an accident by allowing the injured party to obtain compensation by imposing civil liability, as well as satisfying society's needs, by determining criminal blameworthiness,

---

2   ICAO – International Civil Aviation Organization (ICAO), which was formed by the Chicago Convention in 1944.

3   *Establishing the Fundamental Principles Governing the Investigation of Civil Aviation Accidents and Incidents 1994. Official Journal, L 319 of 12.12.1994.*

prosecuting those who have allegedly committed a crime, and holding them accountable.

Traditionally, the unique nature of the aviation industry coupled with the early development of technology, the limited knowledge of human factors, inexperience and restricted investigative means resulted in insufficient analysis of the causes of the accident. The judiciary played a limited role in the investigation of the causes of the accident and in identifying those responsible for the loss of life and damages that resulted. Rapid technological advancements such as the computer animation of the flight and the increased data that can now be captured by the digital flight data recorder (DFDR) and the organizational accident model have now allowed the accident investigation to identify with more certainty the latent and active failures within the organization as well as the factors that have contributed to the accident. As a result of both the advancement in the investigation of aviation accidents as well as the greater demand by modern society for accountability, the judicial authority has an increasing impact on the events subsequent to an aviation accident.

Our Perspective

Our involvement in the litigation proceedings and the criminal trial subsequent to three major aviation accidents, namely the Falcon 900B accident that occurred in Romania in 1999, the Yak 42 accident near Thessaloniki in 1997 and the Helios accident that occurred in Grammatiko, Greece, in August 2005, indicated to us that the findings of the official accident investigation conducted in terms of ICAO Annex 13, the purpose of which is to prevent accidents and not to apportion blame, was relied upon by the prosecution in their case against the accused as a main source of evidence.

A number of aviation accident investigation reports, particularly the causes that are listed as having probably caused the accident (termed 'the probable cause scenario'), have become the basis for criminal action against aviation professionals. This emphasizes the degree to which the investigation and litigation process have become intermingled in a manner that might affect aviation safety, jeopardize the independence of the accident investigation, and lead to injustice.

The accident investigation report has been used in subsequent litigation against aviation professionals and this has been done in an inconsistent manner. Not only do different jurisdictions have different legal systems, the courts have different approaches to adopting the accident report or parts of it in criminal litigation against pilots, ATCOs, engineers and other aviation professionals. The inconsistent use of the official accident investigation, wholly or in part, by the prosecution authorities and the courts during the trial highlights the degree of intermingling between the litigation and the technical investigation process. The contradictory approach results in a perilous situation where pilots, for example, first, may be faced with criminal charges in one country but not in another and, second, will be totally oblivious as to whether statements given during the technical investigation and the final accident investigation report will be used against them in a court of law. It therefore needs to be asked whether justice would be better served by the establishment of an alternative body, having common rules and procedures specifically dealing with the criminalization of aviation professionals.

Aviation professionals may find themselves in a predicament. Should they supply information and assist the technical investigation of an aviation accident, or do they risk incriminating themselves? There are serious consequences to both. On the one hand, not supplying information which is aimed at enhancing safety and preventing future accidents may impede safety, but on the other, supplying such information may possibly result in it being used against the individual in subsequent criminal prosecution, affecting reputation and even liberty. The dilemma experienced by air crew, ATCOs, engineers and other aviation professionals is that of having to choose between not incriminating themselves and enhancing the safety of aviation. In this context, the issues of self-interest, potential litigation and accountability are accentuated, due to the increasing trend of prosecuting aviation professionals. The notion of trust is discussed, but the moral and philosophical issues that this dilemma creates have not been developed in the book. The practical implications are dealt with but it is recognized that a different perspective could offer other insights.

Many international aviation safety organizations and unions of pilots and ATCOs state adamantly that the criminalization of aviation professionals results in their being hesitant to report mishaps and errors and to participate in the technical investigation, and that safety is thus negatively affected:

> Those [SabreTech] prosecutions caused us to take a hard look at the possibility that old types of information might also be lost to the accident investigator. For decades, we have relied on individuals to tell us what happened in an accident – and they usually, sometimes, reluctantly, did so. After the SabreTech prosecutions we feared that what would have been reluctance to co-operate will now become refusal. A pipeline accident in Bellingham, Washington, proved us right. A criminal investigation was immediately launched into the accident, and we have yet to talk to most of the individuals operating the pipeline when it ruptured in June 1999. As a result, serious safety issues and questions about prevention remain unanswered. (Hall 2000)

The two distinctly different investigations conducted in parallel following an aviation accident result in a dilemma for professionals over the manner and degree of their participation, and valuable safety information may be withheld as a result. This is causing increasing concern to unions of pilots, ATCOs and engineers (IFALPA, IFATCA, BALPA and PASYPI, among others), safety agencies and organizations such as Flight Safety Foundation (FSF), Eurocontrol and the International Society of Air Safety Investigators (ISASI), who consider that the trend in criminalization of parties involved in aviation accidents and incidents is impeding aviation safety. To this effect a joint resolution was issued in 2006 by the Flight Safety Foundation, the Civil Air Navigation Services Organization, the Royal Aeronautical Society in England and the Académie Nationale de l'Air et de l'Espace regarding the 'criminalization of aircraft accidents' and 'the growing trend to criminalize acts and omissions of parties involved in aviation accidents and incidents', stating 'that information given voluntarily by persons interviewed during the course of safety investigations is valuable, and that such information, if used by criminal investigators or prosecutors for the purpose of assessing guilt and punishment, could discourage persons from providing accident information, thereby adversely affecting flight safety' (Flight Safety Foundation 2006). In January 2010, the International Society of Air Safety Investigators (ISASI) added their signature to the Joint Resolution (Flight Safety Foundation 2010).

As a result of the above issues, the book will examine the basis of professional negligence resulting in the prosecution of pilots, air traffic controllers and other aviation professionals by determining the legal basis on which they are prosecuted. It will determine whether there are any inconsistencies in the various judicial systems that criminally prosecute aviation professionals. The methodology and processes of official accident investigations conducted in terms of ICAO Annex 13 and EC Directive 94/56 and the scope and level of the technical investigation will be examined, considering other possible limitations as well as any external factors that may adversely affect the investigation or its outcome. It will consider case studies where aviation professionals have been criminally prosecuted after a serious aviation accident or incident, analyse a number of aviation accidents and examine both the technical investigations and judicial investigation and the subsequent criminalization process. The implementation of ICAO Annex 13 will be reviewed to reveal any inconsistencies and gaps that might lead to suggestions for change and to investigate the intermingling between the official accident investigation and the judicial process. How the criminalization of aviation professionals may affect aviation safety will be examined, determining whether a standardized set of rules or a European aviation accident investigation body will better serve the purpose of an accident investigation by providing a uniform standardized process of investigation and discussing the feasibility of a permanent European aviation court or tribunal.

The book provides a chronological overview of cases in which aviation professionals were either criminally charged or convicted and sentenced to imprisonment subsequent to an aviation accident, which provides a comprehensive collection of cases and forms a resource in itself.

Chapter 2
What the Black Box Cannot Tell You – Liability in Law

Aviation accidents have social, political and economic implications and draw great media awareness which ultimately directs attention to errors and omissions of certain parties and/or organizations and fuels public demand for accountability and the need to bring those responsible to justice. Reports of previous incidents in the organization involved increase the public's suspicion that the organization's priority was its financial viability and profitability, not safety; and when supported by evidence of poor safety overseeing by the National Aviation Authority, demands for resignation and political accountability create tremendous pressure on politicians who publicly announce that those responsible will be held liable for their actions.

'Accountability' refers to giving an account for one's actions and is often used to denote responsibility, answerability, blameworthiness and liability. It is a concept that encompasses many forms of accountability such as, inter alia, moral, administrative, political, managerial, market, legal and professional (Jabbra and Dwivedi 1989). Instinctively, we believe that aviation accidents must have been caused by someone's fault or wrongdoing: the party(s) or organization must be identified and blamed.

Legal accountability assigns responsibility for a legal wrong, which may be in the form of a violation of an individual's rights or non-performance of a legal duty. Failure by a person or organization to meet the imputed legal responsibility paves the way for a lawsuit for damages as in cases where an airline is ordered to pay compensation to passengers or to the relatives of the deceased. Liability also applies to alleged criminal acts, making the defendant subject to criminal prosecution, conviction and punishment.

Legal liability is therefore the liability that a court imposes on a party for his acts or inactions (omissions) and for which the court will impose a form of redress, such as pecuniary damages in a civil matter and criminal sanctions in a criminal case. Subsequent to an aviation accident a number of aviation professionals may be faced with both civil and criminal liability. Civil actions may be initiated by the injured party or the relatives of the deceased in order to recover compensation, whilst criminal actions may be commenced by judicial authorities when the accident has resulted in death or in situations of violation of the regulations of EU Ops 1, provisions of the relevant national air navigation order and other applicable legislation.

Legal Theory

Legal liability arises from three general classes of legal wrongs:

- breach of contract for which financial compensation will be sought;
- tort, a civil wrong where a tortfeasor (wrongdoer) breaches a duty imposed by law and causes injury or damage to another person resulting in financial compensation;
- crime, contravening a law (statute), the consequences of which are generally paying a fine and/or imprisonment.

In some cases the law imposes strict liability without the need to prove fault by the wrongdoer, as in when manufacturers are held strictly liable for their defective products. There are also situations where one party may be held liable for the torts committed by another party, such as when an employer is held vicariously liable for the torts of its employees committed during the course of the employment.

There are two main branches of the law, namely civil and criminal. Civil law is concerned with individual's rights and duties, which are enforceable by the individuals themselves. The purpose of civil law is to remedy the wrong and to compensate the victim for the damages suffered as a result of the wrong. Breach of contract and negligence (constituting a tort) are civil wrongs. Criminal law can be said to regulate the conduct of individuals in a society and is therefore concerned with wrongs committed against society at large. The purpose of criminal law is largely to punish the wrongdoer and to deter similar acts.

Even though the purpose of each of these two branches of law and their rules and procedures differ, it often happens that an individual's action or inaction can give rise to both a civil and a criminal action. A pilot who flies his aircraft disregarding the rules of navigation, resulting in the injury of a passenger, may be faced with criminal charges brought against him by the State as well as a civil claim brought by the injured passenger for compensation. An ATCO who speaks on his mobile telephone when responsible for air traffic control, his negligence causing two aircraft to collide, may be faced with criminal as well as civil proceedings.

Criminal law is largely statutory law passed by the legislature. Civil law which is largely case law (common law) is influenced by historical, social and economical factors and the advancement of technology. Well-established and entrenched common law principles of decades ago may still be applicable to situations that arise today. A pertinent example can be illustrated by the case of *The Bywell Castle* decided in 1879, which established the principle that a person who professes to have a certain skill has a duty in law to exercise their duties in accordance with those skills, by stating: 'captains of ships are bound to shew such skill as persons of their positions with ordinary nerve ought to shew under the circumstances' (per Brett LJ at p. 226).

Civil Liability – Negligence

The legal basis for accountability barring terrorism and wilful misconduct, following an aviation accident, is negligence. Simple negligence is the least culpable level of legal liability. Negligence can be defined as the breach of a legal duty to take care, which results in damage, undesired by the defendant to the plaintiff. The following definitions are provided by case law:

In the case of *Blyth v Birmingham Waterworks Co* (1856), per Baron Anderson, it was stated that negligence is the omission to do something which a reasonable man, guided upon those considerations which ordinarily regulate the conduct of human affairs, would do; or doing something which a prudent and reasonable man would not do.

A further definition is that provided in the case of *Lochgelly Iron & Cool Co v M'Mullan* (1934), where negligence was described as the infliction of damage as a result of a breach of a duty of care owed by the defendant to the plaintiff (per Lord Wright).

Liability in tort (negligence) may be imposed as the legal consequence of a person's act or omission to act in accordance with a legal duty imposed on him. When a person suffers loss as a result of negligent conduct, that loss is shifted onto the party who caused the loss by bringing an action in negligence against that party. In nearly all aviation accidents the actions or inactions of those involved will be investigated in relation to any negligent conduct either for ignoring regulations or for failing to exercise due care.

Under English law, for a claimant to prove that the defendant was negligent, it must be shown that:

1. the defendant owed the claimant a duty of care;
2. the damage suffered was a foreseeable result of the wrongful act of the defendant;
3. the defendant breached this duty or failed to conform to the standard of care;
4. that as a result of this breach, the claimant suffered damages that are not too remote and that there is some relation or proximity between the parties (Rogers 2002).

The duty of care was first established in 1932 by Lord Atkin in the case of *Donoghue v Stevenson*, when he stated:

> The rule that you are to love your neighbour becomes in law you must not injure your neighbour; and the lawyer's question, (Who is my neighbour?) receives a restricted reply. You must take reasonable care to avoid acts or omissions which you can reasonable foresee would be likely to injure your neighbour. Who, then, in law is my neighbour? The answer seems to be the persons who are so

closely and directly affected by my act that I ought reasonably to have them in contemplation as being so affected when I am directing my mind to the acts or omissions which are called in question. (per Lord Atkin, p. 580)

The 'neighbour principle' which established the duty of care has since developed. To establish a duty, the defendant must have reasonably foreseen that any careless act or omission on his part may cause damage, injury or loss to the claimant, the defendant must in some way be proximate to the claimant and it must be fair, just and reasonable to impose such a duty (*Caparo Industries Plc v Dickman* [1990]).

When determining the fairness and reasonableness of imposing a legal duty, the courts take into account policy considerations such as arguments that extending negligence liability would open the floodgates to litigation. The courts now consider more recent arguments such as the possible commercial or financial consequences, the prospect of indeterminate liability, the possibility of risk-spreading (for example through insurance) and potential conflicts with rights in property or other social or moral values. In recent years the courts have identified a number of factors relevant to the denial of a duty of care, for example, a duty of care may not exist where, inter alia, (i) the claimant is the author of his own misfortune (*Philcox v Civil Aviation Authority* [1995]), or (ii) a duty of care would lead to unduly defensive practices by defendants seeking to avoid claims for negligence with detrimental effects on their performance of some public duty (*Hill v CC of West Yorkshire* [1988], and *X (minors) v Bedfordshire CC* [1995]).

The courts have clearly stated that the question of how far the duty of care can be imposed in a given situation is more a policy question. In *Hedley Byrne & Co v Heller & Partners Ltd* [1964] the court stated: 'How wide the sphere of the duty of care in negligence is to be laid depends ultimately upon the court's assessment of the demands of society for protection from carelessness of others' (per Lord Pearce, p. 536).

This point is further dealt with in the following two cases. First, in *Capital and Counties plc v Hampshire County Council* (1997), the Court of Appeal held:

> Where the courts have granted immunity or refused to impose a duty of care it is usually impossible to discern a recognition that such a duty would be inconsistent with some wider object of the law or interest of the particular parties. Thus if the existence of a duty of care would impede the careful performance of the relevant function, or if investigation of the alleged negligent conduct would itself be undesirable and open to abuse by those bearing grudges, the law will not impose a duty.(p. 1040)

Second, in *Hill v Chief Constable for West Yorkshire* (1989), Lord Keil of Kinkel states: 'In some instances, the imposition of liability may lead to the existence of a function being carried out in a detrimentally defensive frame of mind' (p. 63).

'Proximity' is shorthand for Lord Atkin's neighbour principle. It means that there must be legal proximity; that is, a legal relationship between the parties from which the law will attribute a duty of care. 'Foreseeability' means whether a hypothetical 'reasonable person' would have foreseen damage in the circumstances. The foreseeability test followed is that expounded in the case of *The Wagon Mound* (1961). In other words, a defendant will only be liable for the damages suffered by the plaintiff if the damages arising from the defendants' breach of duty are not too remote. The test of remoteness of damage is one of foreseeability, namely whether the kind of damages that occurred could have been foreseen by the defendant. It is important to note that it is not a requirement that the exact details or the exact extent or degree of damage or injury should have been foreseen (*The Wagon Mound* 1961). A pilot or ATCO therefore who may be negligent will only be held liable for the resulting damage that he could reasonably foresee.

To establish a breach of duty, generally, it must be shown that the defendant failed to meet the standard of care imposed by the law, which is that of the hypothetical reasonable person. A breach of duty therefore can be said to be the omission to do something that a reasonable man would do, or doing something that a prudent or reasonable man would not do (*Blyth v Birmingham Waterworks Co* [1856]). The reasonable man is a fictitious hypothetical man who 'eliminates the personal equation and is independent of the idiosyncrasies of the particular person whose conduct is in question and who is presumed to be free from both over-apprehension and from over-confidence' (per Lord MacMillan in *Glasgow Corp. v Muir* [1943]). The test is an objective one and does not take into account the personal characteristics of the person whose conduct is in question. The test is what a reasonable man would have done in the defendant's position. The test is not whether the defendant acted reasonably, but whether a reasonable person placed in the position of the defendant would have acted as the defendant did.

Outlined thus far is the general test laid down by the law regarding an ordinary reasonable person. Professionals are judged according to the standard that the law requires of that particular profession. When considering whether a person is negligent and another is injured as a result, the question to be decided is whether the tortfeasor (the wrongdoer) was in breach of his duty of care to the injured party, thus committing a tort. The general principles of tort law are applicable irrespective of whether the tortfeasor is a surgeon (*Bolam v Friern Hospital Management Committee* [1957]), a driver (*Nettleship v Weston* [1971]), an architect (*Voli v Inglewood Shire Council* [1963]), a lawyer (*Saif Ali v Sydney Mitchell & Co.* [1980]), a pilot or any other professional. This indicates that there is an increase over the years in the category of professionals who are being held accountable for their professional negligence.

Where a person practises a profession or holds himself out as having professional skills, the law requires that person to show the amount of competence associated with performing the duties of that profession and if the conduct of that person falls short of that, and someone is injured as a result, he could be found to be acting negligently and therefore be held liable.

It is clear therefore, by applying the general principles outlined above that a pilot, ATCO, engineer or other aviation professional must therefore be judged for his reasonableness through the eyes of a reasonable pilot, ATCO, engineer and so on.

In relation to pilots the courts have held that the standard of care required of a pilot is that of a competent, prudent and qualified pilot. In the case of *McInnerny v McDougall* (1938) the courts held that in the absence of statute, the ordinary rules of negligence apply to the operation of an aircraft and that the pilot is required to exercise that degree of care and skill which a competent, prudent and qualified pilot would use under the circumstances. The courts have also held that a professional is not required to have an extraordinary degree of expert skill, but only the standard degree of competence common to that profession. Justice McNair, in *Bolam v Friern Hospital Management Committee* (1957), stated that:

> Where you get a situation which involves the use of some special skill or competence, then the test as to whether there has been negligence or not is not the test of the man on top of the Clapham Omnibus because he has not got any special skill. A man need not possess the highest of expert skill; it is well established in law that it is sufficient if he exercises the ordinary skill of an ordinary man exercising that particular art. (p. 587)

An American court in the case of *Long v Clinton Aviation Co.* (1950), discussing the standard of skill the law demands of a pilot, said that in the absence of Statute providing otherwise, a pilot is not required to exercise extreme care and caution in the operation of an aeroplane, but only ordinary care in the circumstances. 'Ordinary care' of an aeroplane pilot is doing or failing to do that which an experienced pilot, having due regard for safety of himself and others, would do or fail to do under same or similar circumstance.

In *Saif Ali v Sydney Mitchell & Co.* (1980) Lord Diplock stated that:

> No matter what profession it may be, the common law does not impose on those who practice it any liability for damage resulting from what ... turn out to be errors of judgment, unless the error was such as no reasonably well informed and competent member of that profession could have made it. (p. 220 C-E)

It may be argued that this statement is not necessarily valid in the case of pilots. If one gives a strict interpretation of the word 'judgment', it is evident that it is very much a part of the job of pilots to exercise precise judgment and any marked deviation therefore may amount to negligence.

It can be argued from the cases that the degree of skill and the duty of care imposed on pilots are high and perhaps, higher than those imposed on many other professions. As such it can be said that it would be easier to find a pilot negligent for even the slightest degree of error than it would to find a slight error on the part of many other professionals. The leading statement of the duty of care owed by aircrew is found in the English case of *Taylor v Alidair Limited* (1976), which dealt with a pilot who was dismissed subsequent to an accident in which a very heavy touchdown and the collapse of the nose wheel assembly resulted in damage. The court held that the pilot was not unfairly dismissed and stated:

> there are activities in which the degree of professional skill which must be required is so high and the potential consequences of the smallest departure from that high standard are so serious, that one failure to perform in accordance with those standards is enough to justify dismissal. (per Bristow J., p. 423)

The matter went on to the Court of Appeal which concurred with this statement:

> Not every error of judgment by a pilot constitutes negligence. Similarly, not every negligent act by a pilot will place the airline under a positive duty to dismiss him. But the airline may have to justify its decision not to dismiss in proceedings arising out of any accidents attributable to further errors by the same pilot. (Shawcross and Beaumont 2002, V68)

In an Australian case dealing with the standard of care required of a pilot, Judge Mason in *Australian National Airlines Commission v The Commonwealth of Australia & Canadian Pacific Airlines* (1975) stated that the standard of care to be expected of a pilot is that of a reasonable pilot, being a reasonable man having the additional quality or skill of airmanship. He also raised the issue that the pilot's responsibility increases with the number of lives for which he is responsible. As the above case specifically recognizes that the standard of care required by a pilot includes the skill of airmanship, it is necessary to briefly consider the concept of airmanship.

Airmanship, similar to seamanship, is a vague concept and cannot be easily defined (Kane and Pyne 1995). It would be difficult to get any number of aviators to agree on exactly what constitutes airmanship. It can be said that airmanship is comprised of training, human and operational factors, combined into one single entity. Operational errors and aviation mishaps, of which approximately 80 per cent involve human error (see *Human Factors Training Manual*, ICAO 1998b), are frequently linked to poor airmanship.

The question which follows is whether poor airmanship in relation to the standard of professionalism required of a pilot would constitute a breach of the duty of care, thus amounting to negligence.

Whilst pilots can show poor airmanship in a given situation (for example, bending standard operating procedures and the Minimum Equipment List or MEL), it does not automatically mean that they have also been negligent, even though in certain situations the dividing line can be difficult to define. In today's operation of sophisticated technology such as the fly-by-wire aircraft, the law recognizes that the cockpit crew cannot and are not expected to personally check everything, but omitting to personally check a piece of equipment which malfunctions, or not obtaining information which becomes necessary, could be regarded as poor airmanship. If these omissions are not expected of the ordinary professional pilot, then the pilot concerned may not have acted negligently.

In *Hayes v United States* the court clearly stated that the ordinary rules of negligence apply to aviation accidents (see *Brooks v United States*, cited in *Hayes* at 17) and that in order for the plaintiff to succeed in a negligence claim, he must prove the existence of a duty of care that the defendant owed to him, that the duty was breached by the defendant and that damages resulted from the breach. The court affirmed that it is a question of law whether a duty of care does exist and what the extent of the duty is (see *Shankle v United States* and *City of New Orleans, Etc. v American Commercial, Etc.* cited in *Hayes* at 17), and that it is a question of fact to be decided by the courts whether the duty has been actually breached. On the facts of this case the Supreme Court affirmed the earlier decision, holding that the required test of negligence was met in that the Federal Aviation Authority (FAA) inspector in charge of the flight had a duty to direct the flight examination with due regard for the safety of the aircraft as well as its passengers. It went on to say that this duty was breached by failing to give a pre-flight briefing, by the failure to stop the test after the first attempt to perform the manoeuvre and in negligently allowing a second attempt and that the negligence was the proximate cause of the injuries suffered by the plaintiffs/appellees. The court also held that the safety pilot had a duty to ensure the safety of the flight and that this duty was breached when he failed to stop the inspector and the flying pilot from proceeding with the second attempt at the manoeuvre and that this was a proximate cause of his own injuries as well as of the injuries to others (*Hayes v United States*).

In the case of *Goldman v Thai Airways International Ltd*, the court had to decide whether the pilot had acted recklessly so as to determine whether the airline was entitled to limit its liability in accordance with Article 25 of the Warsaw Convention (1929) which states that:

1. The carrier shall not be entitled to avail himself of the provisions of this Convention which exclude or limit his liability, if the damage is caused by his wilful misconduct or by such default on his part as, in accordance with the law of the Court seised of the case, is considered to be equivalent to wilful misconduct.
2. Similarly the carrier shall not be entitled to avail himself of the said provisions, if the damage is caused as aforesaid by any agent of the carrier acting within the scope of his employment.

A passenger on board a Thai Airways flight from Heathrow to Bangkok with scheduled landings at Amsterdam and Karachi sued the airline for injuries suffered when the aircraft encountered turbulence. When the plaintiff wanted to fasten his seat belt he was thrown from his seat and struck the ceiling. The plaintiff passenger was one of several passengers and crew members who were injured when thrown against the roof. The pilot landed the aircraft at Karachi, the plaintiff was given an injection and then continued his flight to Bangkok. The trial judge held that the plaintiff had successfully brought his claim under Article 25 and therefore there was no limit to the claim. With regards to the pilot's alleged recklessness, the judge found that the pilot violated the specific instructions contained in the flight operator's manual which stated that the 'fasten seat belts' sign should be lit during taxiing, take-off and landing, during all flying in turbulent air and when turbulence can be expected' by not illuminating the seat belt signs ten minutes before entering the specific area (*Goldman v Thai Airways International Ltd* [1983]). The judge quoted the words of Lord Diplock in *R v Caldwell* (1982), who stated,

> In my opinion, a person charged with an offence under section 1(1) of the Criminal Damage Act 1971 is 'reckless as to whether any such property would be destroyed or damaged' if (1) he does an act which creates an obvious risk that property will be destroyed or damaged and (2) when he does the act he either has not given any thought to the possibility of there being any such risk or has recognised that there was some risk involved and has nonetheless gone on to do it. (p. 254)

The judge found that the pilot was reckless in disregarding the safety instructions specified in the manual. With reference to the requirement 'with knowledge that damage would probably result', the judge stated:

> The probability of the result must be read as qualifying the nature of the act, and if the nature of the act is to make the damage probable – I agree it is not possible, but probable – provided the concurrent circumstances for impact or damage are there, then the probability of damage is fulfilled ... (p. 1192)

He concluded that as the accident occurred in that particular area, it was probable that damage would almost inevitably result. As it is not required that 'the damage' suffered is foreseen but that some damage is foreseen the pilot also satisfied this requirement. Based on the facts of the case and on the law as outlined, the trial court held the pilot was reckless in not illuminating the seat belt signs when he should have done so. On appeal, however, the court held that the plaintiff had the burden to prove that his personal injuries resulted from the reckless act or omission of the captain, with knowledge that damage would probably result. As the plaintiff had not successfully proved that the captain knew that damage would probably result he did not discharge this burden and did not prove that the pilot had in fact acted recklessly.

In the UK the court in *Susanne Yvonne Andrews v British Airways* (2008) refused to grant compensation for personal injuries incurred by a cabin crew member who was injured whilst on duty in an aircraft that encountered turbulence during its descent at O'Hare Airport, Chicago. As a result of severe thunderstorms the aircraft encountered some turbulence and the passengers and crew had to have their seat belts on. The pilot had instructed the cabin crew to ensure the passengers had their safety belts on, but no special instruction was given to the cabin crew. The applicant thus continued her duties and was thrown around as a result of the turbulence. The District Court found that as the severe turbulence encountered was unforeseeable – the wind was blowing from the west and the aircraft was north-east of the storm core – the captain was not negligent in failing to instruct the crew to wear their safety belts. The question of foreseeability rested on whether the aircraft was flying downwind of the storm core. The judge adopted the evidence submitted by the expert with the most recent flying experience and whose opinion accorded with the published guidance who said that as the flight path was not under the anvil position in a position downwind of the storm, there was some risk of turbulence but it was not so serious as to require the pilot to order that the crew be seated with their seat belts fastened and therefore there was no risk of severe turbulence. The Court of Appeal concurred with these findings and did not grant the appeal.

It is clear that air traffic services owe a duty of care to anyone who uses or relies on the services they provide. This duty of care emanates from the legal regulations governing the provision of their services as well as from the legal relationship that the controller has with the pilot (*Yates v US* 1974). A breach of this duty will give rise to an action for negligence and the relevant government or air traffic control (ATC) service provider will be the defendant. Generally, the tasks of ATCOs relate to the safe operation of aircraft and maintaining the expeditious flow of air traffic (*Delta Airlines Inc. v US* 1977). In exercising their duties, ATCOs should follow the procedures laid down in official manuals such as the *Procedures for Air Navigation Services, Rules of the Air and Air Traffic Services* (Doc. 4444; ICAO 1987a). It should be noted that in some jurisdictions such manuals and the regulations contained therein carry the weight of the law. Not every breach of the official procedure automatically constitutes negligence, nor will strict compliance automatically preclude negligence as in some cases, it may be reasonably expected of the ATCO to do more than the minimum officially stipulated.

The duty of care owed by controllers has been described as taking reasonable care to give all such instructions and advice as may be necessary to promote the safety of aircraft within their area of responsibility (*Nicole v Simmonds* 1975). ATCOs owe this duty to all aircraft that may be within the zone being controlled. As is often the case, there are many aircraft within that zone at a given time and as such the controller must share his time according to the needs of the moment. An example is given by *Coatney v Berkshire* (1974), where the court said that a controller cannot be expected to check upon the pilot's full compliance when other aircraft call upon his attention.

This duty of care arises because the proximity or closeness of controllers and pilots is determined by the degree of reliance existing in the relationship; in other words, pilots are reliant upon the acts, advice or information provided by controllers.

The difficulty, which often creates great confusion in establishing the legal liability of each individual party, is differentiating the respective responsibilities of pilots and controllers. Hopkins (1995) offers a clarification by stating that the pilot is legally responsible for the safety of the aircraft and its passengers, whereas the controller is legally responsible for the safety of the ATC instructions.

The three main categories of duty that a controller has, that if breached, can lead to potential liability can be described as:

1. a duty to provide information that is accurate and not misleading;
2. a duty to warn of known dangers; and
3. a duty to warn of potential dangers (Bartsch 1996).

ICAO Doc. 4444 (ICAO 1987a) supplemented by each country's legal enactments and the local procedures of each country's ATC system creates the proper manner in which to conduct ATC communication. The corresponding legal duty imposed on pilots to conform and comply with the relevant legislation, regulations, procedures and training, with regard to ATC, is to create a safe flying environment. In addition, a special relationship of trust is created and it is assumed that each party will conform to the relevant procedures and perform their individual duties. However, when there is reasonable cause that makes it evident that either the controller or the pilot is not conforming to his/her duties, then this relationship of trust should no longer be assumed.

In the case of *Nichols v Simmonds, Royal Aero Club of Western Australia and Commonwealth* (1975) Justice Burt stated that in his opinion the negligence of the ATCO was more culpable than the negligence of either pilot. A controller using non-standard phraseologies and words may be faced with a legal action against him if an accident results from consequent miscommunication. If an ATCO knowingly violates safe operating procedures he will be more culpable as this may increase both the likelihood of inducing an error and the chances of serious consequences resulting therefrom.

An example to illustrate possible miscommunication is that of a Canadian Pacific Douglas DC-8 which had landed at Sydney's Kingsford-Smith Airport in 1971 (*Australian National Airlines Commission v The Commonwealth of Australia and Canadian Pacific Airlines* [1975]). The pilot requested permission to backtrack along Runway 16 and the ATCO gave the instruction 'take taxiway right'. The pilot mistook that for 'you can backtrack if you like'. In the resulting confusion a Trans Australian Airlines (TAA) Boeing 727 was cleared for take-off on the same runway. Due to a lump in the runway the TAA crew was unable to see the DC-8. The fin and rudder of the DC-8 was torn off in the collision with the airborne B727's belly but there were no fatalities. The High Court found that both defendants, the controllers and the Canadian Pacific crew, were negligent with contributory negligence on the part of the TAA crew. Justice Mason referred to the failure of the ATCO to keep a proper look-out and for issuing a clearance for immediate take-off without maintaining adequate visual and radio observations as being 'a serious departure from the standards of a reasonable man' (Bartsch 1996, p. 1).

The case clearly demonstrated that an ATCO might be held negligent if he or she provides misleading information upon which the pilot relies and which subsequently causes damage. It also showed that pilots are not relieved of responsibility to maintain situational awareness by gathering information from their own eyes, ears and instruments. The Canadian Pacific crew was found to be negligent for, inter alia, not paying attention to the controller's instruction, not querying or seeking confirmation of that instruction, and in failing to call the surface movements controller promptly after receiving the instruction to do so (Boughen 1994).

The second duty that can give rise to possible legal liability, if breached, is the duty of the controller to warn pilots of known dangers. This could include the duty to provide information regarding, inter alia, mid-air collision, wake turbulence and weather-related hazards.

The controller's duty to warn of a potential mid-air collision centres on the pilot's and the ATCO's knowledge of the facts of the traffic situation. Controllers owe a duty of care to pilots and passengers even in situations where the pilots are generally responsible for their own separation. In addition if a late warning is given by a controller this would not relieve the controller of liability as warnings must be both timely and sufficient to alert the pilot of the extent and magnitude of the potential danger (*Nicole v Simmonds* 1975).

Justice Wallace of the Australian Supreme Court stated: 'In my view, where there is a duty to submit and obey, there is a corresponding duty to, inter alia, warn of danger within the limits of practicability in the performance of the controller's duty and having regard to circumstances prevailing in each particular case' (*Nicole v Simmonds* 1975, p. 655).

In certain cases, the ATCO may have an additional duty beyond that prescribed by the ATC manual. An example is *Hartz v United States* (1965), where improper phraseology was used in a warning given to the pilot of a Beechcraft Bonanza about a departing Douglas DC-7. The court found that the controller's warning of 'prop-wash' (instead of 'wake turbulence') was insufficient to adequately warn the pilot of the degree of hazard created by the DC-7 and that the controller had an additional duty, beyond that prescribed by the ATC manual, to delay the take-off clearance of the Bonanza for as long as reasonably necessary to permit the DC-7's turbulence to dissipate.

The first two duties clearly arise when information is available to a controller and is then passed on to a pilot. Liability may arise if the information was inaccurate, insufficient or untimely. The question arises as to what duty an ATCO has in respect of information that he or she should have known but had not obtained or pursued? When attempting to establish the individual liability of an ATCO or pilot, it should be determined which of the parties was in the best position to evaluate the situation. In the event that such information should be known by the controller but has not been obtained, if the information would have been available by some alternative means to a pilot exercising due care, it may be possible for the controller to avoid liability, as long as the lack of information by the controller was not the primary cause of the resulting accident or was not one of the events in the chain of events that caused the accident or incident.

In *Kack v United States* a student pilot claimed damages against the United States for negligent conduct of the ATCOs on the basis that the employees of the FAA – the ATCOs – failed to provide him with adequate and timely notice of the existence of wake turbulence that caused his aircraft to crash when he tried to land it, failed to provide adequate space between his aircraft and the aircraft which landed before him and caused wake turbulence and failed to warn him of his dangerously low altitude in relation to the wake turbulence hazard that was created by the other aircraft. The District Court, denying recovery, held that controllers do have the duty to warn pilots of the existence of wake turbulence and that the warning was given and would have been timely but for the plaintiff's negligence in failing to maintain the proper altitude; that the controllers did not fail to provide adequate space between the two aircraft and that if the plaintiff had maintained a proper altitude the accident would have been avoided; that the controllers had no special duty to warn the plaintiff of his precariously low altitude as the plaintiff, even as a student pilot, had the primary responsibility for the safe operation of his aircraft. The Appeal Court, affirming the decision of the lower court, stated that the court had correctly held that the pilot has the primary responsibility to see and avoid the hazard of wake turbulence and that the law is clear that under Visual Flight Rule conditions the primary responsibility for the safe operation of the aircraft rests with the pilot irrespective of the traffic clearance. The Appeal Court affirmed that ATCOs do have some duty of care towards pilots and the aircraft they direct and that in some situations this duty may be violated but the facts of the case did not present such a situation and therefore the accident did not occur as a result of the ATCOs' breach of their duty but as a result of the plaintiff's negligence.

In *David R. Hinson, Administrator, FAA, v Hulbert G. Ferger* (1994) the Appeal Court held that in the interests of safety in air commerce and transportation and the public's interest, the administrator's order suspending the respondent's commercial pilot certificate should be affirmed. The court stated that the issue was not whether the ATC could have done more or something different to avert the hazard that the respondent created, but whether the respondent's conduct produced an endangerment that would have existed had he complied with the ATC's instruction. As it clearly did, the respondent had violated sections 91.123 (b) and 91.13 (a) which states respectively:

§ 91.123 Compliance with ATC clearances and instruction.

(b) Except in emergency, no person may operate an aircraft contrary to an ATC instruction in an area in which air traffic control is exercised.

§ 91.13 Careless or reckless operation.

(a) Aircraft operations for the purpose of air navigation. No person may operate an aircraft in a careless or reckless manner so as to endanger the life or property of another.

The general principles of negligence law and civil liability were outlined; however, a deeper examination is required into the principles of criminal liability which can take the form of prosecuting aviation professionals for violations of the relevant regulations, provisions and other aviation legislation and/or the more serious criminal offence of manslaughter in the event that the negligent acts or omissions resulted in death.

All aviation professionals should be aware of the increased danger of facing criminal liability in the event of failing to exercise their duties and responsibilities in accordance with the high degree and standard of care required by the law.

In the words of an administrative law judge in the case of *FAA v NTSB* (1999), '[A]viation is … particularly unforgiving of carelessness or neglect' (p. 26).

Criminal Liability

Aviation professionals can be criminally prosecuted for their negligent, albeit unintentional, acts or omissions as is evidenced by the case of *People v Crossan* in 1927, which is the first reported case of the prosecution of an aviator in which the defendant was convicted of involuntary manslaughter when the aircraft he operated struck and killed two girls.

Article 12 of the Chicago Convention which deals with the Rules of Air states,

> Rules of the air: Each contracting State undertakes to adopt measures to insure that every aircraft flying over or maneuvering within its territory and that every aircraft carrying its nationality mark, wherever such aircraft may be, shall comply with the rules and regulations relating to the flight and maneuver of a aircraft there in force. Each contracting State undertakes to keep its own regulations in these respects uniform, to the greatest possible extent, with those established from time to time under this Convention. Over the high seas, the rules in force shall be those established under this Convention. Each contracting State undertakes to insure the prosecution of all persons violating the regulations applicable.

It is therefore clearly stated that the provisions establishing criminal liability are set out in the domestic legislation of each contracting party, which differs from state to state.

For example, pilots and ATCOs can be criminally liable for contravening, permitting the contravention of or for non-compliance with the relevant air navigation orders (ANO) and Rules of Air. In accordance with the ANOs criminal liability may also be imposed on any person who endangers the aircraft or persons or property in the air and on the ground. Sections 6–9 of the Cyprus Civil Aviation Law 2002 provide that a pilot may be prosecuted if he recklessly or negligently acts in way that endangers the aircraft or any persons or property therein, or operates as a crew member on board an aircraft while drunk, or recklessly or negligently causes an aircraft to endanger any person or any property, or smokes on board the aircraft.

Articles 378-140 of the UK Air Navigation Order 2009, which came into force on 1 January 2010, states that criminal charges may be filed if a person recklessly or negligently acts in a manner likely to endanger an aircraft, and on conviction on indictment will be liable to a fine or imprisonment of a maximum of five years; or any person therein recklessly or negligently causes or permits an aircraft to endanger any person or property, or enters an aircraft when drunk or is drunk on an aircraft and on conviction on indictment for both these offences will be liable to a fine or imprisonment of up to two years; or smokes on board an aircraft if smoking is forbidden.

An example of an endangering offence is from a case that was heard in America in which the court affirmed the FAA's revocation of all airman certificates held by the respondent pilot for, inter alia, operating as pilot in command a Piper PA-32-300 with four passengers on board when the aircraft exceeded the maximum take-off weight permitted, exceeding the maximum baggage weight allowed and a centre of gravity CG outside the allowed range; the aircraft was thus not airworthy at the time of the flight. As a result, the aircraft crashed shortly after take-off and the four passengers were injured (*Marion C. Blakey, Administrator, FAA v Peachie D. Tianvan* [2003]). The pilot had in so doing violated FAA regulations relating to private pilot privileges and limitation; pilot in command; civil aircraft airworthiness; civil aircraft flight manual, marking and placard requirements; careless or reckless operation, certifications, authorizations and prohibitions; and initial and recurrent pilot testing requirements (sections 61.113, 91.7, 91.9, 91.13, 119.5, 135.293).

Another example relates to the pilot's failure to remove the cover of the right engine blower inlet of a Fokker F-27, a regularly scheduled passenger-carrying flight, and failure to assure an adequate pre-flight inspection before commencing the flight (*Joseph M. Del Balzo Acting Administrator, FAA v Ray Edward Delgmant, Jr.*[1993]). Shortly after the aircraft taxied at the airport, smoke entered the cockpit and the cabin, the aircraft stopped and the passengers disembarked. The pilot, in violation of FAR S 91.9 (now recodified as 91.13 (a) which states that no person may operate an aircraft in a careless or reckless manner so as to endanger the life or property of another and s 121.315 (c) requiring flight crews to adhere to approved cockpit check procedures), had his licence suspended. The judge affirmed the violation in respect of the careless or reckless operation of the aircraft and the

FAA appealed. In the appeal, it was affirmed that the pilot has the duty to look at all openings during a walkaround inspection and that this was part of airmanship, as stated by the Director of Flight Operations. Since the pilot failed to look at the opening in that part of the aircraft or did not raise his flashlight high enough to see the cover, the finding of carelessness was supported. In addition, it was held that the pilot had an independent duty to perform his walkaround inspection properly and that he had breached that duty.

A pilot therefore who acts below the standard required of him or her may be negligent and held accountable for violating the ANO, the Rules of Air, and/ or the endangering offences. However, in nearly all the cases where an aviation accident or serious incident involves the loss of life, aviation professionals have found themselves charged with various offences such as, inter alia, involuntary homicide, involuntary manslaughter, professional negligence and interruption of air traffic, and are criminally prosecuted.

Criminal Negligence

Generally, however, a person may not be convicted of a crime unless the prosecution has proved beyond a reasonable doubt firstly, that the accused caused a certain act and that he or she is responsible for that act which is forbidden by criminal law, namely the *actus reus* (conduct, circumstances, consequences), and secondly, that the accused had a defined state of mind in causing that act, namely the *mens rea* (intention, recklessness or negligence) (Smith and Hogan 2002).

Criminal negligence is defined differently by the laws of each country; however it can be said that certain elements of this offence are common, viz., that the actor does not comprehend the consequences of his behaviour and is unaware of the risk he creates, or that he is aware of the risk but chooses to ignore it.

In Canada for example, according to the Penal Code, offences are separated into causing death by criminal negligence, causing bodily harm by criminal negligence, and homicide, which is defined as directly or indirectly by any means causing the death of a human being and which may take the form of culpable and non-culpable homicide. Culpable homicide (S222(4)), which may take the form of murder or manslaughter, is committed when a person causes the death of a human being by, inter alia, means of an unlawful act and by criminal negligence (S222(5) (a) and (b)). Criminal negligence (S219(1)) is defined as doing anything, or omitting to do anything that it is his or her legal duty(S219(2)) to do, showing wanton or reckless disregard for the lives or safety of other persons. To prove that the defendant showed a wanton or reckless disregard for the lives or safety of others, the prosecution must prove beyond a reasonable doubt that (a) the defendant's conduct showed a marked departure from the conduct of a reasonable person in the circumstances; and (b) that a reasonable person in the same circumstances would have foreseen that this conduct posed a risk of bodily harm which is defined as any hurt or injury that interferes with a person's health or comfort and is more than brief or minor. The defendant's individual characteristics are not taken into account when determining what a reasonable person would have done or foreseen.

In Germany, the Penal Code provides the following categories: homicide which carries a prison sentence of 10–20 years; qualified homicide, 15–25 years; extremely grave homicide 15–25 years or life imprisonment; infanticide, two to seven years; and negligent or accidental homicide. A killing which is not murder may be either manslaughter (*Totschlag*) or negligent homicide (*fahrlässige Tötung*). Negligent or accidental homicide with the following aggravating circumstances carries the accompanying penalties: (a) caused by a professional in connection with his job (two to seven years); (b) caused by a vehicle driver with blood alcohol concentration above the legal limits or who is in a drunken state (five to 15 years); (c) caused by a professional in a drunk state in connection with his job duties (five to 15 years); and (e) when the death of two or more persons is caused (five to 15 years).

The French Penal Code categorizes offences according to their seriousness as felonies, misdemeanours or petty offences. Article 121-3[1] states that there is no felony or misdemeanour in the absence of an intent to commit it and that the deliberate endangering of others is a misdemeanour where the law so provides. It goes on to provide that a misdemeanour also exists, where the law so provides, in cases of recklessness, negligence or failure to observe an obligation of due care or precaution imposed by any statute or regulation, where it is established that the offender has failed to show normal diligence, taking into consideration where appropriate the nature of his role or functions, of his capacities and powers and of the means then available to him. In such cases, natural persons who have not directly contributed to causing the damage, but who have created or contributed to create the situation which allowed the damage to happen and who failed to take steps enabling it to be avoided, are criminally liable where it is shown that they have broken a duty of care or precaution laid down by statute or regulation in a manifestly deliberate manner, or have committed a specified piece of misconduct which exposed another person to a particularly serious risk of which they must have been aware.

The Penal Code further provides that causing the death of another person by clumsiness, rashness, inattention, negligence or breach of an obligation of safety or prudence imposed by statute or regulations, in such circumstances constitutes manslaughter punished by three years' imprisonment and a fine of €45,000, and that in cases of a deliberate violation of an obligation of safety or prudence imposed by statute or regulations, the penalty is increased to five years' imprisonment and to a fine of €75,000.[2] In addition, Article 221-7 provides that a legal person may incur criminal liability in such circumstances.

---

1   Act no. 1996-393 of 13 May 1996. Article 1 *Official Journal* of 14 May 1996; Act no. 2000-647 of 10 July article 1 *Official Journal* of 11 July 2000.

2   Article 221-6 (Act no. 2000-647 of 10 July 2000 Article 4 *Official Journal* of 11 July 2000). (Ordinance no. 2000-916 of 19 September 2000 Article 3 *Official Journal*, 22 September 2000 into force 1 January 2002).

The Code also creates the offence of endangering other persons (Chapter III 'Endangering other persons', Articles 223-1 to 223-30). In particular it provides that the direct exposure of another person to an immediate risk of death or injury likely to cause mutilation or permanent disability by the manifestly deliberate violation of a specific obligation of safety or prudence imposed by any statute or regulation is punished by one year's imprisonment and a fine of €15,000 (Risks caused to other persons, Articles 223-1 to 223-2). A legal person may also incur such criminal liability (Article 223-2).

In Taiwan, Article 276 of the Criminal Code specifies that:

1. A person who negligently kills another shall be punished with imprisonment for not more than two years, detention or a fine of not more than 2,000 yuan.
2. A person who in the performance of his occupation commits an offence specified in the preceding paragraph by neglecting the degree of care required by such occupation shall be punished with imprisonment for not more than five years, in addition thereto a fine of not more than 3,000 yuan may be imposed.

Article 284 states that:

1. A person who negligently causes bodily harm to another shall be punished with imprisonment for not more than six months, detention, or a fine of not more than 1,000 yuan; if serious bodily harm results, he shall be punished with imprisonment for not more than one year; detention, or a fine of not more than 500 yuan.
2. A person who in the performance of his occupation causes bodily harm to another by neglecting the degree of care required by such occupation shall be punished with imprisonment for not more than one year, detention or a fine of not more than 1,000 yuan; if serious bodily harm results, he shall be punished with imprisonment for not more than three years, detention, or a fine of not more than 2,000 yuan (Yang 2003).

Provisions in the Italian Penal Code (*Codice Penale*) provide that injury resulting in death occurs when, as a result of a deliberate act of violence not meant to kill, the death of a person occurs (Articles 581 and 582, *Codice Penale*) and is punishable with a sentence of between ten and 18 years (Art. 584). Manslaughter is defined as causing the death of a person without intention and is punished with a sentence between six months and five years, however if the same act causes more than one death, the multiple counts can be added up to 12 years in prison (Art. 589).

Although the classifications and details may vary between them, generally, criminal sanctions are imposed for negligent or reckless conduct that leads to injury, death or property damage.

Manslaughter

Despite the differences in the criminal law of each country, there are generally three common levels of criminal charges:

1. 'Criminal negligence' or 'unintentional /involuntary manslaughter' alleges the creation of a risk to others' lives and that the risk had foreseeable consequences. The person may recognize the danger that his act or omission creates but fails to do anything about it.
2. 'Manslaughter' alleges the defendant knows that the risk of his or her actions may result in death for others, ignores the risk and continues the behaviour anyway.
3. 'Third degree murder' which applies to the USA, holds the defendant responsible for causing the death of another while the defendant was committing another felony.

Generally, there are three forms of unlawful homicide: murder, voluntary manslaughter and involuntary manslaughter. The state of mind of the defendant at the time of committing the act determines the type of homicide.

For murder, the *mens rea* is malice afterthought, meaning either an intention to kill or an intention to commit grievous bodily harm. It will be assumed that in aviation accidents, barring terrorism, no one will have the requisite intention to kill or to cause grievous bodily harm;[3] accordingly a discussion on manslaughter is more pertinent.

Unlawful and dangerous manslaughter occurs where one sets out to commit a less serious offence but kills a person in the process. In this particular offence, death must be caused by an act, not an omission, the defendant must have acted dangerously and the unlawful and dangerous act must have caused the death of another. The *mens rea* is that of the crime constituting the unlawful act and can be either intention or recklessness depending on the definition of the particular offence. To amount to constructive manslaughter the defendant must firstly commit an unlawful act and this must be a criminal offence and have the *mens rea* of intention or recklessness (*R v Franklin* [1883]); secondly, the act must be dangerous. This is objectively judged (*R v Franklin* [1883]); the defendant need not be aware the act is dangerous (*DPP v Newbury* [1977]), the act need not be directed at the victim (*AG's Reference (No. 3 of 1994)* [1997]) and the act must cause the death of the victim.

Criminal negligence occurs when the defendant recognizes the danger that his act or omission creates but fails to do anything about it. Criminal negligence becomes gross negligence when a failure to foresee involves a wanton disregard

---

3   Although under UK law (*R v Woolin* [1999]) where a person foresees either death or grievous bodily harm as a virtually certain consequence of his actions, a jury is at liberty to find intention which would suffice for a murder conviction.

for human life. Gross negligence which is the test for manslaughter has been described as follows:

> In explaining to juries the test which they should apply to determine whether the negligence, in the particular case, amounted or did not amount to a crime, ... in order to establish criminal liability the facts must be such that, in the opinion of the jury, the negligence of the accused went beyond a mere matter of compensation between subjects and showed such disregard for the life and safety of others as to amount to a crime against the State and conduct deserving punishment. (Lord Hewart CJ in *R v Bateman* [1925], pp. 11–12)

Gross negligence, which may take the form of an act or omission, is therefore a failure to exercise a reasonable level of precaution and the defendant may be found guilty if he fails to meet the standard of care expected from a reasonable person of the same profession. To be found guilty, the prosecution must prove that the defendant owed a duty to the deceased to take care; the defendant breached this duty; the breach caused the death of the deceased; and the defendant's negligence was gross – that is, it showed such a disregard for the life and safety of others as to amount to a crime and deserve punishment (*R v Bateman* [1925]).

For gross negligent manslaughter to arise, the jury must be satisfied that the accused has satisfied the degree of fault required for manslaughter as was stated in the case of *Adomako* (1995) namely: 'whether, having regard to the risk of death involved, the conduct of the defendant was so bad as in all the circumstances as to amount in [the jury's] judgment to a criminal act or omission' (p. 71).

The elements for this offence are a duty of care which has the same meaning as that in civil law and the breach of that duty by the defendant. The basic test for gross negligence is an objective one where it is questioned whether the defendant's conduct has fallen below the standards of a reasonable man. The courts will therefore examine the defendant's thoughts, a reasonable person's thoughts and the defendant's acts or omissions.

It was made clear in the *Adomako* case that in order to be guilty of gross negligence manslaughter, there had to be a risk of death.

Corporate Manslaughter

Prosecuting corporations for manslaughter has been fraught with difficulties, mainly due to the fact that it is necessary to show that the corporation has acted through the controlling mind of one of its agents. In order to convict a company for manslaughter the prosecution has had to establish that individual defendants could be identified with the company and that they themselves were guilty of manslaughter. The following are just a few examples of unsuccessful attempts to hold corporations criminally accountable subsequent to accidents resulting in fatalities.

The MS *Herald of Free Enterprise*, a passenger ferry on route to Dover, capsized on 6 March 1987 shortly after departing from the Belgian port of Zeebrugge. The bow doors had been left open and water flooded the car decks, resulting in the death of 192 passengers and crew. In 1987 a coroner's inquest returned the verdict of unlawful killing (BBC News 1987). As a result, five company managers were charged with gross negligence manslaughter and the operating company P&O European Ferries with corporate manslaughter. The judge in *R v P&O Ferries* (Dover) Ltd (1990) stated that a corporation that commits an act fulfilling the prerequisites for the crime of manslaughter through the controlling mind of one of its agents is indictable for the crime of manslaughter. However, the jury was directed to find the defendants not guilty on the basis that there was insufficient evidence that any of the managers had the necessary *mens rea* and that *mens rea* could not be attributed to the company.

Another company that was prosecuted for manslaughter, also unsuccessfully, was Great Western Railways following the 1997 Southall rail disaster in which seven persons were killed. In this case, only the company was charged. The prosecution did not file any charges against any of the directors or managers.

There were other similar disasters – such as the Kings Cross underground fire resulting in 31 deaths, the Clapham rail accident in which 35 people were killed and the Paddington rail disaster in 1999 in which 31 people died – but few resulted in charges being filed and in the successful prosecution of the defendants.

Four corporate manslaughter prosecutions which were successful in the UK are:

- OLL Limited (formerly Active Leisure and Learning Ltd), which was the first company in English legal history to be convicted of the crime of manslaughter in December 1994, subsequent to the deaths of four teenage schoolchildren in a canoeing disaster. The company was fined £60,000 and the owner of the company was sentenced to three years' imprisonment based on the fact that he was directly in charge of the activity centre where the children were staying.
- Jackson Transport (Ossett) Limited, which in 1996 was convicted of corporate manslaughter and fined £22,000. The company director was convicted of manslaughter following the death of an employee who inhaled chemicals and was sentenced to prison for a year and fined £150,000 (BBC News 2001).
- English Brothers Ltd, a construction company, which was convicted of corporate manslaughter in 2001. A director was also charged with manslaughter but after the company pleaded guilty to manslaughter the charges were dropped.
- Teglgaard Hardwood Ltd, which in 2003 was convicted of corporate manslaughter. The director was also found guilty of manslaughter and was sentenced to 15 months' imprisonment, suspended for two years (Welham 2003).

In other European countries, corporate criminal liability is not a recent development. The French Penal Code has provided for this since March 1994. It is specifically stated in the code that, 'Causing the death of another person by clumsiness, rashness, inattention, negligence or breach of an obligation of safety or prudence imposed by statute or regulations, [...] constitutes manslaughter'(Section 11 – Involuntary Offences against Life, Article 221-6) and that a legal person may incur criminal liability for this offence (Article 221-7). Portugal, Spain, Norway, Finland and Denmark have all enacted or amended existing laws to provide criminal punishments against criminally culpable corporations (Crown Prosecution Service 2009). In Italy, for example, a court in Turin sentenced nine owner-managers of an asbestos factory to between seven and eight years' imprisonment with a fine of $12 million compensation award in 1996 after 32 employees were killed and 11 others became ill (Lowery and Wilson 2002). The legal system in Germany also provides for corporate culpability as is evidenced in the case where two German rail managers and an engineer were charged with manslaughter and causing bodily harm through negligence for the deaths of 101 passengers who died in a high speed train accident in 1998 (Lowery and Wilson 2002).

In Australia, the company AAA Auscarts Imports Ltd was convicted and fined £700,000 for the death of an employee who had died after crashing her go-kart into a barrier during her employment duties. However, as the company had already gone into liquidation, no one was held accountable for her death (Fogarty 2009).

However, recent legislation such as the UK Corporate Manslaughter and Corporate Homicide Act 2007 now allows for prosecuting companies and corporations for corporate manslaughter as a result of serious management failures resulting in a gross breach of a duty of care and fatalities. An organization may be found guilty if the way in which its activities are managed causes a death and amounts to a gross breach of a duty of care to the deceased. Juries will examine the management and of the activity resulting in the death, and will consider any processes for managing safety and how these were implemented. Any organizational health and safety breaches as well as the seriousness of such breaches will be examined in order to determine whether the organization's conduct has fallen below the required legal standard. A substantial part of the failure within the organization must have been at a senior level. In accordance with the Act, it is the corporate body that will be prosecuted and not individuals. However, the liability of directors, members and other individuals under health and safety laws or general criminal law remains unaffected and individuals can be prosecuted for gross negligence manslaughter, and for health and safety offences.

Prior to initiating criminal charges, the consent of the Director of Public Prosecutions of England and Wales and Northern Ireland is required. If successfully prosecuted, corporations will be liable to an unlimited fine, a publicity order as well as a remedial order requiring the company to take the necessary steps to remedy the management failure that led to the death.

The first company prosecuted in terms of the new Act was a Gloucestershire-based company charged with corporate manslaughter following the death of a geologist in September 2009. In addition, the company director was also charged with gross negligence manslaughter which carries a maximum sentence of life imprisonment and with failing to discharge a duty contrary to the Health and Safety at Work Act 1974 (Crown Prosecution Service 2009).

Chapter 3
The Greying of the Black Box – Aviation Accident Investigation

The Purpose of an Investigation

Investigating an accident may have a number of different purposes depending on the type of accident, namely to:

1. identify and describe the course of events (what, where, when)
2. identify the direct causes and the contributing factors that led to the accident (why)
3. identify measures to reduce the risk in order to prevent future similar accidents from occurring (learning)
4. investigate and evaluate the basis for potential prosecution (blame)
5. evaluate the question of guilt in order to assess the liability for compensation (pay).

According to Hendrick and Benner (1986) there are ten important factors for accident investigations. Three of these criteria regard the purpose and objectives of an investigation and are that an investigation should be

1. realistic
2. conducted in a non-causal framework resulting in an objective description of the events leading up to the accident
3. consistent.

With regards to the investigation procedures, they submit that the procedures should provide an orderly, systematic framework and set of procedures to discipline the investigators' tasks; be functional; be definitive and be comprehensive. The outputs of the investigation should be readily understandable; the results should be direct in that there is sufficient data to identify the controls and changes required; and the results should satisfy the persons who have initialized the investigation and those who demand results from the investigation. This last point however is debatable as it is very often the case that the investigation results will not please all the parties who are awaiting the results (for instance the airline, the manufacturer, the Civil Aviation Authority, the relatives of the deceased, and so on).

The legal approach to an investigation is to determine the parties who are at fault and to then apportion blameworthiness and liability on them, either in the form of criminal or civil liability. In aviation investigation, the investigation takes on a completely different turn, as the purpose of investigating aviation accidents is to enhance safety by identifying the circumstances that led to the accident and make safety recommendations in order to prevent a recurrence of similar accidents.

It is also clear that the responsibility of investigating an accident rests with different people, depending on the kind of investigation and its purpose. In aviation accidents, this responsibility rests on the relevant accident investigation body in accordance with the rules and procedures set out in ICAO. However, in an investigation to evaluate the potential for criminal prosecution, the responsibility rests with the police and the prosecuting authorities and the courts have the ultimate responsibility for passing the appropriate sentence once liability and blameworthiness have been proved.

The objective of investigating an aviation accident is to establish the course of events leading up to the accident (that is, to identify 'what, where and when'), to determine the direct and root causes or the factors that contributed to the accident (the 'why') and to identify any measures that ought to be taken in order to prevent similar future accidents from occurring.

A complete investigation should identify all the factors that may have had an impact on the sequence of events leading up to the accident and analyse the weight of each of these factors, including the technical/maintenance/engineering system, the ATC, the frontline personnel and their managers, regulators and the government.

ICAO Investigation

A process conducted for the purpose of accident prevention which includes the gathering and analysis of information, the drawing of conclusions, including the determination of causes and, when appropriate, the making of safety recommendations.

Kjellen defines an accident as 'a sequence of logically and chronologically related deviating events involving an incident that results in injury to personnel or damage to the environment or material assets' (Kjellen 2000, p. 376). Doe (1997) defines an accident as 'an unwanted transfer of energy or an environmental condition that, due to the absence or failure of barriers and controls, produces injury to persons, damage to property, or reduction in process output' (p. 184). According to Rasmussen (1977), accidents are caused by the loss of control of physical processes that are able to injure people, and/or damage the environment or property; the propagation of an accidental course of events is shaped by the activities of people, which can either trigger an accidental flow of events or divert a normal flow (Rasmussen 1977). Another definition is that provided by Hendrick and Benner, who submit that an accident is a process in which a perturbation 'transforms a dynamically stable activity into unintended interacting changes of state with a harmful outcome' (Hendrick and Benner 1986, p. 438).

The terms 'accident' and 'incident' are defined in Annex 13 to ICAO (ICAO 2001) as follows:

Accident

An occurrence associated with the operation of an aircraft which takes place between the time any person boards the aircraft with the intention of flight until such time as all such persons have disembarked, in which:

a. a person is fatally or seriously injured as a result of:
    - being in the aircraft, or
    - direct contact with any part of the aircraft, including parts which have become detached from the aircraft, or
    - direct exposure to jet blast,
        1. *except* when the injuries are from natural causes, self-inflicted or inflicted by other persons, or when the injuries are to stowaways hiding outside the areas normally available to the passengers and crew; or
b. the aircraft sustains damage or structural failure which:
    - adversely affects the structural strength, performance or flight characteristics of the aircraft, and
    - would normally require major repair or replacement of the affected component,
        1. *except* for engine failure or damage, when the damage is limited to the engine, its cowlings or accessories; or for damage limited to propellers, wing tips, antennas, tires, brakes, fairings, small dents or puncture holes in the aircraft skin; or
c. the aircraft is missing or is completely inaccessible.

Note 1. For statistical uniformity only, an injury resulting in death within thirty days of the date of the accident is classified as a fatal injury by ICAO.
Note 2. An aircraft is considered to be missing when the official search has been terminated and the wreckage has not been located.

Incident

An occurrence, other than an accident, associated with the operation of an aircraft which affects or could affect the safety of operation.
Note. The types of incidents which are of main interest to the International Civil Aviation Organization for accident prevention studies are listed in the *Accident/Incident Reporting Manual* (ICAO 1987b).

Serious incident

An incident involving circumstances indicating that an accident nearly occurred.
Note 1. The difference between an accident and a serious incident lies only in the result.
Note 2. Examples of serious incidents can be found in Attachment D of Annex 13 and the
ICAO Accident/Incident Reporting Manual (ICAO 1987b).

A close examination of the definition of a 'serious incident' clearly shows that the
only difference between that and an 'accident' is in the result.

The Legal Framework of an Aviation Accident Investigation

The investigation of international aviation accidents and serious incidents is
governed by the accident investigation standards and recommended practices
of the International Civil Aviation Organization, (ICAO), which was formed
by the Chicago Convention in 1944. Member states are required to investigate
international accidents according to the procedures established by ICAO (Article
43 of the convention). The convention applies only to civil aircraft, not to state
aircraft, and it is one of the most important aviation instruments.

In the event of an accident to an aircraft of a contracting State occurring in
the territory of another contracting State and involving death or serious injury, or
indicating serious technical defect in the aircraft or air navigation facilities, the
State in which the accident occurs will institute an inquiry into the circumstances
of the accident (Article 26).

The State where the accident occurs has the responsibility to immediately
preserve the aircraft wreckage and its contents and to initiate the investigation, but
it has the option to invite another government to participate in the investigation.
Other States, the State of Registry, the State of Manufacturer and Design, the
State of the Operator and a State with an interest because of citizens on board,
are entitled to participate in the investigation by the appointment of 'accredited
representatives' and technical advisers. Treaties and other special agreements
between countries will often include a provision allowing agents of a particular
government to participate in the investigation of foreign accidents.

Annex 13 to the Convention (ICAO 2001) deals with the procedures to be
adopted in the event of an aviation accident or incident and contains 'Standards'
and 'Recommended Practices' which provide the background for the investigation.
The aim of Annex 13 is to standardize the procedures of reporting aircraft accidents
and incidents; to establish procedures ensuring the participation of experts in
accident and incident investigation; and to ensure the expeditious publication of
important safety and airworthiness information.

It is clearly stated that 'The sole objective of the investigation of an accident or
incident shall be the prevention of accidents and incidents. It is not the purpose to
apportion blame or liability' (Annex 13, Chapter 3.1).

Even though it is specifically mentioned that the purpose of this investigation differs from a normal legal investigation, the purpose of which is to determine criminal and or civil liability, it does not ensure that in practice, the evidence and results of the investigations are not used in subsequent legal consequences and litigation. Concurrent to the accident investigation carried out in terms of Annex 13, police and judicial investigations will also be carried out in order to determine what offences were committed, the exact nature of the offences and the parties who have allegedly committed any such offences. The exact details of the accident need to be established in order to assist the victims in establishing their claims. The person or persons who are allegedly blameworthy for the accident and the legal basis of their liability need to be determined.

The evidence, data and other specific details gathered in the course of the investigation, are also significant to the police authorities and the plaintiffs when establishing their claim. Annex 13, however, stipulates that the investigators shall not make the information available to those persons 'unless the appropriate authority for the administration of justice determines that their disclosure outweighs the adverse domestic and international impact such action may have on future investigations' (Chapter 5.2).

The accident investigation authority has independence in conducting the investigation and it has unrestricted authority over its conduct. The investigator-in-charge has unrestricted access to the wreckage and full control over it.

Once the investigation has been completed, a final report must be published containing all relevant factual information relating to the circumstances of the accident (Chapter 6).

An analysis of this information leading to an assessment of the causes as well as safety recommendations intended to reduce the likelihood of a similar accident occurring in the future are also included. A draft of this report is first circulated to all States which participated in the investigation for their comments. Any comments made should then be taken into account by the State drafting the report. The report may then be amended or it may have the dissenting comments attached to it before the final report is issued.

At an international level, Annex 13 lays down the international standards and recommended practices relating to aircraft accident and incident investigation. At a European level, in an effort to provide the competent authorities with an appropriate legal framework within which to conduct an investigation of civil aviation accidents and incidents, the European Community adopted a directive that established the principles of Annex 13 to the Chicago Convention into European law (European Council 1994). Council Directive 94/56/EC, which establishes the fundamental principles governing the investigation of civil aviation accidents and incidents, came into effect on 21 November 1994. The directive applies to investigations into civil accidents and incidents which occur in the territory of the European Community and accidents which occur outside the territory which involve aircraft registered in the EC when an investigation is not carried out by another State.

A number of important changes are introduced by the directive. In accordance with the Chicago Convention, a permanent and 'independent' accident and investigation body is established in each State (Article 6). This introduces a change as previously the accident investigators were mainly employed by the aviation regulatory authority. In addition, a clear distinction is made between the judicial inquiry, aimed at establishing liability, and the technical investigation, the status of which is stepped up. Another change brought about by the directive is the provision of powers that enable the investigators, in co-operation with the authorities responsible for the judicial inquiry to have, inter alia, free access to the accident site, the aircraft and all the other evidence that is available, immediate access to flight recorders, access to the results of examination of the bodies of victims or of tests made on samples taken from the bodies of victims, etc.

Article 7(2) of the directive further provides that the investigating body shall make public the final accident report in the shortest possible time, and it stipulates that where possible this should be done within 12 months of the date of the accident. Another change is the provision of powers that enable free access to the accident site and all the other evidence that is available.

The purpose of the directive is clearly stated to be *to improve* air safety by facilitating the expeditious holding of investigations, the sole objective of which is the prevention of future accidents and incidents and that it is not designed to apportion blame or liability. The directive also clearly establishes the principle that a safety recommendation must in no case create a presumption of blame or liability for an accident or incident. Article 7.1 states that 'The [investigation] report shall state the sole objective of the investigation … and contain, where appropriate, safety recommendation'.

This clearly reiterates the purpose of an accident investigation as stipulated by Annex 13; however, it needs to be examined whether in practice the technical investigation is used to apportion blameworthiness.

In relation to the legal framework surrounding an aviation accident investigation, the cases examined in the book will examine whether the accident was conducted by an independent accident investigator in accordance with ICAO Annex 13; whether the provisions of EU Directive 94/56 were taken into account and whether the purpose of the technical investigation in relation to not apportioning blame was met.

The directive is very similar to Annex 13; however, its mandatory nature, which requires Member States to bring into force laws, regulations and administrative provisions, provides a uniform legal framework for investigating aviation accidents in Member States. In particular, it provides a specific obligation on Member States to investigate, to determine the status of the investigation, to conduct the investigation in the most expedient way, and to publish a report of the investigation. It is important to stress that the directive provides that Member States are required to define a legal status for the technical investigation of the accident and to ensure co-operation with the judicial enquiry (Article 5.1). It is therefore up to each State to establish an 'independent' accident and investigation body or entity to investigate civil aviation accidents and incidents in order to avoid any conflict of interest and any possible involvement in the causes of the occurrences being investigated. The accident investigation committee should be totally impartial, owing no allegiance to the government or to the industry. Every case should be decided in relation to the air safety accident concerned and the lessons to be learnt therefrom, aiming solely to prevent future similar accidents.

At a domestic level, individual States provide for accident investigation by enacting domestic legislation, largely constructed within the framework of the guidelines laid down by ICAO. The regulations of any domestic legislation must conform to the international requirements of Annex 13, and the EU directive which applies to all 27 Member States. The domestic laws have very similar wording reflecting the philosophy promulgated in the international treaty and in the European Directive in relation to the purpose of investigating an aviation accident.

It is very clearly stipulated in each legal stratum that the purpose of an aviation investigation is to improve safety and prevent the recurrence of accidents in the future. It is also specifically stated that is not the purpose of the investigation to apportion blame or liability.

It is this thread that forms the background to examining the investigation of accidents, the final reports compiled and the ultimate use of the reports in subsequent legal proceedings.

Purpose of the Technical Investigation

The ICAO *Manual of Aircraft Accident Investigation* (ICAO 2000) refers to the purpose of an accident investigation by stating that the primary purpose of the group system is to establish the facts pertinent to an accident by making use of the specialized knowledge and practical experience of the participating individuals with respect to construction and operation of the aircraft involved and to the facilities and services that provided services to the aircraft prior to the accident. It goes on to ensure that undue emphasis is not placed on any single aspect of the accident to the neglect of other aspects which might be significant to the investigation, and that, whenever it is possible to establish a particular point by means of several methods, that all those methods have been resorted to and the results co-ordinated.

Of the 190 ICAO Contracting States, fewer than 20 States have notified ICAO of differences existing between their national regulations and practices, and the International Standards and Recommended Practices of Annex 13. Most Contracting States have specific wording that incorporates the philosophy expounded by Annex 13. An example is Section 7 (1) of the Transport Safety Investigation Act 2003 (Australia) which states:

> The main object of this Act is to improve transport safety by providing for:
> (a)   the reporting of transport safety matters; and
> (b)   independent investigations into transport accidents and other incidents that might affect safety; and

(c)   the making of safety action statements and safety recommendations that draw on the results of those investigations; and

(d)   publication of the results of those investigations in the interests of transport safety.

Section 7 (3) of the Transport Safety Investigation Act 2003 (Australia) states:

> The following are not objects of this Act:
> (a)   apportioning blame for transport accidents and incidents;
> (b)   providing the means to determine the liability of any person in respect of a transport accident or incident;
> (c)   assisting in court proceedings between parties (except as expressly provided by this Act);
> (d)   allowing any adverse inference to be drawn from the fact that a person is subject to an investigation under this Act.

Therefore, accident investigation bodies are now increasingly investigating serious incidents in the same manner as they investigate accidents. Judicial authorities are therefore also increasingly scrutinizing serious incidents and the circumstances surrounding them, looking for acts or omission resulting in the endangering offences stipulated in the relevant ANOs. This can be illustrated by the case of an Olympic Airways A340 flying over Paris en route to New York which entered a violent thunderstorm that caused serious damage to the aircraft and a diversion to Paris. This serious incident occurred as a result of the crew not switching on the weather radar. The prosecuting authorities investigated the actions of the crew but failed to file charges for endangering the aircraft, its passengers and crew. Olympic Airways, however, filed charges against the crew demanding the cost of the diversion and for the damages of the aircraft.

The definitions given of some terms are specific and clear, such as that of a safety 'investigation', which clearly states that the purpose of an investigation is to prevent accidents by determining the cause(s) and making safety recommendations resulting from the analysis of information and data gathered.

Many definitions used in the context of accidents and their investigation, due to their imprecise and ambiguous meanings, cause a lot of confusion and are unfortunately often misleading. In addition, the basic concepts and terms inherent in the investigation of accidents are not afforded commonly accepted definitions. This applies particularly to the concept of 'cause'. For many years, there has been much discussion and disparity surrounding the determining of the 'causes' of accidents. The 'causes' of the accident were linked to errors, acts and omission that opened the window for the judicial authorities or other enforcement agencies to conduct an investigation and in many cases to take action against those parties related to the errors, acts and omissions.

Cause, or Probable Cause

Rimson (2002, pp. 3–6) provides the following analysis of the term 'cause'. The first reference to the term was in the American Air Commerce Act of 1926 requiring the Department of Commerce to: '(e) investigate, record and make public the causes of accidents ...'. In the amendment to the Act nearly eight years later the term 'probable cause' was used. It stated that 'the Secretary of Commerce shall ... make public a statement of the probable cause or causes of the accident ...'. In 1938 the Civil Aeronautics Act established a Safety Board within the Civil Aeronautics Authority, having the duty to 'investigate such accidents and report to the Authority the facts, conditions, and circumstances relating to each accident and the probable cause thereof; and make such recommendations to the Authority as, in its opinion, will tend to prevent similar accidents in the future'. In 1958 the Federal Aviation Administration (FAA) and the Civil Aeronautics Board (CAB) were established. The CAB had the responsibility for 'the promotion of safety in air commerce' and a specific duty of the board was to investigate such accidents and report the facts, conditions and circumstances relating to each accident and the probable cause thereof. In 1966 the Department of Transportation (superior to the FAA and the National Transportation Safety Board [NTSB]) was established. The duties of the NTSB included 'determining the cause or probable cause of transportation accidents'. A further development arose in 1974, when the NTSB was established (P.L. 893-633, 88 Stat. 2166-2173) as an independent agency, which stipulated that its duties were, inter alia, to 'investigate or cause to be investigated (in such detail as it shall prescribe), and determine the facts, conditions, and circumstances and the cause or probable cause or causes of accidents'.

It is evident from the above that United States investigative agencies were required to determine, initially, the 'cause', then the 'probable cause' and later the 'cause or probable cause' or even the 'cause or probable cause or causes', without ever being given a comprehensive statutory definitions of 'cause' or 'probable cause'. This left a tremendous gap resulting in various interpretations of what constituted a 'cause' and a 'probable cause'.

One interpretation of 'probable cause' is that by the Director of the Civil Aviation Authority (CAA) Air Safety Board, Jerry Lederer, who stated:

> We, therefore, endeavor to state how the accident happened and why. The 'why' is our conclusion expressed in terms of probable cause and contributing factors.... It has been our endeavor to stick to a practical pattern which establishes the proximate cause as the probable cause and sets up the underlying or more remote causes as contributing factors. (Flight Safety Foundation 2002).

A further complication arises in that the terms 'proximate cause' and 'probable cause' which are legal terms carrying specific meanings. The first of these, the 'proximate cause' is a specific legal term unlikely to appear in an accident report but it certainly may be used in a court of law.

The two terms are defined as follows in their legal applications (*Black's Law Dictionary* 1990, pp. 804, 1219):

Proximate Cause
- That which, in a natural and continuous sequence, unbroken by any efficient intervening cause, produces injury, and without which the result would not have occurred.
- That which is next in causation to the effect, not necessarily in time or space.
- The proximate cause of an injury is the primary or moving cause, or that which, in a natural and continuous sequence, unbroken by any efficient intervening cause, produces the injury and without which the accident could not have happened, if the injury be one which might be reasonably anticipated or foreseen as a natural consequence of the wrongful act.
- An injury or damage is proximately caused by an act or a failure to act, whenever it appears from the evidence in the case, that the act or omission played a substantial part in bringing about or actually causing injury or damage; and that the injury or damage was either a direct result or a reasonably probable consequence of the act or omission.

Probable Cause
- Reasonable cause; having more evidence for than against.
- A reasonable ground for belief in certain alleged facts.
- A set of probabilities grounded in the factual and practical considerations which govern the decisions of reasonable and prudent persons and is more than mere suspicion but less than the quantum of evidence required for conviction. An apparent state of facts found to exist upon reasonable inquiry (that is, such inquiry as the given case renders convenient and proper), which would induce a reasonably intelligent and prudent man to believe, in a criminal case, that the accused had committed the crime charged, or, in a civil case, that a cause of action existed.
- The evidentiary criterion necessary to sustain an arrest or the issuance of an arrest or search warrant.

There are a number of different legal definitions of 'proximate cause' and 'probable cause' such as, inter alia, direct result, natural consequence, reasonable anticipation, reasonable inquiry, reasonably probable, foreseeability, and so on. When the investigators attempt to apply objective methodologies to achieve their primary objective which is to determine what caused the accident, this inevitably results in a very obscure and perplexing situation. The determining of the causes of an accident is an inherent goal of any investigation, however, there is no single established definition to assist the investigators in using scientific, validated, standard methodologies to produce verifiable conclusions. With no precise, clear definition against which to measure their conclusions, it is therefore impossible for investigators to determine the causes or probable causes of accidents or incidents.

Amongst some of the more widely used terms by investigators to denote this concept of 'causes' are 'causal factors' (Doe 1997), 'determining factors' (Kjellen and Larsson 1981), 'contributing factor' (Hopkins 2000), 'safety problems' (Hendrick and Benner 1987) and 'active failures and latent conditions' (Reason 1997).

According to Hopkins (2000, p. 2), 'one thing is said to be a cause of another if we can say *but for* the first, the second would not have occurred', whereas Leplat (1997, p. 8) states that 'to say that event X is the cause of event Y is to say that the occurrence of X is a necessary condition to the production of Y, in the circumstances considered'. A recommendation made by Kletz (2001) is that one should avoid using the term 'cause' in accident investigation, and one should instead talk about what might have prevented the accident. This is a view that we favour as, in the investigation of an aviation accident and in the writing of the report, by emphasizing who caused the accident rather than what might have prevented it, the investigators assign blame, albeit in an indirect manner. By identifying the 'cause' of the accident, the conclusion is drawn that the event itself is evidence that some person or persons did something that caused the accident to occur or omitted to do what was necessary to avoid the accident.

As it was so aptly put,

> It [Causation] is usually between a consequent and the sum of several antecedents; the concurrence of them all being requisite to produce, that is, to be certain of being followed by the consequent. In such cases it is very common to single out only one of the antecedents under the denomination of Cause, calling the others merely conditions ... The right to give the name of causes to one of them exclusively of the others. (Mill 1843/1872, pp. 326–7)

Assigning blame involves the subjective evaluation of the acts or omissions of persons involved in an accident or incident. In most cases investigators, from their personal experience, know what the actor 'should have done' in a given situation, and assume that it was not done in the correct manner because of the occurrence of the accident or incident. In many cases this subjective evaluation or judgments are evidenced by the choice of words such as, inter alia, 'failed to', 'did not do', 'improperly', and 'incorrectly'.

A study of NTSB aviation accident investigation conducted in the late 1990s (NTSB 1999b) recommended that the statement of causation should clearly state the primary event or failure that led to the accident and that it should be expanded to also include all related causal factors, ranked in terms of their contribution to the event, in accordance with methods that should be stipulated in the NTSB's procedures. It further stated that the NTSB should no longer have a one-line probable cause statement in the report, but that the statement should be a comprehensive one that reflects the fact that an accident is as a result of multiple errors or failures (RAND 1999).

Annex 13 to the ICAO standard (ICAO 2001) specifies merely that an accident report should 'List the findings and causes established in the investigation. The list of causes should include both the immediate and deeper systemic causes' (Conclusions, App-2, p. 3).

It further states:

> 3.2.1 Causes are those events which alone, or in combination with others, resulted in injuries or damage. ...
>
> 3.2.3 Some States list the causes, usually sequentially as they occurred, without attempting to prioritize the causes. Other States would prioritize the causes by using terms such as primary causes and contributing causes.
>
> 3.2.4 When certain of a cause, a definite statement should be used; if reasonably sure of a cause a qualifying word such as 'probable' or 'likely' should be used.

It is evident that, despite such guidance given by ICAO, there are still cases where the report provides 'probable cause(s)' of an accident and in so doing, indirectly point the blame at some persons. As long as the report meets the ICAO standard, there is no reason to specifically state the 'probable cause(s)' of an accident.

There seems to be a growing consensus that to include 'probable cause' in the report is outdated. Many believe that emphasizing a single cause may even be detrimental to gaining a complete understanding of what happened (Fenwick 2006) and that non-pejorative language is more beneficial to the making of a complete safety report (McKellar 2006).

The term 'probable cause' has a different meaning attributed to it in a legal and in a technical sense. Judicial authorities seem to place great importance on this term as there are cases where they relied heavily on the probable cause scenario to initiate legal action against pilots and ATCOs as illustrated by the Olympic Airlines Falcon 900 B accident in 1999 and the Yak-42 accident in Thessaloniki in 1997.

The case studies chosen for examination will consider firstly the use of this term in the final accident report to determine if there is a move away from using the term 'probable cause(s)' as is advocated by the ICAO manual and secondly the reliance, if any that is given to the probable cause scenario by a court of law.

Irrespective of the approach that the accident investigators use, it is imperative that all approaches would reveal the same probable cause. It is also crucial that investigators conducting the technical investigation in accordance with Annex 13 be consciously aware at all times that it is not their role to assign blame and extra care should be taken not to selectively accept facts that support blameworthiness or to use terms that in any way assign blame.

The ICAO *Human Factors Training Manual* (ICAO 1998/2005) states that the investigation of major catastrophes in large-scale, high-technology systems has revealed these accidents to have been caused by a combination of many factors, whose origins could be found in the lack of consideration given to human factors during the design and operating stages of the system, rather than in operational personnel error. Examples of such catastrophes include the accident at the Three Mile Island (Pennsylvania, USA, 28 March 1979) and the Chernobyl nuclear power plant (Ukraine, USSR, 26 April 1986), the Challenger space shuttle disaster (Florida, USA, 28 March 1977) and the Bhopal chemical plant accident (Bhopal, India, 3 December 1984). Large-scale, high-technology systems like nuclear power generation and aviation have been called 'sociotechnical systems', in reference to the complex integrations between their human and technological components. Management factors and organizational accidents are key concepts in socio-technical system's safety. The terms 'system accident' and 'organizational accident' reflect the fact that certain inherent characteristics of socio-technical systems, such as their complexity and the unexpected interaction of multiple failures, will inevitably produce safety breakdowns. In socio-technical systems, remedial action based on safety findings goes beyond those who had the last opportunity to prevent the accident, i.e. the operational personnel, to include the influence of the designers and managers, as well as the structure or architecture of the system. In this approach, the objective is to find *what*, rather than *who*, is wrong.

After the crash in the Florida Everglades of the ValuJet plane, Flight 592, in May of 1996, William Langewiesche (1998), categorizing the accident as a 'system accident', said the following:

> We can find fault among those directly involved – and we probably need to. But if our purpose is to attack the roots of such an accident, we may find them so entwined with the system that they are impossible to extract without toppling the whole structure ... Beyond the question of blame, it requires us to consider that our solutions, by adding to the complexity and obscurity of the airline business, may actually increase the risks of accidents. (pp. 81–98)

The investigation process has been greatly affected and improved by the work conducted by Professor James Reason (1997), who argues that accidents are not isolated events that occur as infrequent one-off events, but that they are in fact the consequences of particular sets of circumstances in which active and latent failures, at times combining with external environmental factors, result in the failure of a system.

Reason's concept is based on his fundamental belief that during an investigation, the investigator should adopt a total system approach to safety in which two kinds of failures, namely both latent and active failures, as well as the various stages in a systematic system failure, must be examined. According to Reason, errors are seen as consequences and not as causes, and the origin of errors is not so much in human nature but in systematic factors that include recurrent error traps in the workplace and the organizational process giving rise to them. A serious shortfall of examining only the human factors in an investigation is that it isolates unsafe acts from their system context. High-technology systems have many defences and safeguards; some engineered, others relying on people and others depending on procedures and administrative controls that aim to protect potential victims from local hazards. In reality, each defensive layer is like slices of Swiss cheese with many holes that are continuously opening and closing and moving their position. The holes in any one slice of cheese will not automatically result in an accident; however, when the holes in many layers line up causing a trajectory of accident opportunity (Reason 2000, pp. 768–70) this is often a recipe for an accident.

The holes in the defences arise as a result of both active failures and latent failures and nearly all accidents involve a combination of these two factors. Active errors occur at the point of contact between a human and some aspect of a larger system (for example a human–machine interface) and are generally readily apparent such as pushing an incorrect button or ignoring a warning light. Active failures are sometimes referred to as errors at the 'sharp end', namely the crew, the pilots and the ATCOs. In other words, errors at the sharp end are noticed first because they are committed by the person closest to the resulting occurrence.

Latent errors (on latent conditions), in contrast, refer to less apparent failures of organization or design that contributed to the occurrence of errors. Latent errors are those at the other end, the 'blunt end' – referring to the many layers in the system affecting the persons at the sharp end. Latent conditions are the 'resident pathogens' within the system. They arise from decisions made by designers, policy writers and top-level management.

Latent conditions can be transformed into error-provoking conditions within the workplace, for example, time pressure, understaffing, inadequate equipment, fatigue and unworkable procedures and design deficiencies. Latent conditions are often dormant within the system for many years before they combine with active failures to create an accident opportunity. They can be identified and remedied before an adverse event occurs. If this is understood, it will lead to a proactive rather than reactive risk management.

Accident investigations can enhance aviation safety and lower the current rate of accidents when they are able to penetrate the 'inner loops' of Reason's model and detect and rectify incorrect decisions by corporate managers and unsafe acts before the occurrence of a major accident or incident. Accidents such as the crash of ValueJet Flight 592, in which all 110 people on board were killed, could have perhaps been avoided if the NTSB conducted an in-depth investigation into the large number of incidents that occurred prior to the crash, including in-flight fires, landing gear malfunctions and the hiring of inadequately trained pilots, all related to organizational failures and defects in the operation of the airline. The cases examined in this book will illustrate whether the accident investigation has penetrated the 'inner loops' of Reason's model by identifying active and latent failures in the organization as opposed to just identifying the errors and mishaps of those at the 'sharp end'.

Significant changes to ICAO Annex 13 were introduced in 1994 and it is now an international requirement that organizational and management information be formally addressed in the accident report. ICAO recommends that the Reason Model should be used when addressing this issue. Many investigation bodies have now adopted a systems safety approach to the investigation.

Aviation accidents are the result of many factors and involve many individuals operating at different levels within a multi-level complex system. Adopting the new approach to accident investigation that is advocated by Reason and recommended by ICAO results in the focus moving away from the individual performing the final error in the chain of events leading up to the accident, and moves towards investigating actions, omissions, decisions, practices and policies within the organization. These decisions often have a more significant role in the occurrence of the accident than the final error(s) made by the pilot or ATCO. This highlights the importance of moving away from the probable cause scenario and accident investigators should critically investigate the whole organizational system, ranging from the regulatory authorities to the decisions of the board of directors, post-holders and all employees.

An inherent part of the investigation is to derive safety lessons from previous accidents. However, learning from previous mistakes also includes learning from other industries and methods of transport (Braithwaite 2004). Braithwaite (2004) provides two examples of multimodal investigation agencies that have been formed in the transport industry, namely, the NTSB and the Transport Safety Board of Canada (TSB) that provide many advances such as the sharing of resources.

As aviation systems become safer, they become increasingly complex which may result in latent defects/conditions being overlooked and perhaps becoming apparent as safety hazards by other triggering events. An investigator therefore, has to be able to examine not only the actions of the individuals involved in an accident or incident, but also the error-producing conditions that may have an impact on their actions.

Since most serious accidents are caused by a number of inter-related causal factors, the investigation of such accidents should be conducted by an investigative team comprised of various disciplines and supported by the appropriate and formal methods of accident investigation.

Members from the International Society of Air Safety Investigators (ISASI) would agree that 'principles and rules of procedure are not systematically organized, and that generally accepted rules of procedure for analyzing, predicting or explaining the accident phenomenon are not available to the accident investigator' (Benner 1975). The ICAO manual that investigators use contains procedures for organizing and co-ordinating the investigation as well as the reporting of investigative findings. However, the principles regarding the scope and development of the hypothesis are not well organized or documented. A further difficulty that investigators face is that accident investigation methods for establishing the validity of their hypothesis are not well defined and are not satisfactorily documented. This may result in an inefficient and incomplete investigation. Additionally, if each accident is perceived as an unscheduled scientific experiment performed to test a hypothesis or theory, the experiment and all the costs of performing it will be futile without a hypothesis or theory to evaluate.

A further issue that may affect the investigation of an accident, the independence of the investigating body, needs to be discussed.

One of the most crucial aspects of an accident investigation board is its independence from any other government or other agency, body or persons in order to allow the board to conduct its investigation in an unbiased manner striving to establish and to disseminate the probable causes of an accident so that future accidents are prevented.

This independence is now a legal requirement in accordance with European Directive 94/56/EC (European Council 1994). However, there are still cases where one could question whether or not the accident investigation is conducted in an unbiased and independent manner. The following scenario is a recent example that raises this issue.

On 1 January 2007, an Indonesian Adam Air B737 with 96 passengers and six crew lost contact with ATC at 35,000 ft and crashed into the ocean. The official investigation was conducted by the Indonesian National Committee of Transport Safety (KNKT). The founder and chairman of Adam Air (formerly Adam Sky Connection Airlines) is also a speaker in Indonesia's House of Representatives which has a say in determining the budget of the KNKT, the very body that will be investigating the accident (*Air Accident Digest* 2007). Evidently, the above facts raise serious questions regarding the impartiality of the investigation which may be mitigated by appropriate national legislation.

Most accidents are the result of many inter-related causal factors, and not from just one single cause. All the actors or decision-makers influence the work process and the outcome of an event and may directly or indirectly influence the accident scenario and this intricacy should be taken into account in choosing the method for investigating a particular accident.

The amount of research conducted regarding the investigation of aviation accidents is encouraging. A study examining the operations of the NTSB over 30 years (RAND 1999) suggests the following four areas that need immediate action. Firstly, the investigative procedures and methods need to be modernized to take into account the complexity of the accidents in light of modern aircraft design and operation. Secondly, the available resources need to be increased, in respect of both personnel and facilities for testing and training staff. Given that the party system is a primary part of the investigative process, the third suggestion is that methods to enhance the party process to provide access to independent analytical and engineering resources during the investigation, such as other agencies and laboratories, universities and independent experts, should be considered. Fourthly, the statement of the 'probable cause' of the accident should be expanded to include all other causal factors listed in order of priority.

Process of an Investigation

Accepting that an aviation accident is caused by a chain of events, current investigation processes also consider the complex inter-relationships between the actions of individuals and the task and organizational factors and the effect that these may have had on human performance, as well as on the safety of the aviation system as a whole. Investigations are initiated usually subsequent to an event involving some kind of damage, harm, destruction, loss, injury, death, cost or crime.

The normal procedure of an investigation is to:

1. establish the scope and level of the investigation;
2. collect evidence;
3. review the evidence for completeness;
4. analyse the evidence and draw conclusions;
5. provide a report on the results of the investigation; and
6. make recommendations based on the findings of the investigation.

Annex 13 refers the reader to the ICAO *Manual of Aircraft Accident Investigation* for the organization and conduct of the investigation (ICAO 1970). Whilst there is nothing specific in the Foreword to the manual with regard to the actual process of investigation, it provides a guide for accident investigators, enabling them to follow a uniform system of investigating an aviation accident.

Throughout the investigation there is an ongoing process of reviewing the evidence gathered as it comes to light. Many sub-investigations take place during the course of an investigation. Continually reviewing the evidence and sharing the information gathered with all the sub-groups involved plays a vital role in ensuring that time, effort and cost are not squandered on unnecessary collection of evidence.

Often, when arriving on the scene of an accident that may have a number of different possible scenarios as to the cause of the accident, an investigator goes through an initial process of elimination.

In this regard, the *Manual of Aircraft Accident Investigation* (ICAO 2000) warns against drawing premature conclusions and stresses that each investigation should make use of an elimination technique whereby, according to the circumstances, certain areas can be eliminated early on in the investigation process as being possible causes of the accident; consequently, other areas requiring extensive, in-depth investigation become apparent.

Reviewing the evidence collected for correctness and completion permits the investigation to progress onto the next stage which is the final analysis of the evidence. This will allow the investigator to establish how and why the accident occurred, by reaching logical conclusions from the factual data gathered and only from evidence obtained during the investigation.

The analysis of the data once it has been gathered is perhaps the most difficult phase in an accident investigation as very few guidelines are offered by ICAO. The ICAO report format deals mainly with the writing of the report and not with the analysis of the data. Many of the reports written over the years spark off much controversy and debate and are not universally acceptable.[1] Very clear guidelines relating specifically to the analysis of data are crucial and long overdue.

As the purpose of conducting an investigation of an aviation accident is to prevent future accidents, the final report includes a number of safety recommendations. The safety recommendations must be supported by the evidence obtained from the investigation and other related sources. However, there is no framework in place to ensure that the safety lessons are learnt or that corrective actions have been implemented.

The final stage of the investigation is to draft a report proportionate to the level and scope of the investigation. However, gaps and lacunae, vagueness and incompleteness in reports, inadequate gathering of data, incorrect manipulation of data, the application of unsound rationale and non-exploration of alternative propositions will not only frustrate the investigation, it will in effect, result in the drafting of poor recommendations. Consequently, the purpose of an accident investigation which is to prevent similar accidents from occurring through the recommendation of effective changes may be hampered.

Level and Scope of an Investigation

Prior to commencing any form of investigation, it is crucial that the level and scope of the investigation be clearly defined. This will often depend on factors such as, inter alia, the amount of resources available to the investigator, the allocation of time and workload and any pressure constraints.

Some of the problems investigators face in the absence of a clear theory are: 'How do you establish the scope of your investigation? How far back in time must you delve – an hour, a day, a year, two years, five? What rules of procedure or what principles establish the beginning or end of the accident? How is one assured of enough facts in an investigation, and how are the facts to be reported distinguished from the facts that are not to be reported? What rules or principles govern these decisions? (Benner 1975).

Without clearly defined theories and principles on which to base the investigation and guide and shape their activities, the investigators are faced with a very difficult role. It is therefore extremely important for investigators of an accident to have a

---

1 See, for example, the discussions of the air accidents at Munich in 1958 and Cali in 1994 in RAE (1964) and Stewart (1986).

theoretical basis from which to work. A key factor in the investigation is the safety benefits that are expected. Many national air safety investigation agencies adopt policies that afford levels of investigation in relation to the benefits they hope to derive from the investigation.

An important question to be considered is whether all aviation accidents or incidents should be investigated. An initial response may be that this should be so, however, the answer may lie in the degree of investigation that is justified and is appropriate.

Traditionally, many accident investigation branches conducted an investigation into all accidents and incidents. Nowadays, however, many bureaus are selective in the accidents or incidents that they investigate. There are two main reasons for the adoption of a selective approach. The first is that as a result of limited resources, it was thought better to concentrate all possible resources on in-depth investigations that would contribute the most to aviation safety. The second is the realization that no real benefit to aviation safety was gained from investigating accidents and incidents that recurred. This selective investigating policy is largely based on various pre-selected criteria, such as, inter alia, incidents or accidents that affect fare-paying passengers and that incite the most public interest as well as the type of aircraft and type of operation involved.

An example of a selective approach adopted is that of the Bureau of Air Safety Investigation (BASI)[2] as it was called before it merged with other Australian Transport Safety Agencies in July 1999 to form the Australian Transport Safety Bureau (ATSB):

> In recent years, the Bureau has adopted a policy of selective investigation, similar to many of our equivalent organisations in other countries. The traditional approach in Australia had been to investigate everything, no matter how minor. However, many categories of air safety occurrence are repetitive in nature, such as ground loops involving aircraft with tail wheel undercarriages, and no new prevention knowledge is gained by continuing to investigate such events. However, the law requires that all accidents and incidents must be reported. Because BASI receives all these reports, it retains the ability to monitor trends, and can initiate an investigation into safety issues raised – for example, by a number of relatively minor occurrences. While these events individually would not warrant full investigation, considered as a group they may be indicative of broader systemic safety deficiencies … (Mayes 1997, p. 110)

In practice ATSB does not distinguish operationally between accidents and incidents – they are all 'safety occurrences'. The objective of selective investigation is to concentrate the ATSB's resources on in-depth investigations which offer the greatest potential to enhance air safety. BASI has developed and refined various

---

2   The agency of the Australian government responsible for the investigation of accidents and incidents occurring to civil aircraft in Australia and its territories.

criteria to decide which events will be looked at most closely – one of these is a primary emphasis on the safety of fare-paying passengers in any category of operation – high-capacity regular public transport (RPT), low capacity RPT and charter, and other commercial operations involving fare-paying passengers.

This very significant change in most accident investigation bureaus is the shift from primarily reactive organizations investigating accidents and incidents after they occur, to organizations that are proactive and concerned with preventing threats to safety. In this respect, additional resources are dedicated to identifying deficiencies in the aviation system that have the potential, combined with the right combination of events and circumstances, to becoming significant factors in accidents and incidents. In addition to determining what went wrong at the sharp end, viz., the cockpit, the control tower, cabin or maintenance area, focus is also placed on identifying any underlying factors in the aviation system that might have contributed to the occurrence. For example, a rejected take-off followed by an evacuation may be relevant in identifying latent factors such as poor communication, inadequate training and supervision and so on.

One of the most notable selective investigations that took place was the investigation of the level burst rate around London Heathrow airport. A large number of incidents were reported, but no accident occurred from the failure of pilots or ATCOs to maintain adequate separation between aircrafts. The UK Air Accident Investigation Branch (AAIB) chose to conduct an in-depth investigation into the matter that resulted in the implementation of a number of new ATC policies and phraseologies, the redrafting of Standard Instrument Departures (SIDs) and a large campaign to make pilots aware of the problem. Evidently, this correctly applied selective approach, indicative of the new proactive approach to aviation safety, did enhance aviation safety.

In relation to the size and scope of investigating an accident, the ICAO *Manual of Aircraft Accident Investigation* (ICAO 2000) emphasizes that the enormity of the task and the scope of the investigation be assessed early to ensure efficient planning of the investigating team, allocation of skills and organization of the tasks involved.

The time and resource constraints imposed on the investigating authorities and their investigators may lead to tremendous pressure which in turn may result in a job not done well and in a sub-standard investigation. Having a formal recognized methodology will undoubtedly lead to a highly efficient and more just investigation that would be on a par with other investigations.

After having decided on the level and scope of the investigation, its progress should be continually monitored and critically reviewed. Any changes, be it widening the scope and increasing resources, often as a result of the public interest or the parties involved, or reducing the scope according to the safety benefits expected, should be swiftly and efficiently implemented.

When one examines the history of accident investigation, it becomes evident that there is a trend to carry out a deeper investigation than just identifying technical failures or the human errors by those at the far end. The ICAO *Manual of Aircraft Accident Investigation* does not state when the investigation should be stopped. It only refers to the working groups by stating that their activities cease when their group reports have been completed and submitted to the investigator-in-charge. Reason (1997) suggests that investigators should stop an investigation when the causes identified are no longer controllable. Inevitably, various parties will stop at different points. A company should trace the causes of an accident back to their own management systems, whereas supervisory authorities or permanent investigation boards should also identify any weaknesses in the regulatory system that could have contributed to the accident.

Safety Recommendations

A major purpose of investigating aviation accidents is to make recommendations that will help prevent the recurrence of such accidents. However, there are many problems related to this. It is important to note that a major difference arises in the investigation of an accident and in the making of safety recommendations. Whilst the former is based on a retrospective task – establishing what has happened – the latter has an element of prediction as it aims to influence future behaviour.

It is evident that the safety recommendations stem from the cause(s) identified by the investigators. Investigators therefore make judgment calls and draw conclusions about what they have determined are the causes of the accident. However, in order to prevent something from recurring it is essential to first have a very clear understanding of what happened and why it happened. Only then can proper recommendations be made.

In addition to the problems surrounding the 'causes' of an accident, there are many deficiencies outlined (Benner 1992) in safety recommendations that raise a number of questions regarding the effectiveness of the recommendations made by aviation accident investigators.

Initially, it was an easier task to make safety recommendations as usually only one cause was identified for each accident. With the realization that accidents were a result of numerous causes, more than one recommendation was made. The practice of making safety recommendations was further influenced by the notion of making recommendations to various parties. As a result, the official accident investigation report often provides many recommendations.

Making safety recommendations does not ensure that the investigator has correctly defined the problem or risk or that the proposed recommendation will fix the problem and prevent future accidents. The individualistic approach of each investigator determines how they identify proposed actions to fix the problem as well as how many actions are proposed. There are no formal systematic, methodical or validated techniques for the investigator to apply that will enable him to arrive at recommendations ensuring the prevention of future similar accidents.

An important lacuna in making safety recommendations stems from the fact that there is no training provided for doing so. This should be included in the investigation manual as part of the investigators' training courses. Another gap relates to follow-up practices. Research has shown that follow-up largely deals with the implementation of recommendations and not with the effectiveness in solving the problems they address. There is no validation process for the recommendations, to determine if they were implemented or to assess whether the problems addressed were in fact permanently solved.

The Role of Accident Investigators

The success of each investigation rests to a large extent on the quality of those conducting the investigation. In order that the investigation be conducted in an effective manner, the accident investigators must be professionals, properly trained and be equipped with the required personal skills and physical attributes.

The ICAO *Manual of Aircraft Accident Investigation* (ICAO 2000, Part I.3.3) provides some insight into the requisite qualities of an investigator by stating that as the aircraft accident investigation is a highly specialized task, it should only be undertaken by trained personnel who have qualities including, inter alia, an inquisitive nature, dedication, diligence, patience, perseverance, logic, humility, integrity and respect for human dignity. Additionally, the investigator should possess a good sound working knowledge of aviation and factors which affect operations as a whole, as well as good technical skills.

It is not sufficient to nominate, as the occasion arises, a person with specialist aviation knowledge as the investigator, for accident investigation is a specialized task itself.

Investigations often take place under much pressure and constraints, sometimes under physically challenging circumstances. The investigation kit should always be complete and ready to be taken on site. The investigator needs to ensure that they are physically fit and that they have received the appropriate vaccinations for diseases likely to be incurred such as, for example, tetanus and hepatitis.

Another very important factor in investigating is the sensitive nature of the work which often requires the investigator to obtain statements and pertinent information from people who have just been involved in an accident and who are in a state of shock and severely affected by the experience they have encountered. Sensitivity, understanding and tact have to be employed at all times by the investigators.

The clarity and transparency of the investigator's role is of utmost importance. The investigator must also ensure that he establish an open and frank line of communication with all involved, especially with the people who are directly involved and who can provide the necessary information and details, always ensuring confidentiality and stressing that a no-blame approach will prevail at all times during the investigation.

Due to the tragic nature of serious accidents involving many people, the media will often appear at the accident site. It is very important that investigators receive media awareness training in order to ensure an effective interaction with the media, causing minimum disruption to the accident site and the investigation and permitting the media to accurately cover the story. The case studies in this book will examine the role and influence, if any, that the media has on the investigation of an aviation accident. Even though the act of investigating is continuously developing, resulting in very few accidents remaining unsolved, there is a need for further changes in the system such as in the training of investigators (Braithwaite 2002b).

Some of the responsibilities of the investigator are highlighted in the ICAO *Manual of Aircraft Accident Investigation*, which states:

> When called to the scene of the accident the investigator should endeavor to arrive as soon as possible; similarly, in his dealings with witnesses and other people concerned in the accident, he should be prompt in attending appointments and correct in his manner, regardless of how he may feel personally. Above all the investigator must be accurate and factual; he must observe, interpret and record clearly and accurately at all times, because his record of what is seen, heard and done, may well prove to be the only record available, the analysis of which may have far-reaching effects on individual people, aircraft and equipment and aviation safety as a whole. (ICAO 2000, Appendix 1, p. 2)

Clearly, the investigator has a daunting but crucial task. Government investigators are assisted by a number of legislative enactments that give them numerous powers, often placing them in a more advantageous position than others connected to the accident.

The investigator's role is to determine what happened by identifying facts, conditions and circumstances. Any vagueness that arises can be eliminated by gathering additional facts, data and information. Once it has been determined what happened, the scenario and the hypothesis should then be tested and proved.

The ICAO *Human Factors Training Manual* (ICAO 1998b, p. 2-4-4, para. 4.2.5) stresses the fact that humans do not act alone, but are part of larger, more complex system and that when a catastrophe has occurred; the investigators must ensure that all the elements of the system are investigated when determining why the accident occurred. It specifically states that 'the investigation of Human Factors in aircraft accidents and incidents should form an integral part of the entire investigation and resultant report' (p. 2-4-9, para. 4.3.1).

The International Society of Air Safety Investigators (ISASI) code of conduct (ISASI 2004) states that in maintaining the highest standards of objectivity, each member shall:

> 3.1 Ensure that all items presented as facts reflect honest perceptions or physical evidence that have been checked in so far as practicable for accuracy.

> 3.6 Avoid speculation except in the sense of presenting a hypothesis for testing during the fact-finding and analysis process.

It is the last point that has great significance as it stresses the need to avoid speculation and states that in cases where this is done, the hypothesis should be tested. It does not, however, require the testing of more than one hypothesis to ensure that all possible explanations are exhausted.

Investigators gain access to confidential information and it is imperative not only to the actual investigation, but to aviation safety at large, that such information is not misused. This issue is specifically dealt within Annex 13 (ICAO 2001, Paragraph 5.12) which states:

Disclosure of Records

The State conducting the investigation of an accident or incident, wherever it occurred, shall not make the following records available for purposes other than accident or incident investigation, unless the appropriate authority for the administration of justice ... determines that their disclosure outweighs the adverse domestic and international impact such action may have on that or any future investigations.

(a)   all statements taken from persons by the investigation authorities in the course of their investigation;

(b)   all communications between persons having been involved in the operation of the aircraft

(c)   medical or private information regarding persons involved in the accident or incident;

(d)   cockpit voice recordings and transcripts from such recordings; and

(e)   opinions expressed in the analysis of information, including flight data information.

These records shall be included in the final report or its appendices only when pertinent to the analysis of the accident or incident. Parts of the records not relevant to the analysis shall not be disclosed.

Paragraph 5.12 continues with a note. The note draws attention to the fact that the information contained in the records listed could be utilized inappropriately for subsequent disciplinary, civil, administrative and criminal proceedings. The note continues with somewhat of a warning: 'If such information is distributed, it may, in the future, no longer be openly disclosed to investigators. Lack of access to such information would impede the investigative process and seriously affect flight safety.'

Chapter 4
Knowing and Doing

There are many cases in which aviation professionals have been criminally prosecuted subsequent to an aviation accident or serious incident and in this chapter we examine a number of cases of legal proceedings following an aviation accident in which pilots, ATCOs and other aviation professionals were prosecuted for their alleged role in the occurrence of the aviation accident.

Specific cases were chosen that involved serious accidents resulting in the criminal prosecution of pilots, ATCOs and other aviation professionals. The official technical accident investigation and available legal documentation were examined. The case study approach is one whereby cases are investigated in order to answer specific questions. Cases provide a range of different kinds of evidence which must be abstracted and collated in order to get the best answers to the research questions. A range of different kinds of evidence from documents (such as, inter alia, the official accident reports, the proceedings in the litigation, testimonies, court transcripts) data and interviews can be collected from cases. This approach was chosen as it uses highly qualitative data collection techniques. These enable a deep understanding of the case in question. Consideration was given to the limitations of the value of the case study approach, such as the question of how far understanding of a specific case can be transferred to other situations and it is understood that the question of reliability is a limitation of the approach chosen.

This method was best suited to examine the intermingling of the judicial and technical investigations, the use of the technical report and evidence from the technical investigation by a court of law. It was also considered best suited to examine the following issues: how far the accident was investigated in accordance with ICAO Annex 13 (ICAO 2001) and EU Directive 94/56 (European Council 1994); the scope and level of the investigation as well any external factors, if any, which may have affected the technical investigation; whether the final report of the investigation included a probable cause theory and crew statements and testimony. In addition, the judicial investigation and/or any other investigations conducted subsequent to the accident were looked at to determine the charges filed against pilots, ATCOs and other aviation professionals, the use of the technical investigation report and sensitive aviation data such as the cockpit voice recorder (CVR) and flight data recorder FDR in a court of law; the court's proceedings and decision, the appeal and the time span between the accident and judgment.

The cases are presented in chronological order.

British Airways Trident 3B and Inex-Adria Aviopromet DC-9 Mid-air Collision – Zagreb, Croatia (1976)

Perhaps one of the most well-known cases of criminalization of aviation professionals is that subsequent to the mid-air collision over Zagreb in 1976.

On 10 September 1976, the world's deadliest mid-air collision with the highest death toll at the time occurred when a British Airways Flight 476 Trident 3B, with nine crew members and 54 passengers en route from London to Istanbul, and an Inex-Adria Aviopromet Flight 550, a DC-9 with five crew and 108 passengers scheduled to fly from Yugoslavia to West Germany, collided in mid-air over Zagreb at 11.15 am local time. All 176 people on board both flights were killed.

In 1976 the Zagreb Air Route Traffic Control Center (ARTCC) was the second busiest in Europe. It had 30 ATCOs who had to cope with traffic that required many more controllers. The problematic modern radar system which was installed in 1973 was being used only as back-up and as a result Zagreb ARTCC relied on procedural control whereby pilots transmitted their positions at specified points along the airways which were then being monitored by the radar system. Zagreb airspace was divided into three layers, a lower, middle and upper section. At the time of the accident, the shift supervisor, three upper-section controllers and two middle-section controllers were on duty.

The technical investigation attributed the accident to the failure to provide the required separation of the aircraft, untimely recognition of conflict separation and application of imprecise measures for prevention of the collision. It lists a number of acts and omissions of the upper-section assistant controller as the main contributing factors of the accident.

Immediately after the accident the judicial investigation commenced. By noon of the same day of the accident, all five controllers were in custody being interrogated. All were later released, except the controller who was the upper-section assistant controller at the time of the accident, who remained in custody until the trial. He was the youngest member of the Zagreb staff and was on his third consecutive day of 12-hour shifts. Charges were filed against all the controllers in accordance with Articles 271-271 of the Penal Code of Yugoslavia for endangering railway, sea or air traffic and threatening the lives of men or property. The trial commenced on 11 April 1977 before a judge and the five members of the Grand Council of the Zagreb District Court. The upper-section assistant controller at the time of the accident was the only one found guilty and sentenced to seven years' imprisonment. After a petition and accusations that he was used as a scapegoat, he was released on 29 November 1978 after serving 27 months in prison (Weston and Hurst 1982).

Air France A320 – Habsheim, France (1988)

On 26 June 1988, a brand new fly-by-wire[1] A320 aircraft, Flight 296, as part of an air show in Habsheim, France, was to perform a series of flights on behalf of the Mulhouse Flying Club, overflying the Mulhouse-Habsheim airport twice, first at low speed, gear down at 100 feet and then at high speed in clean configuration. The aircraft took off at 14:41 and climbed to 1,000 feet above ground level. The crew initiated the descent three minutes inbound to Habsheim airfield. The first officer informed the captain that the aircraft was reaching 100 feet at 14:45:14. Eight seconds later the aircraft descended to 50 feet and then to 30–35 feet. Go-around power was added, the A320 continued and touched trees at the end of the runway with a 14 deg. pitch attitude and then sank slowly into the forest. A fire broke out, three passengers died in the accident and over 50 were injured. This was the first ever accident involving an A320.

The A320 was one of a new generation of highly sophisticated fly-by-wire computerized aircraft aimed to revolutionize aircraft manufactured up to that time. The air show was an important marketing tool to promote the aircraft. There were 500 orders placed for this aircraft at the time of the accident. The A320 put its manufacturer, Airbus, years in front of their competitors in terms of technological advancement and aircraft protection systems set to advance aviation safety. There would have been serious consequences to Airbus if any faults with the aircraft's new fly-by-wire flight control systems or the full automatic digital engine computer were to appear. On the other hand, confidence in the new computerized A320 would ensure commercial victory for Airbus as well as the French administration, a shareholder in the Airbus consortium. The day after the accident both France and Britain suspended operation of the A320 fleet. The accident attracted world media attention and the developments were closely followed by aviation experts and safety organizations. The French media in particular, aware of the tremendous financial and political consequences which could have resulted if the safety of the A320 was being questioned, provided continuous coverage of the developments of both the technical and judicial investigations initiated subsequent to the accident.

Shortly after the accident, the French Minister of Transportation, the company Air France and the manufacturer, Airbus Industrie, publicly declared that there was no problem with the aircraft. This statement was based on the initial information obtained from the automatic flight data printout.

The official accident investigation was conducted by the French Bureau d'Enquêtes et d'Analyses (BEA), in accordance with ICAO Annex 13. The BEA stated that the probable cause of the accident was the very low flyover height, lower than the surrounding obstacles; very slow speed, reducing to reach maximum

---

1 Fly-by-wire – the term used to describe new aircraft that had the data regarding the flight controls (the ailerons, rudder, elevators) electronically transmitted to the hydraulic jacks and engines from computers that calculated the pilot's flight instructions.

possible angle of attack; engine speed at flight idle and the late application of go-around power, which led the aircraft to impact the trees. The report further states that if the descent below 100 feet was not deliberate it may have been the result of not taking proper account of the visual and aural information intended to give the height of the aircraft (BEA 1990).

A critical analysis of the wording of this section indicates that it clearly refers to all actions and omissions of the pilot, thus indirectly pointing to blameworthy parties. The probable cause theory was based on the FDR readouts, CVR transcript, crew statements and a video taken by a spectator at the air show who had recorded the flight. The captain had his licence revoked and was removed from flying duties.

Parallel to the technical investigation, a judicial investigation was also launched. French national law provides that the judicial authority, when it is deemed that a possible criminal offence has taken place, will conduct a separate investigation from the official technical investigation conducted under the provisions of Annex 13. It further provides that the judicial authorities have total control over the wreckage and documents as they remain under the control of the judicial authority (Supplement to annex 13; ICAO 2003). The FDR and CVR therefore remain in the custody of the judiciary for examination by independent experts; however, in this case they were taken undamaged from the aircraft two hours after the accident by the civil aviation authorities and kept for ten days until they were confiscated by the investigating magistrate. When they were eventually returned, the black boxes (on which the official report was based) showed a number of anomalies which resulted in the authenticity of the black boxes being doubted and led to speculation that they were tampered with or may have even been replaced (Rogers 1998).

Five people were accused of manslaughter by the Court of Colmar in France; the two pilots, the president of the Habsheim air club, a security officer of Air France, and the head of flight operations for authorizing the crew to descend to 100 feet instead of the minimum 170 feet required by the relevant regulations. The appointed experts as well as the Disciplinary Committee concluded that the crew did not intentionally fly below the regulatory minimum. They therefore lacked the essential element of intention and were held not to be legally responsible for this. The court attributed responsibility for this on the Director of the Operations of Air France who programmed the height for the flight.

During the trial the prosecution relied heavily on the data from the CVR and FDR which were admissible in court. The trial became a struggle between the defence, who disputed the findings of the FDR data, the prosecution and the expert witnesses. The lower court did not accept the possibility that the flight recorders could have been tampered with and denied the request by the captain's counsel to have the flight data recordings annulled.

On 14 March 1997 (nearly nine years after the accident) the Court of Colmar (Tribunal de Grande Instance 1997) imposed a sentence on the captain of six months' imprisonment and a further 12 months suspended on probation and a sentence of 12 months suspended on probation on the co-pilot. The other defendants also received prison sentences suspended on probation. The co-pilot accepted the sentence and continued his employment with Air France.

The captain, on whom the major responsibility for the accident was placed, appealed. The appeal was started in January 1998 at the Appeals Court of Colmar (Cour d'Appel de Colmar 1998). Again, the disputed black boxes were used as evidence. In April 1998, the Court of Appeal declared the captain guilty of manslaughter and bodily harm and increased the original sentence to ten months' imprisonment and a further ten months on probation.

In May 1998 (ten years after the accident) the Swiss Institute of Police Forensic Evidence and Criminology (IPSC) submitted its official report regarding the authenticity of the black boxes. The IPSC report stated that the boxes used in the trial against the captain were not the ones taken from the aircraft. The IPSC analysed the photographs taken from the accident showing a man carrying the black boxes. It concluded that the digital flight data recorder DFDR taken from the aircraft had straight white stripes on its side perpendicular to the edges and that the DFDR presented at the trial had angled white lines on its side and therefore the DFDR presented at the trial was not the DFDR taken from the scene of the accident (Rogers 1998).

The captain then filed a claim with the highest court of France, the Supreme Court, in order to have the first trial annulled for evidence tampering.

There were many doubts as to the authenticity of the recorders used in the trial. The analysis of the CVR data was given to the Acoustics Department of the Gendarmerie, a government body; the role of checking the authenticity of the data tapes was given to an organization who reported to the DGCA (the French civil aviation authority); the CEV (the Flight Test Centre), which also reports to the DGA, was named to verify the acceleration data; the engine manufacturer was asked to check the engines despite the fact that an engine malfunction was suspected; three engineers from the company that distributed the flight recorders were asked to verify there was no data forgery. The evidence of crucial data was therefore given to involved parties which could thus have had serious implications. In addition, Airbus greatly protested against having the analysis conducted by independent organizations outside France, fearing that their competitors might ensure that the analysis may be biased (Rogers 1998).

The public prosecutor in this case did not comply with his legal duty to order the serial numbers of the CVR and DFDR to be recorded. Nor did he appoint a judicial police officer as he should have done to accompany the recorders to the investigating magistrate after they were duplicated by the BEA Accident Enquiry Bureau. The CEV Test Flight Centre also failed to record the serial numbers of the CVR when it received it, raising serious questions and suspicion. It was also shown that the DFDR was illegally 'lent' to Air France from 26 July to 17 August 1988 by one of the prosecution experts. The handling of the black boxes in this case was not done in accordance with French law which is very clear and specific with regards to flight recorders (Rogers 1998).

Air Inter A320 Flight 148 – Mont Sainte-Odile, France (1992)

On 20 January 1992 an Air Inter A320, Flight 148, on a scheduled domestic flight departed from Lyon Saint-Exupery International Airport, France. The aircraft was scheduled to land at Strasbourg but crashed near Mont Sainte-Odile, whilst on approach for landing. The accident was caused by the aircraft's wrongly programmed flight control unit (FCU), a consequence of the crew's failure to notice that the FCU was in the incorrect vertical speed mode when programming the angle of descent. The excessive descent took the aircraft below its minimum safe altitude which resulted in the aircraft's crashing into the cloud-covered mountains. At the time of the accident it was not mandatory for French aircraft to be installed with a Ground Proximity Warning System (GPWS) and therefore the crew had no warning of the imminent impact. Of the 96 passengers and crew on board, five crew members and 82 passengers were killed.

The technical investigation was conducted by the BEA in accordance with ICAO Annex 13 (ICAO 2001) and EU Directive 94/56 (European Council 1994) and the final report was released in November 1993.

The final report attributed the accident to the following:

> The crew was late in modifying its approach strategy due to ambiguities in communication with air traffic control; as the controller's radar guidance which did not place the aircraft in a position allowing the pilot flying to align it, the crew was faced with a sudden workload peak in making necessary lateral corrections, preparing the aircraft configuration and initiating the descent; the key event in the accident sequence was the start of aircraft descent at the distance required by the procedure but at an abnormally high vertical speed and the crew's failure to correct this abnormally high rate of descent due to a number of possible reasons outlined. The accident was made possible by the crew's failure to notice that the resulting vertical trajectory was incorrect. This failure was attributed to a number of acts and failures by the crew. In addition, the report stated that the ergonomic design of the auto-pilot vertical modes controls, which it believed tends to increase the probability of certain errors in use, particularly during a heavy workload, could have contributed to the creation of the accident situation. (BEA 1992)

Following the judicial investigation conducted by the French prosecuting authorities which was conducted parallel to the technical investigation, charges of involuntary injuries and involuntary manslaughter were laid against the director general of the French Civil Aviation Authority, the manager of the civil aviation authority (DGAC), Air Inter and Airbus Industries, the manager of Air Inter, the manager of Airbus Industries, the former Air Inter deputy director general and the military ATCO on duty at the time.

The trial commenced in the Colmar Correctional Court, 14 years after the accident. The court found no definite causal link between the accident and the failings of which the four former Air Inter and DGAC employees were accused of, such as not ensuring aircraft were installed with an alarm system that would have warned the pilots that they were close to the ground. The six defendants were eventually cleared of all criminal charges. Airbus and Air France (Air Inter was the domestic subsidiary of Air France) were found liable for damages and had to pay compensation to the relatives of the people who died in that accident.

ValueJet MD DC-9-32 Accident – Florida, USA (1996)

On 11 May 1996 a MD DC-9-32, ValuJet Flight 592, a scheduled flight from Miami, Florida, to Atlanta, Georgia, crashed in the Florida Everglades at a speed of 500 miles an hour, shortly after take-off from Miami International Airport, at 2:04 pm local time after one hour four minutes' delay. At 2:10 the crew noticed what they believed to be an electrical problem. The pilot apparently attempted to return to Miami for an emergency landing. At 2:14 the aircraft disappeared from radar. Improperly packed oxygen generators ignited, leading to an uncontrollable fire which burned through control cables and filled the cabin with smoke. The aircraft was damaged beyond repair. All the 105 passengers, the pilot, the co-pilot and three flights attendants died. The NTSB determined that the fire in the Class D cargo compartment was the result of the actuation of one or more oxygen generators improperly carried as cargo from the failure of SabreTech to properly prepare, package and identify the chemical oxygen generators before presenting them to ValuJet for carriage; the failure of ValuJet to properly oversee its contract maintenance programme and the failure of FAA to require smoke detection and fire suppression systems in Class D cargo compartments (NTSB 1997).

The US Federal and Florida State Prosecutors brought criminal charges, 110 counts of manslaughter and 110 counts of third degree murder, against ValuJet's maintenance contractor, SabreTech, SabreTech's maintenance supervisors and two mechanics who worked on the plane. In addition, SabreTech was charged with violation of hazardous material regulations, failing to train its employees on proper handling of hazardous materials, placing a destructive device on board an aircraft, conspiracy to falsify records and making false statements. SabreTech's maintenance supervisor and two mechanics who worked on the plane were charged with conspiracy and making false statements.

ValueJet was never prosecuted but SabreTech was the first American aviation company to be criminally prosecuted for its role in an American airline crash. SabreTech settled the state charges by agreeing to plead no contest and to a state charge of mishandling hazardous material; the company agreed to donate $500,000 to an aviation safety group and a charity. SabreTech was found guilty on the mishandling hazardous materials and improper training charges. SabreTech's maintenance supervisor and the one mechanic were acquitted on all charges. The second mechanic failed to appear in court and is still currently missing. SabreTech was fined $2 million and ordered to pay $9 million in restitution.

In 2001, an appeal was lodged in the United States 11th Circuit Court of Appeals and SabreTech was acquitted of the federal charges based on its wilful mishandling of the oxygen generators as they could not find intent to harm. The conviction for improper training was upheld and SabreTech was given a $500,000 fine, three years' probation and no restitution.

Aerosweet Yakovlev-42 – Thessaloniki, Greece (1997)

On 17 December 1997, a Yakovlev 42, Flight AEW-241 operated by Aerosweet Airlines of Ukraine, on a regular scheduled passenger flight from Odessa International Airport, Ukraine, to Macedonia International Airport Thessaloniki Hellas, was performing a VOR/ILS approach for runway 16. Executing the missed approach procedure, due to not having the runway in sight, the aircraft followed a path of significant deviation from the anticipated one and crashed into the mountainous terrain of Katerini, killing all 74 people aboard the aircraft (Hellenic Republic Ministry of Transport and Communications 1998).

Subsequent to the accident the official accident investigation took place in accordance with ICAO, Annex 13 (ICAO 2001). The official accident investigation was conducted by the Hellenic Republic, Ministry of Transport and Communications, Aircraft Accidents Inquiry Council and a final report was published. Accredited representatives from Russia and Ukraine participated in the investigation. The probable cause of the accident was stated as being the crew's failure to adequately plan and execute the missed approach, utilize the Macedonia Airport radio-navigational aids, declare an emergency when they lost orientation and maintain cockpit discipline.

The report included conclusions in the format of findings, causes and contributory factors as well as recommendations. The causes outlined in the report attributes the accident to the acts and omissions, mainly of the flying crew. In the section dealing with the contributory factors, item five states 'the insufficient evaluation by the approach control, under the aforementioned circumstances of the difficulties encountered by the flight crew in following procedures and clearances which prevented the controllers to offer any available assistance by their own initiative in order to prevent, probably, the accident' (Hellenic Republic Ministry of Transport and Communications 1998, Section 3.3, p. 85).

The technical accident investigation relied heavily on the CVR and ATCO's transcripts as well as the information obtained from the Thessaloniki military radar in order to identify the reasons that led the aircraft to deviate from the standard missed approach procedure. The CVR had to be read and translated as the internal cockpit communication between the crew was in Russian. The CVR was read three times by three different experts. The read-outs and the translations of the transcripts had a number of serious inaccuracies which provided misleading information. As the wreckage of the aircraft was found two days after the accident in a mountainous area, the crash site was not properly secured and vital instruments such as the aircraft altimeter were obtained and removed from the site by relatives of the deceased passengers. These instruments were presented during the criminal trial prosecuting the two ATCOs.

The ATCOs participated in the technical investigation by voluntarily supplying pertinent information and providing statements regarding their role, particularly during the missed approach phase of the flight and these statements are included in the final report.

The accident occurred at night and in bad weather conditions. Search and rescue operations lasted for two days. During the search and rescue operations a Greek Hellenic Air Force Hercules crashed into high ground, killing all five members on board the aircraft. This delay in finding the wreckage site as well as the accident of the Hercules C130 drew tremendous pressure from the media and the public. The level of air traffic control safety around Thessaloniki airport as well as search and rescue capabilities was greatly criticized. Relatives of the passengers were at the airport for the duration of the entire search and demanded that justice be done to punish the guilty party(s) as well as the resignation of a number of high-ranking political figures.

In this climate, the Thessaloniki judicial authorities initiated their investigation which ran parallel to the technical investigation. Two ATCOs where charged with involuntary manslaughter and the disruption of the safety of air transport by the Greek prosecuting authorities. In this case the prosecution alleged that the ATCOs fell below the standard of care required of ATCOs and that their failure to take positive steps that a reasonable ATCO would have taken in those particular circumstances, resulted in negligence.

On 6 October 2000 the trial started in the Thesssaloniki courts.[2] During both, the criminal proceedings the CVR transcripts, the findings of the technical report as well as the animation of the flight path including the CVR conversations, were admitted in court and formed important evidence against the ATCOs. The court concluded that, based on the evidence presented to the court, the charges of involuntary manslaughter and disruption of air traffic services were proved beyond a reasonable doubt. The two air traffic controllers were found guilty and sentenced to five years' imprisonment.

Judge Persiteridou stated:

> In order to be found guilty of manslaughter, in the case where the negligence of the accused is not intentional, in terms of Art 302, para 1 of the Criminal Code the following elements must be present.
>
> (i) the accused must not have exercised the required objective judgment and attention that the average reasonable man in the same circumstances would have exercised

---

2   First instance court, Thessaloniki, No. 20200.

(ii)　having the personal skill, knowledge and capabilities to have foreseen and to have avoided the punishable result and

(iii)　the causal connection between the acts and / or omissions and the result.

(p. 631, translated by the authors)

Both ATCOs appealed; however, in December 2002 their appeal was dismissed. Their sentences were reduced to four years and four months each. One of the ATCOs suffered mental illness as a result.

LAPA Flight 3142 – Buenos Aires, Argentina (1999)

On 31 August, 1999 LAPA Flight 3142, a B737, was a flight from Buenos Aires to Córdoba, Argentina, operated by the Argentinean airline LAPA. The plane crashed at the Aeroparque Jorge Newbery in Buenos Aires at 20:54 local time, shortly after take-off. The crash resulted in 65 fatalities, 17 people severely injured and several people with minor injuries, making it one of the deadliest accidents in the history of Argentinean aviation.

The aeroplane departed the airport properly. The pilot then aborted the take-off, crossed a highway and skidded across a golf course (NTSB 1999a). It was later determined that the flaps were not correctly set for take-off and that a warning horn was ignored.

The Civil Aviation Accidents Board of Investigations (Junta de Investigaciones de Accidentes de Aviación Civil – JIAAC) conducted the official accident investigation in accordance with ICAO Annex 13 and attributed the accident to the pilot's failure to configure the aircraft correctly for take-off. The contributing factors were, inter alia, lack of crew discipline, excess conversations irrelevant to the flight and moments of significant emotional intensity between the pilots; personal and/or family and/or economic problems or other issues of both pilots that interfered with their operational manner and their discussion of very personal and non-work-related affairs; insufficient psychological screening of pilots; aggravation of the captain's previous negative in-flight behaviour by his personal situation; previous negative flight characteristics of the first officer; lack of immediate recognition by the pilots of the relationship between the type of audible alarm and the improper take-off configuration, and the failure to employ the flaps correctly for take-off and the design of the alarm system (Sitiosargentina. com n.d.).

A judicial investigation was also initiated subsequent to the accident, overseen by a federal judge who received the preliminary report of the JIAAC. In May the judge was replaced by another judge, who ordered a search of LAPA headquarters and their operations room at Aeroparque, seizing the files of the company's pilots (Clarin 2000). The final JIAAC report given to the judge was questioned as it attributed the blame for the accident solely on the pilots. The newspaper *La Nacion* reported that the judge investigating the case had asked the air force to send him the files that prompted the report's conclusions as he wanted all the allegations to be based upon and supported by documents (Capiello 2000).

In May 32 people were indicted, including the president of LAPA, the former head of the air force, the former head of the National Division of Aeronavigability, the former head of the Division of *Habilitaciones,* the former *titular* of the National Institute of Aeronautical and Space Medicine, and the former head of the Command of Aerial Regions. In addition assets of the president of LAPA and 11 others, valued at 60 million pesos, were also confiscated, but this order was later annulled by the Federal Court of Appeal in November 2000 (Zommer 2000).

In December 2000, formal charges were laid against four LAPA officials, the president, the director general, the operations manager and the human resources manager, for criminal negligence leading to death and three members of the air force, the head of the Command of Aerial Regions; the (retired) director of empowerment and promotion and the (retired) director of the National Institute of Aeronautical and Space Medicine, for dereliction of duty in public office.

In March 2001, the judge in charge of the investigation resigned and the case was given to another judge and then another judge in November 2001.

On 15 July 2002, the second session of the Federal Court of Appeals confirmed the charges filed against the president, the director general and the operations manager of LAPA but did not confirm the accusations against the human resources manager. The court revoked the accusations against the three members of the air force and also revoked the dismissal of the accusations against two of the operations manager's predecessors at LAPA, as well as the head of the Boeing 737 division of LAPA. Additionally the court recognized the lack of merit of four LAPA flight instructors (*La Nacion* 2002). *La Nacion* comments that:

> The central point of the resolution of [the three] Congressmen ... is the analysis of the Captain's professional background. Beginning with this evaluation, they sustained, 'one can affirm the existence of negligent actions of those persons (the accused) who, in one way or another, allowed the Captain to be in command of an airliner'.

The judges understood that, taking it as a given that one of the basic principles of aeronautical activity is safety, 'one ought not pass over nor minimize the errors committed by the crew during initial exams or follow-ups (skill re-certification exams), whether in flight or in a simulator, which provide observations like those that appeared in the dossier of the deceased Captain' (*La Nacion* 2002). Thus, they enumerated a long series of errors and examples of inattentiveness committed by the pilot during his exams. According to the material contained in the file that was incorporated into the judicial review, it was noted as early as April 1994 the captain 'appeared slow' and that 'he should improve his command of lists and procedures ... He passed his pilot exam with the minimum score' and was subsequently certified by his instructors. In that same year, his file claimed that he needed to improve his in-cockpit co-ordination and his use of the checklists. 'One evaluation shows that he was uninformed about his appropriate role; as a consequence of this, he does not lead well and there is a lack of security and co-ordination in the cockpit,' according to his file (*La Nacion* 2002).

On 17 October, federal officials requested renewed accusations against the three members of the air force, on the basis that at the time of the accident they did not have a revised and approved operations manual provided by the Command of the Aerial Regions, and against the human resources manager on the basis that he knew that the captain of the flight in question did not have a valid licence as it had expired (*La Nacion* 2002). In December 2003, the second session of the Federal Court confirmed the accusations against the three members of the air force accusing them of the crimes of 'abuse of authority and failure to fulfil the responsibilities of public office' based on the fact that 'the evaluations taken of the crew were totally insufficient to present a clear profile of the subjects'. In addition, the court charged the human resources manager saying that:

> Human behaviour does not occur in a vacuum, but is rather a reflection of the corporate and regulatory environment in which it takes place. For the Congressmen, there was a 'clear relationship' between the courses that the Captain had not completed, and 'the violations that occurred in the cockpit' on that fateful day, a fact that was not caught by the managers who controlled the process. (*La Nacion* 2003)

On 10 September 2004, the accused were required to stand trial in a public jury trial proceeding. On 9 June 2005, the Federal Court of Appeals rejected the nullification motions that several of the accused had proposed, and again ordered them to stand before a jury trial. On 5 July 2005 the judge formed a tribunal to try the nine accused. They were six LAPA officials, the ex-president of LAPA, the director general, two operations managers, the head of the B-737 Line at LAPA, the human resources manager of LAPA and three members of the Argentinean air force, the ex-Commander of Aerial Regions, the ex-director of Aeronautical *Habilitacion* and the ex-director of the National Institute of Aeronautical and Aerospace Medicine (Rodriguez 2005).

On 23 July 2005, one of the three air force members accused is reported to have committed suicide (Pagina/12 2005). On 28 February 2006, the request by the two former members of the air force that the tribunal dismiss the charges against them because of the statute of limitations, was accepted as the crime for which they had been accused had a maximum sentence of two years and four years had already lapsed since the first accusations and the end of the trial (Infobae.com 2006).

Olympic Airway Falcon 900-B – Bucharest, Romania (1999)

On 14 September 1999, a Falcon 900B owned by the Greek government and operated by Olympic Airways, with a Greek government delegation including the Minister in Charge of European Affairs on an official visit to Romania, departed Athens at 18:16 UTC. During climb, after the flaps and slats were retracted, the 'PITCH FEEL' light was illuminated and the captain disengaged the autopilot, checked the forces on the control column and re-engaged the autopilot. The 'PITCH FEEL' warning light remained continuously on during cruise and descent until the slats were extended. The Falcon reached a cruising altitude of FL400 until 47 minutes from take-off, when a normal descent to FL150 was initiated, with the autopilot engaged in vertical speed mode. During descent the indicated air speed (IAS) increased from 240 knots to 332 knots and approaching FL150, the first officer requested a further descent. Just before FL150 the ATC re-cleared the flight to continue descent to FL50. One second later the autopilot disengaged and thereafter the aircraft was manually flown by the captain. Between FL150 and FL140, for approximately 24 seconds, the aircraft experienced ten oscillations in pitch axis varying from +4.7 g and –3:26 g. At about FL130, after the aircraft recovered from the oscillations, an emergency was declared and the aircraft landed at Bucharest Otopeni Airport. The cabin interior was completely destroyed and seven passengers were killed.

Subsequent to the accident the Romanian accident investigation board (the Inspectoratul Avietiei Civile) of the Romanian Ministry of Transport Civil Aviation Inspectorate conducted the official accident investigation and compiled a report that was published on 1 August 2000. This investigation was conducted in accordance with the provisions of Annex 13 (ICAO 2001), the EU Directive 94/56/CE (European Council 1994) and the Romanian legislation of investigation of air accidents.

The report included conclusions in the format of findings and causal factors as well as recommendations. The investigation identified the following causal factors as stated at Paragraph 3.2: the inadequate risk assessments of the pitch feel malfunctions; the overriding of risk assessments of the pitch feel malfunctions; inappropriate inputs on the control column at high speed and with Arthur unit failed in 'low speed' mode, leading to pilot-induced oscillations; seat belts not fastened during flight phase. It is evident from the way the report is written that it attempts not to apportion blame on any party(s); however, it can be seen that the actions stipulated, such as maintaining high speed during descent when the pitch feel malfunction was illuminated, are all actions or omissions of the pilots. The section of the report that deals with the analysis of the initiation of the oscillations, which were what led to the accident, provides the most probable scenario. The most probable scenario highlights the possible actions of the pilots as the main reason causing the oscillations and hence the accident. This probable scenario was submitted to the accident investigation board by the manufacturer of the autopilot. Due to the limitations of the FDR, which is the primary computer that records data pertinent to an accident investigation, the manufacturer used data that was obtained from a secondary computer. The manufacturer used computations and mathematical calculations in order to establish the most probable scenario which was then submitted to the Romanian accident investigation board. It is interesting to note that the probable scenario was submitted by the manufacturer of the autopilot, the behaviour of which may have played a vital role in the occurrence of the oscillations.

The accident investigation board did not make any further attempts to have an independent evaluation of the autopilot performance, nor did it have the technical resources to verify and validate the computations, mathematical calculations and tests performed by the manufacturer.

A detailed examination of the report revealed that the serial number of a secondary computer which was relied on during the investigation was the same serial number as a computer which was taken from a Falcon 900-B aircraft operated by Amway Corporation which had suffered oscillations with the autopilot disengaged during descent in visual meteorological conditions whilst attempting to land at Grand Rapids, Michigan, USA, about three weeks after the Falcon accident. On that occasion, as a result of the oscillations, a cabin crew member was seriously injured (Flight Safety Foundation 2001). As both computers had the same serial number, it was suspected that data from the second accident was used to support the probable cause scenario submitted for the first accident. When this was questioned during the trial, the manufacturer stated that this was an error on their behalf. The accident investigation board, not performing a flight test with the faulty part of the pitch feel system (potentiometer) of the aircraft in order to positively confirm the probable scenario theory submitted by the manufacturer, was criticized in the trial. As there was no safety risk posed in performing such a test the defence attorneys repeatedly questioned the scope of the technical investigation. The technical investigation was not able to use data retrieved from the CVR as the CVR was found destroyed immediately after the accident. This limited the investigation as vital data obtainable from the CVR which would have revealed the actions of the crew based on the cockpit communication between them was not available.

The above reveals a crucial deficiency in the technical investigation process in relation to the scope and level of the investigation, which is left to the discretion of the chief investigator and the resources available. Despite the deficiencies, it can be said that the purpose of the technical investigation, to provide recommendations aiming to prevent future accidents, was generally achieved.

In the section entitled 'Additional Information' at 1.18.1 the report included the statements of both pilots as well as the statements of the flight attendant. This illustrates the fact that the pilots freely participated and voluntarily provided pertinent information in order to enhance safety. On the other hand, a very important fact is that these statements were used later in subsequent criminal proceedings against the pilots.

At that time Greece had not yet adopted EU Directive 94/56. When the official report was published, it was submitted to the Aviation Accident Review Board which allowed all the interested parties to make representations against the findings in accordance with Greek legislation. As a result of the parties' presentations, minor changes were made to the official report and a further report on the accident was published.

This accident caused the death of the Foreign Minister, his son and five journalists, and involved a presidential aircraft used by the president and other ministers: it provoked a public outcry, media frenzy and a major internal political crisis in Greece. In addition, the technical problems of this aircraft were known and there were a number of reports that had resulted in the grounding of the aircraft due to the pitch feel technical malfunction prior to the accident. This led to tremendous pressure by the public, the media and politicians to identify the blameworthy parties and hold them accountable.

As a result, the Transport Minister of Greece directed the Greek civil aviation authority to conduct its own investigation into the accident. Subsequent to the report submitted by the civil aviation authority, both pilots had their licences suspended but these were reinstated subsequent to their successful appeal in the Administrative Court.

A further parallel investigation by the judicial authorities was initiated by a public prosecutor who appointed two aviation experts to conduct the investigation. The judicial investigation, whose role is to determine the responsible parties and to file criminal charges against them, adopted the manufacturer's probable scenario and criminally charged the pilots, Olympic Airways and eight engineers. The pilots were charged with manslaughter as a result of their alleged criminal negligence. It was alleged that the pilots had induced the oscillations that created positive and negative G-forces on the aircraft leading to the death of the passengers, and that they operated the aircraft outside the prescribed procedures, in particular maintaining high speed during descent without taking into account the pitch feel malfunction and failing to switch the seat belt sign on during descent as prescribed by the aircraft's flight manual.

The trial began on the 13 May 2002 in the first instance court. The following reports were submitted to the court and accepted as admissible evidence:

1. the final report compiled by the two aviation experts on behalf of the prosecuting authorities
2. the report compiled by the aviation accident review board
3. the official accident investigation report conducted by the Romanian authorities.

This clearly shows that the Romanian report, which was not supposed to be used in any way to apportion blame, was accepted by the court as evidence. The other two reports that were largely based on the findings and the probable scenario that the technical Annex 13 report adopted were accepted by the court and used as evidence during the trial. This leads to the finding that the Romanian accident investigation conducted with the limitations as outlined above provided the basis for the judicial authorities to prosecute the pilots.

With the adoption of these reports by the courts, the trial became a battlefield with the prosecution supporting the findings of these reports and the defence trying in vain to dispute the technical findings of these reports. It was evident during the trial that the judges could not fully understand a lot of the highly technical and scientific evidence submitted and, as a result of this, the pilots were in a very disadvantageous position. By a majority of two to one the court accepted the most probable cause scenario as outlined in the official investigation report and found the captain guilty, sentencing him to five years' imprisonment, and acquitted the co-pilot and the engineers.

On appeal, the court rejected the most probable cause scenario and reduced the sentence to 35 months, suspended for three years, holding the captain guilty for failing to switch the seat belt sign on 'On top of descent' as required by the flight manual, despite the fact that he complied with the Olympic Airways Standard Operating Procedures requiring the seat belt sign to be switched on five minutes prior to landing. It is interesting to note that the company policy had been approved by the Greek civil aviation authority. The pilot then appealed to the Supreme Court and the case has not been concluded eight years after the accident.

Singapore Airlines Boeing 747 – Singapore Chiang-KaiShek Airport, Taiwan (2000)

On 31 October 2000, a Singapore Airlines Flight SQ006, a scheduled flight from Singapore Chiang-KaiShek (CKS) Airport, Taiwan, to Los Angeles International Airport, entered the incorrect runway during rain and strong winds brought about by a typhoon. The B747 was destroyed by its collision with the runway construction equipment during the take-off roll and by post-impact fire. Four crew members and 70 passengers of the 179 on board were killed in the accident. The aircraft attempted a take-off from a runway that had been closed for repairs and crashed into concrete barriers and heavy construction machinery (NTSB 2001a).

The Taiwan Aviation Safety Council (ASC), an independent government organization of Taiwan, investigated the accident in accordance with ICAO Annex 13 (ICAO 2001) and the civil aviation law of China. Immediately after the accident, the CVR was removed from the aircraft by the prosecuting authorities and they released the CVR to the ASC on 1 November 2000. A full copy of the CVR transcript is provided in the final report. The crew provided a number of statements to the ASC investigators and extracts of their interviews are also included in the final report.

In the final report the ASC divides its findings into three categories, namely: probable causes, risks and other findings. They identify a number of unsafe acts of the crew, to findings in relation to the risks and to other findings. The final report alleging pilot error was disputed by the Civil Aeronautics Administration, Singapore Airlines and the International Federation of Air Line Pilots (IFALPA). The CVR was removed from the aircraft by the prosecuting authorities and they released the CVR to the ASC on 1 November 2000.

Following the accident, the pilots were detained in Taiwan and were only allowed to return to Singapore in December. Concerns about their detention and the increasing criminalization of pilots were expressed by many safety organizations and pilot unions. IFALPA made a number of requests to the Taiwanese government to allow the three pilots to return to Singapore. Fearing an international outcry and strained diplomatic and economic ties, the Ministry of Justice consulted the Ministry of Foreign Affairs and the Ministry of Transportation and Communications before deciding whether or not to proceed with a criminal investigation into the accident. The investigation into the accident was conducted by the Taiyuan District Prosecutor's Office who stated that, as a sovereign state, Taiwan had a right to apply its criminal laws to the accident and that it was humiliating to Taiwan and inimical to its sovereignty not to do so (Chuang 2000). In this case the need to exercise its national sovereignty played an important part in the ultimate decision to continue with a criminal investigation into the accidents.

In accordance with Article 276 of the Criminal Code the captain and co-pilot were charged with negligent killing. Their indictments were suspended for three years and they were not permitted to fly an aircraft to Taiwan for a year (Chuang 2002). The pilots were released from their employment with Singapore Airlines. The third co-pilot was not indicted as his duties only began once the aircraft was airborne and therefore he had not played any role in the attempted take-off of the aircraft. In 2002 the judicial authorities decided to drop the indictments of the captain and the co-pilot.

Scandinavian Airlines (SAS) MD-87 and Cessna Jet – Milan Linate Airport, Italy (2001)

On 8 October 2001 a Scandinavian Airlines (SAS) MD-87 aircraft with 110 people on board and a Cessna jet with two pilots and two passengers collided in heavy fog on a runway at Linate Airport in Milan. The SAS was cleared to taxi to Runway 36R for departure. At approximately the same time, the Cessna business jet was cleared to taxi via taxiway Romeo 5, but mistakenly entered taxiway Romeo 6, entered runway 36R and at that point was impacted by the SAS which had been cleared for take-off. Both aircraft broke up, skidded to the right of the active runway, and impacted an airport baggage hangar, which partially collapsed. All 110 persons on board the SAS, the four persons on board the Cessna and another four persons on the ground were killed.

The official accident investigation was conducted by the Italian accident investigation body, the Agenzia Nazionale per la Sicurezza del Volo (ANSV) in accordance with ICAO Annex 13 (ICAO 2001) and EU Directive 94/56 (European

Council 1994). The judicial authorities obtained the MD-83 CVR and FDR, and the technical investigators did not have access to the original tapes but were provided with a copy of the readouts. The other aircraft was not equipped with the CVR and FDR. The investigators were not able to get testimony from the ground, tower or the supervisor controllers as they made themselves unavailable pending the criminal investigation that was initiated after the accident (ANSV 2004). It is extremely important to note that the tower controllers did provide testimony to the judicial authorities and that these statements were then taken from the judicial authorities and used by the technical investigators to complete their investigations (ANSV 2004, para. 2, Analysis).

The report outlines the findings, which are divided into operational conditions prior to the accident, before-collision impact findings and post-impact findings, and then stipulates the causes of the accident. Investigators found that the immediate cause for the accident was the runway incursion in the active runway by the Cessna and an inoperative ground radar system contributed to the accident. The report found that the system at Milano Linate airport 'was not geared to trap misunderstandings, let alone inadequate procedures, blatant human errors and faulty airport layout' (ANSV 2004).

A parallel criminal investigation was immediately launched. A magistrate from the Milan Tribunal (Procurator della Repubblica) whose territorial jurisdiction covered the airport area was in charge of the judicial investigation. A safety expert who was a pilot and a member of the ANSV assisted in the judicial investigation and in compiling the judicial report. The final judicial report was very similar to the final report of the technical investigation, thus endorsing the findings and the identified causes of the accident.

Eleven aviation officials were charged with negligence and multiple manslaughter charges; the former director of ENAV (Italy's air traffic services provider) and five other officials from ENAV: the acting air traffic controller from ENAV, two officials from Italy's national agency for civil aviation (ENAC) and officials from Linate's airport management (SEA).

The 11 defendants were tried in two different sections. The first section dealt with charges against the Linate air traffic controller (ENAV), the former director of ENAV, the former managing director of Linate Airport (ENAC) and the former manager responsible for Linate and Malpensa Airport, from ENAC. On 16 April 2004 the four officials accused were sentenced to jail terms ranging from six and a half to eight years. The former director of the Linate Airport was sentenced to eight years' imprisonment. The former CEO of Italy's air traffic control agency ENAV and the person who oversees Milan's two airports was sentenced to six and a half years' imprisonment each. The air traffic controller who was on duty at the time was sentenced to eight years' imprisonment: a sentence that was more than twice that recommended by the prosecutor. These are reportedly the heaviest penalties handed down by the courts in industrial accident cases (Thomas 2007). The former director of Linate Airport received the recommended sentence and the other two received less than the recommended sentence.

The second section was concerned with the criminal proceedings against the general manager of ENAC, the manager of Linate Flight Assistance Centre and his local supervisor, the central safety supervisor of Linate Airport, an official from ENAV and the two managers from the airport management company (SEA). The general manager of ENAC was convicted and given a sentence of four years and four months, the manager of Linate Flight Assistance Centre and his local supervisor three years and ten months and the central safety supervisor of Linate Airport and the official from ENAV three years and four months.

The two managers from the airport management company (SEA) were found not guilty and acquitted. The prosecution then appealed their acquittal and the Appeal Court in 2006 convicted them and sentenced them each to three years' imprisonment.

Three of the ENAV defendants plea-bargained a three-year sentence before the appeal began which was ratified by the Territorial Court. The official from ENAV did not enter a plea bargain. His sentence became final, being confirmed on appeal.

The sentence of general manager of ENAV of four years and four months was confirmed. The sentence of the ATCO who was on duty was reduced to three years (entirely remitted) while the sentence of the former CEO of Italy's air traffic control agency ENAV was upheld. The former director of the Linate Airport and the person who oversees Milan's two airports were both acquitted.

The general manager of ENAC, the ATCO on duty (ENAV), the former director of Linate airport and the two managers of the SEA then appealed to the Supreme Court, the Cassation Court. The prosecution appealed the acquittal of the former director of Linate Airport and the manager overseeing Milan's two airports on behalf of ENAC. The Supreme Court, in February 2008, upheld the convictions of the general manager, the ATCO and the former director of Linate Airport and overturned the acquittals of the former director of Linate Airport and the manager overseeing Milan's two airports on behalf of ENAC. The court acquitted the two SEA managers.

During the first degree trial the court relied on the evidence which was provided by the same expert who was a member of the ANSV and who had assisted in the judicial investigation, called on behalf of the prosecution. He also assisted the prosecutor in the appeal. The court did not consider any other views provided by experts on behalf of the defence (Barra 2009).

Crossair Avro RJ100 – Zurich, Switzerland (2001)

On 24 November 2001, Crossair Flight 3597, an Avro RJ100, departed from Berlin-Tegel Airport, Germany, for Zurich-Kloten Airport. When the aircraft was descending to 4,000 feet, it turned right for the final approach to Runway 28. The weather was poor with intermediate snowfall and a previous aircraft, an Embraer, reported having seen the runway at 2.2 nautical miles. Shortly after the captain had reached the minimum descent altitude, he reported that he could see the ground. A few seconds later the radio altimeter called 500 feet which was followed by another radio altimeter call 'minimum'. The captain ordered a go-around, but this was too late. The aircraft crashed killing 21 passengers and three crew members.

The technical investigation was conducted by the Swiss AAIB, the Büro für Flugunfalluntersuchungen, in accordance with ICAO Annex 13 (ICAO 2001). In addition the United Kingdom, as the state of manufacture, and Germany, as the home country of some of the deceased passengers, assigned accredited representatives to the investigation.

The final Swiss AAIB technical report attributed the accident to pilot error. They determined that the accident was attributable to the fact that, on the final approach, the flight crew deliberately continued the descent under instrument flight conditions below the minimum altitude for the approach without having the necessary prerequisites and that the flight crew initiated the go-around too late. The report also stated the following as causal factors: The commander deliberately descended below the minimum descent altitude of the standard approach without having the required visual contact to the approach lights or the runway and the co-pilot made no attempt to prevent the continuation of the flight below the minimum descent altitude. A number of contributory factors were identified: inter alia, there was no system available at Zurich Airport triggering an alarm if a minimum safe altitude was violated and the airline failed to make the correct assessments of the commander's flying performance or, in the case where weaknesses were perceptible, they did not take the appropriate corrective measures (BFU n.d.).

BFU issued eight safety recommendations to the Bundesamt für Zivilluftfahrt (BAZL) on 10 April 2002, including crew pairing criteria and GPWS installation on all new aircraft. All the recommendations made in the report were adopted and put into practice.

In 2004, the Swiss Federal Prosecutor's Office opened a criminal investigation of negligent manslaughter and grievous bodily harm in connection with the accident on the basis that the pilots knew that they were exceeding the regulatory limits. As a result of the judicial investigation, six former managers of Crossair, including the operations chief, the chief trainer, the former chief executive officer of Swiss International Airlines and the former chairman of Crossair, were prosecuted.

The trial commenced at the Federal Criminal Court in Bellinzona, Switzerland. The prosecution requested suspended imprisonment for all indicted, particularly a sentence of two years for the chairman and the former CEO and sentences of between 12 and 18 months for the four middle managers at the time of the accident (Stocker 2008).

During the two-week trial, the prosecution argued that the management established a dictatorial rule and alleged that they intimidated pilots and encouraged them to ignore flight safety regulations. The prosecutor argued that the pilot should have been removed from his flying duties as he had did not have a clear record. It was also alleged that the management did not instil a safety culture in the airline but that they maintained a culture of fear; that pilots felt that they could not report incidents, that they were encouraged to take risks and that pilots felt pressurized to fly in unsafe conditions instead of cancelling flights. The lack of additional training of the pilots was also faulted as it was alleged that previous incidents regarding the pilot were known. Witnesses testified in court regarding the pilot's record. A Lufthansa flight instructor submitted on behalf of the defence that the pilot had not been involved in any major incident prior to the accident and that there was no need for additional training; whereas a prosecution witness testified that as the co-pilot in a previous flight with the pilot she had experienced him making a risky landing at the difficult airport of Lugano, but that she was frightened to report this as a result of the prevailing culture of fear.

The court described these allegations as unfounded and on 16 May 2008 the court found the accused not guilty and acquitted the former CEO, the chairman and the four Crossair middle managers. The court awarded damages to the six defendants totalling about SFr 850,000 ($814,000) (Swissinfo.ch 2008).

Piper – Winnipeg, Canada (2002)

On 11 June, 2002 a Piper aircraft with six passengers on board was damaged when taking off from a private airstrip near Pennsylvania (NTSB 2003a). The pilot had flown one group of fishermen from Winnipeg into Gunisao Lake at 6 am and picked up another group to fly them into Winnipeg. The aircraft was scheduled to land shortly after 9 am. On the return flight, approximately 40 miles from Winnipeg, the fuel gauges on the aircraft started to drop quickly. One of the engines failed at about 15 miles from Winnipeg and the pilot restarted the engine by activating the cross-feed on the fuel system. During the first approach he was unable to see the runway due to low visibility and initiated a missed approach. As he was attempting a second approach both engines failed. The aeroplane then struck a tree and a power line located about 500 feet beyond the end of the runway, shearing the right wing from the fuselage, descended back to the ground, nosed over and then came to rest inverted. The pilot was forced to land the plane on a busy Winnipeg street. Several passengers were injured and one of the passengers died from his injuries after the accident.

The accident was investigated by the Canadian Transportation Safety Board (TSB) in accordance with ICAO Annex 13 (ICAO 2001). The findings of the board with regards to the causes and factors contributing to the accident were:

- the pilot did not correctly calculate the amount of fuel required to accomplish the flight and did not ensure that the aircraft carried sufficient fuel for the flight
- the ILS approach was flown above the glide slope and beyond the missed approach point, which reduced the possibility of a safe landing at Winnipeg and increased the risk of collision with terrain

- during the missed approach, the aircraft's engines lost power as a result of fuel exhaustion, and the pilot conducted a forced landing at a major city intersection
- the pilot did not ensure that the aircraft was equipped with the required autopilot.

The report also refers to findings regarding risks in that:

> The company did not provide an adequate level of supervision and allowed the flight to depart without an autopilot; the company operations manual did not reflect current company procedures; the company did not provide an adequate level of supervision and allowed the flight to depart without adequate fuel reserves; the company did not have a safety system in place to prevent a fuel exhaustion situation developing. (Transportation Safety Board of Canada 2003)

In addition the aviation enforcement division of TSB investigated the accident and the pilot made three statements. Following the investigation he was charged and found guilty of two breaches of the Canadian Aviation Regulations, namely failing to have a functioning autopilot and not having sufficient fuel to comply with instrument flight rules IFR (*R. v. Tayfel* (M.) [2009]).[3]

Criminal charges were later filed and the pilot was accused of one count of criminal negligence causing death, four counts of criminal negligence causing bodily harm, and one count of dangerous operation of an aircraft.

The legal basis for the charges were the offence criminal negligence, which is doing anything or omitting to do anything that is a legal duty to do, showing wanton or reckless disregard for the lives or safety of other persons (*Canadian Criminal Code*, S 219 (1) (2) Criminal Negligence), and the offence of dangerously operating an aircraft by operating an aircraft in a manner that is dangerous to the public, having regard to all the circumstances, including the nature and condition of that aircraft or the place or air space in or through which the aircraft is operated (Section 249(1)(*c*) Dangerous Operation of an Aircraft). In 2007 the trial began; it lasted eight days, a fairly short trial perhaps because many facts were agreed upon and much of the evidence was submitted without objection.

The court, considering the conduct of the accused as the pilot in command and how he executed his duty to ensure that the aircraft had enough fuel for the scheduled flight, submitted that

> As the pilot, he had a duty under both the Canadian Aviation Regulations and the company operating policies ... to ensure that there was sufficient fuel on the flight to arrive at the destination, to cover contingencies such as inclement

3   Available at http://www.canlii.org/en/mb/mbca/doc/2009/2009mbca124/2009mbca 124.html [accessed: 15 April 2006].

weather, vectoring (waiting to land if it is busy at the destination airport) and, in addition, to carry a mandated fuel reserve. The amount of reserve fuel is determined by the weather conditions: visual flight rules (VFR) apply when flying in good weather, that is when the pilot will have visual contact with the ground, and instrument flight rules (IFR) apply when flying in cloudy weather. (Beard J., in *R v Tayfel* [2007] at para 47)

The trial judge found that the accused's conduct both in failing to ensure that there was adequate fuel on board to safely complete the flight and in the manner in which he responded when it became clear that there was a problem with the fuel constituted both criminal negligence and dangerous operation of an aircraft (at para 11).

In what is believed to be one of the very few cases in which a commercial pilot has been found guilty of criminal negligence in an aviation accident in Canada, the pilot was found guilty on four counts of criminal negligence causing bodily harm and dangerous operation of an a aircraft subsequent to the accident that occurred (CBC News 2007). The pilot received a two-year conditional sentence, 240 hours community service and a daily curfew, and also had his licence suspended for 45 days (Rollason 2009a). In her decision the judge stated that 'this decision is a signal to pilots and small commercial airline owners and operators that a corporate culture of bending or ignoring the aeronautics regulations to get the job done at the cost of reduced safety to passengers and others is criminal behavior' (Rollason 2009c).

Providing an analysis of the relevant law the trial judge stated that the offence of criminal negligence causing death requires proof of a modified objective intention, taking into account the circumstances but not the personal characteristics of the accused. Regarding the issue of whether the accused's actions constituted a wanton or reckless disregard for the lives and safety of others, she provided '[t]he best compendium definition' of such actions is as follows (at para. 38):

> For the *accused's actions or omissions to constitute wanton or reckless disregard for the lives or safety of others, that conduct must be a marked and substantial departure from what we would expect of a reasonable person in such circumstances;* because the conduct must show heedless, reckless disregard for the lives or safety of others, a small error or a momentary lapse in care, that results tragically in death or bodily harm is not sufficient conduct to constitute criminal negligence. The greater the risk of death or bodily harm occurring from the type of conduct engaged in by the accused, the more likely it is that engaging in such conduct shows wanton and reckless disregard for the lives and safety of other persons. [emphasis added]

Explaining the difference between criminal negligence and dangerous operation of an aircraft which she equated to the difference between criminal negligence and dangerous operation of a motor vehicle, she states that the former requires a '"marked and substantial or significant" departure from the standard of a reasonable driver' and the latter requires a 'marked departure' (at para. 40). Supporting this, she provides a summary of the elements of criminal negligence causing death as follows (at paras 43–4):

- the conduct of the accused was both a marked and a substantial departure from the conduct expected of a reasonable person in the circumstances; criminal negligence requires more than just carelessness or a small or momentary lapse in care – the conduct of the accused must be a marked departure from the conduct of a reasonable person and must also be a substantial departure;
- the accused, by his conduct, showed a wanton and reckless disregard for the lives and safety of other persons, meaning a heedless or unrestrained disregard for the consequences of your actions; 'reckless' meaning an indifference to the consequences of your actions. For the accused's actions to constitute wanton or reckless disregard for the lives or safety of others, that conduct must be a marked and substantial departure from what we would expect of a reasonable person in such circumstances, and that conduct must show a heedless, unrestrained, reckless disregard for the lives or safety of others – a small error, or a momentary lapse in care, that results tragically in death or bodily harm, is not sufficient conduct to constitute criminal negligence; the greater the risk of death or bodily harm occurring from the type of conduct engaged in by the accused, the more likely it is that engaging in such conduct shows wanton and reckless disregard for the lives and safety of other persons.

The court then goes on to submit that this is proved by applying an objective test in that if the act or omission constituted a marked and substantial departure from that which is expected of a reasonable person in those same circumstances, and that if there is a wanton and reckless disregard for the lives or safety of others, this would constitute criminal negligence whether or not the accused recognized the obvious and serious risk to the lives and safety of others.

Referring to the accused's submission that he had made a mistake of fact, the court provides the law regarding the element of a mistake of fact in relation to criminal negligence as follows: a mistake of fact occurs where the accused made an honest mistake of fact about an essential ingredient or circumstance of the offence; and that mistake of fact is a defence to all of these charges only if the mistake is honestly held by the accused and is reasonable in all of the circumstances known to the accused.

Applying the law as outlined, the trial judge found the accused guilty of all counts in that that the accused's conduct caused the death of one passenger and serious injuries to four passengers (at para. 142); that the accused's actions were a marked and substantial departure from what is expected of a reasonable and prudent person in the same circumstances as the accused; that the accused's conduct was not a small error or a momentary lapse in care; that he showed a heedless, reckless disregard for the lives and safety of others, including the other passengers on the aircraft and people on the ground and in so doing his conduct showed a wanton and reckless disregard for the lives and safety of other people; and that any mistake of fact alleged by the accused was not reasonable in all of the circumstances known to the accused at the time.

In December 2009, the Manitoba Court of Appeal (in *R v Tayfel* (M.) [2009]) unanimously ruled that the previous convictions of criminal negligence causing death and four counts of criminal negligence causing bodily harm be overturned and that the conviction of dangerous operation of an aircraft be upheld. The court found that the pilot's conduct did not show a complete disregard for the consequences of his actions and stated that:

> However flawed his conduct was in addressing the sufficiency of the fuel for the flight, I am of the view that this conduct, when considered in the context of all the evidence, is not conduct that meets the very high threshold of wanton or reckless disregard for the lives and safety of other persons ... (Hamilton, J.A., at para 89, *R. v. Tayfel* (M.) [2009])

The Appeal Court reiterated that the civil standard of negligence is the starting point to assess whether there has been a marked and substantial departure in determining the *mens rea* element of criminal negligence based on the requisite objective test which usually involves expert evidence as to the relevant standard for the conduct in question. Based on the expert evidence provided by both the Crown and the defence with regards to what other pilots would have done in the same circumstances, the trial judge considered this evidence and concluded that the accused's conduct did not meet the standard of a reasonable and prudent pilot and that the conduct was a marked and substantial departure from that standard. However, with regards to whether the trial judge erred in law in finding the accused guilty of criminal negligence the judge refers to two cases heard in the Supreme Court of Canada subsequent to the trial's decision (*R v Beatty* [2008]). To prove the *actus reus* of criminal negligence it must be proved that beyond a reasonable doubt that the accused was under a legal duty to do something; that he failed to fulfil that duty by his omissions, and that in failing to fulfil the duty he showed a wanton or reckless disregard for the lives or safety of other persons. The court stated that the pilot was undoubtedly under a legal duty to ensure that there was sufficient fuel in the aircraft for the flight and that he breached that duty. However, the issue with respect to the *actus reus* element was whether the trial judge erred in that the accused showed a wanton or reckless disregard for the lives or safety of other persons. Providing and explanation of the terms, the court cited *R v Waite* reflex (1986): 'The word "wanton" means "heedlessly." "Wanton" coupled as it is with the word "reckless", must mean heedless of the consequences or without regard for the consequences' (at p. 341). The court then concluded that on reading the trial judge's explanation of the law and how she applied it that she had analysed the law in reverse as she imported into the *actus reus* enquiry the enquiry of the *mens rea* element.

Despite this error, however, the question was whether the findings of the trial judge supported a conclusion that the *actus reus* of the offence of criminal negligence was proved beyond a reasonable doubt. The court concluded that this was not done in that the accused's conduct could not be considered in isolation from all the evidence related to the day in question. With the exception to the manner of calculating the fuel and his decision to fly VFR for an IFR flight the accused's conduct could not be criticized. As he did address safety issues before and during the flight, his conduct cannot be said to have shown a complete disregard for the consequences of his actions. As the findings of the trial judge did not support the conclusion that the *actus reus* of the offence of criminal negligence was proved beyond a reasonable doubt, the convictions for criminal negligence causing death and criminal negligence causing bodily harm were set aside.

Regarding the accused's appeal of his conviction for dangerous operation of an aircraft the court found that while the accused honestly believed he had sufficient fuel for the flight, he did so knowing that it was sufficient only for a VFR flight. The trial judge's conclusion that this decision was not a momentary lapse but a marked departure from the standard of a reasonable and prudent pilot was not mistaken and the verdict of guilty for the offence of dangerous operation of an aircraft was upheld.

DHL B757 and Bashkirian Airlines Tu-154 Mid-air Collision – Uberlingen, Germany (2002)

On 1 July 2002, a DHL Boeing 757 cargo plane collided with a Bashkirian Airlines Tupolev-154 near Uberlingen on the northern shore of Lake Constance, in southern Germany over the Swiss–German border. Flight 2937 was a chartered flight carrying 60 passengers and nine crew members. Forty-five of the passengers were Bashkortostan schoolchildren being taken to a resort in the Costa Dorada area of Spain as a prize for winning a competition.

Both aircraft were level at FL360, under Swiss air traffic control (Zurich). One controller who was monitoring two frequencies and two radar scopes was responsible for the entire traffic in the Zurich airspace whilst the other controller on duty was resting in another room for the night. This was against the regulations, but had been a common practice for years and was known and tolerated by management. The controller was guiding one aircraft for an approach on one frequency and had to control four aircraft, including the Bashkirian Tupolev and the DHL cargo plane on the other frequency.

Approximately 50 seconds before the collision, Swiss ATC instructed the Russian pilot to descend by 1,000 feet to avoid collision with the Boeing. No response was registered by the Russian crew. A few seconds later, a second descent instruction was made by the Swiss controller and the Tupolev crew acknowledged the instruction. The pilot of the Tupolev initiated its descent about 25 seconds before the collision; however, the Traffic Collision Avoidance System (TCAS)[4] instructed them to climb. At nearly the same moment, the Boeing's TCAS in response to the threat of a collision with the TU-154 instructed the pilots to descend. The Boeing initially followed the TCAS instructions and initiated a descent, but could not immediately inform the controller due to the fact that he was dealing with the Tupolev. The Tupolev pilot disregarded the TCAS instruction to climb and instead began to descend, as instructed by the controller, thus both planes were now descending. As he was unaware of the TCAS-issued alerts, the controller then repeated his instruction to the Tupolev crew to descend, giving them incorrect information as to the position of the DHL plane. At the time of the accident, maintenance work was being carried out on the main radar system, affecting monitoring and communication.

The aircraft collided at almost a right angle. The tail fin of the Boeing struck the left side of the Tupolev fuselage over the wing emergency exits. The Tupolev's left wing sheared off 80 per cent of the Boeing's tail fin and immediately broke up into four pieces. The Boeing lost control and battled for another 8 km before crashing into a wooden area. Each engine was found several hundred metres away from the wreckage. The debris scattered over an area nearly 40 km wide. Seventy-one people died, 69 in the Bashkirian aircraft and two in the Boeing Aircraft.

The mid-air collision within Swiss airspace which is considered to be one of the busiest crossing points within the European air traffic system, invoked media attention not only within Europe, but on a global level, questioning the safety of Swiss ATC and demanding an immediate explanation of the accident. The deaths of the 45 children who were on a school trip added to the demands for accountability. The Swiss government, recognizing the urgency to reassure the public of the safety of the Swiss airspace and in response to public and political sensitivity, took a number of steps to improve aviation safety. One of the actions was to recognize that the accident had systemic causes and could not be attributed solely to the actions of the pilots or ATCOs involved.

The official accident investigation was carried out by the German accident investigation body, the Bundesstelle für Flugunfalluntersuchung (BFU) in accordance with ICAO Annex 13 (ICAO 2001) and EU Directive 94/56 (European Council 1994). The immediate causes of the accident were stated as being the imminent separation infringement that was not noticed by air traffic control in time, and that the instruction for the Tupolev to descend was given at a time when the prescribed separation to the Boeing aircraft could not be ensured any more. In addition, the Tupolev crew followed the ATC instruction to descend and continued to do so even after TCAS advised them to climb.

The accident investigation also considered possible systemic failures, conforming to recent investigation practices which consider an accident as an

---

4   The TCAS alerts pilots of other aircraft in the vicinity to the presence of an aeroplane in order to avoid a collision.

organizational accident and try to identify possible weaknesses in the system that may have contributed to the accident or serious incident. The report identifies the following systemic causes:

- the operational and procedural instructions of the TCAS manufacturer and the operators were not standardized, they were incomplete and partially contradictory;
- the management and quality assurance of the air navigation service company did not ensure that during the night all open workstations were continuously staffed by controllers;
- the practice of one controller working and the other resting during low traffic was tolerated.

The approach taken by the Swiss government focused on identifying the systemic failures of the ATC and aviation safety system. It embraced the modern approach of investigating aviation accidents by considering an air accident as an organizational failure and not the failure of the pilots and ATCOs involved. The official technical investigation report implemented the amendments of ICAO Annex 13, requiring the investigators to take into consideration all organizational and systemic failures when investigating an aviation accident. The report makes 19 recommendations of which 11 refer to systemic and organizational deficiencies of the ATC provider, Skyguide.

A criminal investigation of Skyguide began in May 2004 after the publication of the technical investigation report and the investigation was based largely on the BFU final accident report which criticized the fact that there was only one controller on duty at the time (Winiger 2007). In August 2006 Swiss prosecutors laid 71 charges of negligent homicide and negligently disturbing public transport against eight Swiss Skyguide employees, namely three ATC managers, the ATSEP project leader for maintenance work at the airport at the time of the accident, an ATSEP employee, the ATCO on duty at the time of the accident, the ATCO supervisor and a technical systems manager.

The trial commenced in Bulach, a small town north of Zurich Airport, in an 'improvised courtroom prepared in a community centre', amidst high media presence. Attacks on the defendants were feared following the fatal stabbing of the ATCO who was on duty at the time of the accident, and tight security measures were implemented. The eight defendants were brought into the court room via a back room. The court was comprised of three judges and an expert was invited to speak. The questions asked by the judges were based mainly on the accident investigation report, relevant Skyguide manuals and on a report by an Austrian aviation expert (Winiger 2007). The prosecution requested jail terms of six to 15 months on conviction. In September 2007 the District Court of Bulach found the three ATCOs managers guilty of the offences charged with and sentenced them to one-year prison sentences, suspended for two years, plus court costs. The TSEP project leader was also found guilty and received a fine suspended for two years and court costs. The other four Skyguide employees were found not guilty and cleared of any wrongdoing. The four Skyguide employees who were found guilty decided not to appeal their sentences. Two of the four convicted employees went back to work at Skyguide assuming different duties and the other two took early retirement (Skyguide 2007).

It is noteworthy that in this case the court acquitted the ATCOs and focused more on the wrongdoing of management, finding the four managers blameworthy.

Tuninter ATR 72 – Italian Coast (2005)

On 6 August 2005 a Tunisian Tuninter ATR 72 flight from Bari, Italy, scheduled to fly to Djerba, Tunisia, ran out of fuel and after gliding for approximately 16 minutes, ditched in the ocean off the Sicilian coast. This resulted in the deaths of 14 passengers, the airline engineer and the senior flight attendant. A day prior to the flight, when the aircraft arrived in Tunis, it had 790 kg of fuel left in the fuel tanks. During maintenance the fuel quantity indicator (FQI) was changed and a FQI for an ATR-42 aircraft was mistakenly installed in the ATR-72. As a result the amount of fuel on board the aeroplane now indicated 3,050 kg of fuel instead of 790 kg and during the preparation of the flight to Bari, a further 465 kg fuel was added. When the aircraft landed at Bari only 305 kg were left in the tanks but the incorrect indication led the crew to believe that they had sufficient fuel left. In preparation for the flight to Djerba, a further 265 kg of fuel was added. The flight FQI indicated that the aircraft had 2,700 kg of fuel whereas in fact it only had 570 kg. The aircraft ran out of fuel, both engines quit and the aircraft was ditched. Twenty-three people on board the aircraft survived.

The Italian ANSV conducted the investigation into the accident in accordance with ICAO Annex 13 (ICAO 2001) and the relevant EU directive (European Council 1994). The complex task of investigating a ditching accident required co-ordination between the ANSV and a number of other agencies, including the judiciary. The technical investigation faced many obstacles imposed by the judicial authorities who initiated their own investigation in accordance with Italian national law. As a result of the two parallel investigations and the legal, procedural and methodological differences, the ANSV were unable to obtain access to documentation and to the CVR and FDR, which were seized by the judicial authority and kept in their possession until it was ruled by the judicial authority that they be taken to the ANSV headquarters for the read-out. The data obtained from the read-out was then sequestrated by the judicial authorities and the tapes removed. The ANSV was not given a copy of the CVR data until later. A copy of the FDR raw data was made available to the ANSV for further decoding and analysis. In addition, the ANSV was not permitted to supply the data to the foreign accredited representatives who had a right to have access to that data, in accordance with ICAO Annex 13.

The accident was also analysed by using the Reason Model provided as an analysis instrument in ICAO (1998b) and ICAO (1998a). Using this 'Organization Accident' model as it is termed, errors and omissions committed by front-line employees (pilots, ATCOs, engineers), which are called 'active failures', can trigger an accident if they are combined with pre-existing factors and conditions termed 'latent failures'. In this case the active failures were identified as being committed by both the ground mechanics the day before the accident while searching for and replacing the FQI and by the crew who did not verify and accurately complete the aircraft documentation which would have alerted them to the anomalous situation regarding the amount of fuel on board. Some of the latent failures identified were, inter alia, inadequate maintenance and organization standards, the absence of quality assurance systems, flight data monitoring program and a safety management system (ANSV 2007, para. 2.13).

The final ANSV report attributes the ditching to both the engines flaming out as a result of fuel exhaustion and determines that one of the contributing factors leading to the accident was the incorrect replacement of the fuel quantity indicator. The report also identifies a number of failures on behalf of the crew, the ground mechanic and the airline (ANSV 2007).

As with previous accidents that have taken place in Italy, a judicial investigation is initiated immediately after an aviation accident. The judicial authorities seized the CVR, FDR and ATC communication disks and any other pertinent documentation related to the accident. Even though Italy has not filed any differences with ICAO in relation to ICAO Annex 13, the judicial authorities did not conform with the provisions of Annex 13 in that the judiciary took full control of the CVR and FDR, an accredited representative from Tunisia was not permitted to take part in the investigation and Tuninter was banned from having access to the first ANSV findings and recommendations (Director of the Tunisian Civil Aviation Authority 2007).

In the aftermath of the accident, the pilots were initially seen as heroes for successfully ditching the aircraft and saving the lives of 20 passengers and three crew; however, that was soon to change as the judicial authorities conducted their own criminal investigation into the accident. Prosecutors stated that the crew was blameworthy as they did not follow the required emergency procedures and that the captain panicked and started praying aloud instead of attempting to fly the aircraft to the nearest airport at Palermo (*Aviation Human Factors Industry News* 2009). The judicial authorities based this conclusion on their interpretation of what they heard from the CVR transcript when the captain is praying just before ditching the aircraft. Clearly, the judicial authorities placed great reliance on the CVR transcript.

In this case the media played a negative role in the aftermath of this accident. The afternoon that the judicial authorities released the content of the CVR to parties involved in the criminal proceedings, a copy of the CVR transcript was released to the media who covered it extensively both in audio and print form of the CVR transcript (ANSV 2007). While the media first praised the pilots for successfully ditching the aircraft, soon after the release of the CVR transcript to the media they were seen as those responsible for the death of 16 people and the focus was now on bringing them to justice and holding them accountable.

The prosecution authorities charged nine people with multiple manslaughter charges and with causing a disaster. Nearly four years after the accident, on 23 March 2009, the Italian court in Palermo convicted the seven people charged to a total of 62 years. A very important piece of evidence that was admitted in court, to the detriment of the pilot, was the CVR in which the captain is clearly heard praying seconds before ditching the aircraft into the Mediterranean Sea, calling for the help of 'Allah and Muhammad his prophet' (*Aviation Human Factors Industry News* 2009).

The captain and co-pilot were sentenced to ten years' imprisonment. The director general and the technical chief were sentenced to nine years while the airline's head of maintenance, the chief mechanic and the maintenance squad leader received eight-year sentences. Two members of the airline maintenance crew were acquitted (ANSA 2009).[5]

This case has caused a global outcry amongst pilots, pilots unions and aviation safety organizations. IFALPA have publicly stated that the very harsh sentences are unwarranted based on the facts of the case, and calls on the Italian government to enact necessary legislative amendments to laws having a detrimental effect on air safety (IFALPA 2009a). Many speculate that the harsh decision of the Italian court was discriminatory as the pilots were foreign and the crew was Muslim.

Helios Airways B737-300 – Grammatiko, Greece (2005)

On 14 August 2005, an Helios Airways Boeing 737-300 on its way to Prague, via Athens, crashed into the mountain side of Grammatiko, north of Athens, killing all 121 passengers and crew aboard the aircraft. The aircraft departed Larnaca, Cyprus, at 09:07 and was cleared to climb to FL340. As the aircraft climbed through 16,000 feet, the captain contacted the company operations centre and reported a take-off configuration warning and an equipment cooling system problem. Several communications between the captain and the operations centre took place in the next eight minutes concerning these problems and ended as the aircraft climbed through 28,900 feet. Thereafter, there was no response to radio calls to the aircraft. During the climb at an aircraft altitude of 18,200 feet, the passenger oxygen masks deployed in the cabin. The aircraft levelled off at FL340 and continued on its programmed route. At 10:21, the aircraft flew over the KEA VOR, then over Athens International Airport and subsequently entered the KEA VOR holding pattern at 10:38. At 11:24, during the sixth holding pattern, the Boeing 737 was intercepted by two F-16 aircraft of the Hellenic air force. One of

---

5 Available at http://www.iasa.com.au/folders/Breaking_News/Snippets_/index.htm (accessed 2 July 2009).

the F-16 pilots observed the aircraft at close range and reported at 11:32 that the captain's seat was vacant, the first officer's seat was occupied by someone who was slumped over the controls, the passenger oxygen masks were seen dangling and three motionless passengers were seen seated wearing oxygen masks in the cabin. No external damage or fire was noted and the aircraft was not responding to radio calls. At 11:49, he reported a person not wearing an oxygen mask entering the cockpit and occupying the captain's seat. The F-16 pilot tried to attract his attention without success. At 11:50, the left engine flamed out due to fuel depletion and the aircraft started descending. At 11:54, two MAYDAY messages were recorded on the CVR. At 12:00, the right engine also flamed out at an altitude of approximately 7,100 feet. The aircraft continued descending rapidly and impacted hilly terrain at 12:03 in the vicinity of Grammatiko village, Greece, approximately 33 km north-west of the Athens International Airport. All 115 passengers and six crew members on board were killed in the accident. The aircraft was destroyed (AAIASB 2006).

The Air Accident Investigation and Aviation Safety Board (AAIASB) of the Hellenic Ministry of Transport and Communications investigated the accident following ICAO practices and in accordance with Annex 13 (ICAO 2001), EU Directive 94/56 (European Council 1994) and Greek legislation. The final report was published in November 2006. The report did not state the 'probable cause(s)' of the accident, but the 'direct and latent causes' of the accident.

It stated that the direct causes were:

1. Non-recognition that the cabin pressurization mode selector was in the MAN (manual) position during the performance of the Preflight procedure, the Before Start checklist and the After Take-off checklist.
2. Non-identification of the warnings and the reasons for the activation of the warnings (Cabin Altitude Warning Horn, Passenger Oxygen Masks Deployment indication, Master Caution).
3. Incapacitation of the flight crew due to hypoxia, resulting in the continuation of the flight via the flight management computer and the autopilot, depletion of the fuel and engine flame-out, and the impact of the aircraft with the ground.

The latent causes were:

1. Operator's deficiencies in organization, quality management and safety culture.
2. Regulatory authority's diachronic inadequate execution of its safety oversight responsibilities.
3. Inadequate application of crew resource management principles.
4. Ineffectiveness of measures taken by the manufacturer in response to previous pressurization incidents in the particular type of aircraft (AAIASB 2006).

The AAIASB also made a number of recommendations and stated the following factors as having contributed to the accident; omission to return the cabin pressurization mode selector to the AUTO position after non-scheduled maintenance on the aircraft; lack of cabin crew procedures (at an international level) to address events involving loss of pressurization and continuation of the climb despite passenger oxygen masks deployment; and ineffectiveness of international aviation authorities to enforce implementation of action plans resulting from deficiencies documented in audits. It is evident, based on the above latent causes, that, had the pilots survived, they would have been criminally charged.

On the same day of the accident judicial investigations into the accident were launched by the Greek and Cypriot judicial authorities. Statements were immediately taken from the two engineers who performed the non-scheduled maintenance of the aircraft prior to its departure. Two days later, their statement and personal details were revealed by the media, resulting in their hasty departure from Cyprus. During the technical and judicial investigation, any further statements were made in the UK, in the presence of their lawyers.

The tragic accident causing the deaths of 121 persons from a very small community had a devastating impact on the whole of Cyprus and Greece. There was a great demand from both the media and the public to identify the responsible parties particularly in light of the general feeling that there would be a cover-up as the airline belonged to the biggest tourist company involving both economic and political interests.

Figure 4.1   Relatives demanding justice

As a result the president of Cyprus, in an unprecedented move, made a public statement on 29 August 2005, aiming to appease the public and to outline what procedures would follow. He stated that with regard to the investigation of the accident, the following enquiries would take place:

1. an official accident investigation by the Greek authorities
2. an investigation by the Cyprus Air Accident and Incident Investigation Board
3. an investigation to establish the possibility of human factors and the direction of further investigation to apportion blame (this would be done subsequent to the official report having concluding its findings)
4. an independent investigation with the assistance of experts and consultants from the EU to identify any possible responsibility on the part of the Ministry of Communications and Works, the Department of the Civil Aviation Authority or any persons responsible for the audits conducted of the airline
5. a police investigation in order to identify any criminal acts or omissions of the airline or any other persons
6. an independent public enquiry appointed by the Council of Ministers.

Figure 4.2   Letter of the President to deceased's relatives stating that action will be taken to bring to justice those responsible for the accident

It is evident that by outlining what enquiries would follow as well as stipulating the manner, extent and the sequence of the investigations, the President intervened into both the technical and the judicial investigations. The technical investigation conducted by the Greek authorities, whose purpose is to enhance safety and not to apportion blame, was made the basis of all further investigations, including the judicial investigations. During the process of the technical investigation the Greek chief investigator was in direct contact with the Cyprus Minister of Communication and Works and the President, keeping them abreast of the investigation.

On 10 May 2006 the Council of Ministers approved the appointment of an independent investigative committee to investigate 16 specific points set down by the Council of Ministers. It was headed by a former Supreme Court judge who was assisted by two Greek expert appraisers.

The final report of this committee was submitted to the Cabinet and then to the attorney general. It was widely believed by the public that this committee was specifically set up to decide on whether blameworthiness can be apportioned to any party(s), that it was empowered to name the guilty parties and that based on its conclusions, the attorney general would decide whether or not to initiate criminal proceedings against those parties identified in the report. However, the attorney general clarified the point that the committee was not a court and that neither the official accident investigation report compiled by the Greek AAIASB, nor the report of this committee would lead to criminal charges without an investigation by the police. He also added that the official accident report was useful to the police because it could point them in the right direction.

In light of the fact that the public inquiry did not have the power to bind authorities, the public questioned the basis of setting up the committee in the first place. The government spokesman who wanted to clarify the position and to appease the relatives' fears that no one would be brought to justice, stated that the mandate of the commission was to establish potential criminal, disciplinary or administrative liability. He stressed the fact that it would only note where such liabilities lie, as from that point onwards, it would be up to the judicial authorities to investigate specific charges.

One hundred and nineteen charges of manslaughter and causing death through a reckless, careless and dangerous act were filed in the Nicosia District Criminal Court against the chairman of the board of directors and CEO of Helios, the chief pilot, the general manager of Helios, the operations manager and the airline, Helios Airlines.

It is interesting to note that even though 121 people were killed as a result of the accident, only 119 charges were filed against the accused as the two pilots who were also killed were considered to have had some responsibility for the accident.

In February 2010 the Greek judicial authorities, despite the fact that four individuals as well as the Helios airlines as a legal entity are already on trial at the Nicosia Criminal Court, proceeded with charges against the same individuals but included the two engineers. It is the first case in which criminal trials in two jurisdictions are being initiated against aviation professionals subsequent to an air accident.

Gol Boeing 737 and Embraer Jet Collision – Amazon Jungle, Brazil (2006)

On 29 September 2006 at 4:57 Brasilia standard time, a Gol Airlines B737, Flight 1907 collided in mid-air with an Embraer Legacy business jet. The Gol Airlines flight departed Manaus-Eduardo Gomes International Airport, at 3:35 local time on a scheduled passenger flight to Brasilia, with continuing service to Rio de Janeiro.

The Embraer Legacy departed at about 2:51 and at 4:02, the transponder of the Legacy was no longer being received by ATC radar. The controller made an initial 'blind call' and a further six radio calls attempting to establish contact and then instructed the crew to change frequencies. No replies were received. At 4:48, the crew of the Legacy made a series of 12 radio calls to ATC attempting to make contact. The crew heard the 4:53 call, but the pilot did not understand all of the digits, and requested a repeat. No reply from ATC was received. The pilot made seven more attempts to establish contact. Both the Gol Boeing 737 and the Legacy were now on a head-on collision course at the same altitude. Because the transponder of the Legacy was not functioning properly, the TCAS equipment on both planes did not alert the crews. At FL370, over the remote Amazon jungle, both aircraft collided. The left winglet of the Legacy (which includes a metal spar) made contact with the left wing leading edge of the Boeing 737. The impact resulted in damage to a major portion of the left wing structure and lower skin, ultimately rendering the 737 uncontrollable. The B737 was destroyed by in-flight break-up and impact forces. The Legacy's winglet was sheared off and damage was sustained to the vertical stabilizer tip. The crew made numerous further calls to ATC declaring an emergency and their intent to make a landing at the Cachimbo Air Base. At 5:02, the transponder returns from the Legacy were received by ATC. At 5:13, an uninvolved flight crew assisted in relaying communications between the Legacy and ATC until the aeroplane established communication with Cachimbo tower. The damaged Legacy made a safe emergency landing at Cachimbo Air Base with heavy damage. Wreckage of the Boeing 737 was found about 14 hours after the incident in a heavily wooded area near the area of the reported collision. All 154 passengers and crew aboard the Boeing 737 were killed as the aircraft crashed into an area of dense rainforest, while the Embraer Legacy, despite sustaining serious damage to its left wing and tail, landed safely with its seven occupants uninjured (CENIPA 2008). This was South America's worst aviation disaster but was subsequently surpassed by the TAM Airlines Flight 3054 accident which killed all 199 people on board in July 2007.

Immediately after the Legacy jet had landed at the Cachimbo Air Base, the crew were interviewed by officials from both the air force and the Brazilian agency responsible for the regulation and the safety oversight of civil aviation, the Agência Nacional de Aviação Civil (ANAC) and were later detained. Both the

CVR and the FDR were seized from the Legacy jet and sent to Sao Paulo and later to Canada for the read-out and analysis of the data (Bleyer 2006).

The accident was investigated by both the Brazilian air force Centro de Investigacao e Prevencao de Acidentes Aeronauticos (CENIPA) as the military controls civil aviation traffic in Brazil and the US National Transportation Safety Board (NTSB) in accordance with the provisions of ICAO Annex 13 (ICAO 2001), representing the state of the manufacturer (Boeing), the state of registry, state of operator of the Legacy and state of the manufacturer of the avionics equipment installed in both planes (Honeywell). The final report was issued on 10 December 2008.

In mid July 2007 the Brazilian Congress concluded an inquiry conducted by the lower house. IFATCA, the International Federation of Air Traffic Controllers' Associations, issued a response to the statements made in front of the Brazilian Congress by the chief commander of the Brazilian Air Force and the commander of the ANAC that the ATCO controlling the Legacy flight had made a mistake resulting in the mid-air collision with the Gol Airlines B737. They contended that both the pilots and the controllers were victims of the system design of the air traffic and flight equipment in use. IFATCA also urged the Brazilian authorities not to engage in a 'counterproductive' blame and to take the necessary remedial actions in the interests of safety (IFATCA 2006).

The CENIPA report released in December 2008 states that the following contributed to the accident:

- the air traffic controllers originally issuing an improper clearance to the Legacy, and not catching or correcting the mistake during the subsequent hand-off to Brasilia Centre or later on;
- the errors in the way the controllers handled the loss of radar and radio contact with the Legacy;
- the Legacy pilots' failure to recognize that their transponder was inadvertently switched off, thereby disabling the collision avoidance system on both aircraft, as well as their overall insufficient training and preparation (CENIPA 2008).

The NTSB stated that the accident was probably caused by the two aircraft following ATC clearances which directed them to operate in opposite directions on the same airway at the same altitude resulting in a mid-air collision and the loss of effective air traffic control was the result of a combination of numerous individual and institutional ATC factors reflecting systemic shortcomings in ATC concepts. The report further states that the undetected loss of the TCAS functionality as a result of the inadvertent inactivation of the transponder on board the Legacy and the inadequate communication between ATC and the Legacy flight crew were factors that contributed to the accident (NTSB 2006b).

The two American pilots were detained in their hotel for 71 days. They had their passports revoked by a magistrate and were threatened with charges of involuntary manslaughter. The pilots were finally allowed to leave on 15 December, after being formally charged with the offence of 'endangering air safety'. Three ATCOs also faced criminal charges and a fourth controller was charged with the more serious crime of knowingly exposing an aircraft to danger (Aero-News.net. 2007).

In 2007, a judge overturned the Brazil court ruling demanding the pilots travel to Brazil for the trial and therefore if and when the trial commences they will be permitted to provide evidence from the United States.

The charges against two ATCOs were dismissed and in 2008 a judge dismissed the charges against the two American pilots. However, in January 2010, the Appeals Court overturned the first ruling, stating that they should face the charges (Fox News 2010).

There was much media coverage of the accident both locally and abroad. The president of the Association of Aircraft Pilots and owners testified before Congress and in the press and prior to the release of the report from the technical investigation, pointing to the pilots and blaming them for causing the accident. There was speculation that the ATCOs were also responsible for the accident and there was a public outcry against the air traffic system, criticizing the military's complete control of the Brazilian air services as well as calls for the resignation of military officials thought to be accountable for the accident (Downie 2007). After the TAM Airlines accident in July 2007 mentioned above, the president of Brazil fired the Minister of Defence, who had been in charge of the air traffic services in Brazil, and appointed a former Supreme Court president to replace him (BBC News 2007).

Following the Gol–Legacy jet collision, a crisis in the troubled Brazilian ATC broke out. In the aftermath of the accident, controllers, who are also military personnel, went on strike, protesting against, inter alia, their working conditions and poor equipment; this resulted in delays and protests from passengers. On 30 March 2007, 100 ATCOs left their posts causing many delays and nearly caused a complete stop in the country's air traffic as all departures across Brazil were suspended (Reuters 2007).

Pilot unions such as IFALPA and ALPA, as well as safety organizations, reacted strongly to the criminalization of the pilots and the ATCOs and their indictments in light of insufficient evidence and protested against the precedent that this would set. In a press release IFALPA stated that:

> There should be no criminal liability without intent to do harm. Brazilian law must respect this fundamental principle in all cases. Since there has not been any factual support advanced for a finding that there was any intent by the Legacy crew to place their aircraft in danger, there should be no basis for prosecution under Brazilian law and therefore, Judge Mendes' ruling is flawed and counter productive to the improvement of air safety. (IFALPA 2009b)

Subsequent to the accident in 2007, the two pilots were initially charged with unintentionally committing a crime against the safety of the national air transport system. However, in 2009 the Federal Public Prosecutor's Office filed new charges against the pilots alleging a crime intentionally committed against the safety of the national air transportation system (Batista n.d.). These charges were based on the evidence given by two experts who identified two types of conduct by the pilots that allegedly caused the accident. Their opinion was based on the analysis of the accident conducted by CENIPA dated December 2008. They point out two mistakes that still had not been identified: the pilots omitted information that the Legacy jet had no authorization to over-fly an area considered to be special airspace, and at no time during the flight did they turn on the TCAS. The TCAS is an instrument that provides information to the pilot regarding the existence of other nearby aircraft in order to avoid collisions. In critical situations, when the risk of collision is imminent, the TCAS issues warning signals and indicates evasive movements capable of guaranteeing a safe distance. The two experts maintained that the pilot of the Legacy had a mandatory requirement to report the fact that the aircraft did not have the approval for reduced vertical separation minimum RVSM and that the transcripts of the conversation between the crew and ATC indicated that this was not reported. Secondly, they reported that the pilots did not, at any time during the flight switch on the TCAS.

This case raises many complex legal and political issues, putting a strain on the relations between Brazil and the USA. As there is no extradition treaty between the two countries, it remains to be seen if and how the prosecution of the pilots will be enforced in practice.

Garuda Boeing 737-400 – Yogyakarta Airport, Indonesia (2007)

On 7 March 2007, 06:57 local time, Garuda Indonesia Flight 200, a Boeing 737-400, registration PK-GZC, an early morning service scheduled to fly from Jakarta to Yogyakarta, overran the runway upon landing at Yogyakarta Airport, Indonesia. Of the 140 persons on board, 119 survived. One flight attendant and 20 passengers were killed and a flight attendant and 11 passengers were injured. The pilot in command (PIC) was the pilot flying, and the co-pilot was the pilot non-flying. The PIC intended to make an instrument landing system (ILS) approach to Runway 9 at Yogyakarta and briefed the co-pilot accordingly. The aircraft was cleared for a visual approach, with a requirement to proceed to long final and report runway in sight. Although the crew acknowledged the visual approach clearance, they continued with the ILS approach but did not inform the ATCO. The descent and approach were conducted in visual meteorological conditions.

At 07:55:33 the PIC descended the aircraft steeply in an attempt to reach the runway, but in doing so, the airspeed increased excessively. As the aircraft was being flown at speeds that were in excess of the wing flaps' operation speed, the co-pilot elected not to extend the flaps as instructed by the PIC. During the approach, the GPWS alerts and warnings sounded 15 times and the co-pilot called for the PIC to go around. The PIC continued the approach with flaps five degrees, and the aircraft attained the glide slope. The aircraft crossed the threshold, 89 feet above the runway, at an airspeed of 98 knots faster than the required landing speed for flaps 40 degrees and touched down at an airspeed 87 knots faster. Shortly after touching down, the co-pilot called, with high intonation, for the PIC to go around. The aircraft overran the departure end of Runway 9, to the right of the centreline at 110 knots. The aircraft crossed a road, and impacted an embankment before stopping in a rice paddy field. The aircraft was destroyed by a post-crash fire (NTSC 2007).

The accident was reported widely in the world media and aviation safety in Indonesia was questioned. As five of the perished passengers were Australian citizens the accident received great coverage in Australia. Media reports and governmental statements demanded an expedient and complete investigation into the accident. In June 2007, the European Union banned all Indonesian airlines from its airspace; the ban was lifted for four airlines, including Garuda, in 2009.

The official accident investigation was conducted by the National Transportation Safety Committee of Indonesia (NTSC 2007) in accordance with ICAO Annex 13 (ICAO 2001). The report outlined its findings which are categorized into operational-related issues, regulatory oversight, airport- and maintenance-related issues and other factors. The committee lists as the causes:

- the less than effective crew communication and co-ordination which compromised the safety of the flight;
- the excessively high airspeed and steep descent by the PIC during the approach;
- the crew's failure to abort an unstabilized approach;
- the PIC's failure to act on the 15 GPWS warnings and the two calls from the co-pilot to go around;
- the first officer's failure to take control of the aircraft and
- the inadequate simulator training by Garuda.

While clearly pointing to pilot error, the report also criticizes the airline for its lack of training and the Directorate General of Civil Aviation (DGCA) for its lack of oversight of the airline. At the time of the crash the DGCA had carried out only one safety and security audit on Garuda since 1998 and the results of the audit were disseminated.

Concerns have been expressed regarding the scope and level of the final investigation. IFALPA in a press release of February 2008 criticized the report for being incomplete. Many serious questions regarding the crew's actions prior to the accident were unanswered, particularly the underlying reasons for the reported behaviour of the PIC. IFALPA added that additional investigation was required to identify the underlying factors which contributed to the actions of the crew (IFALPA 2008).

Following the release of the official technical investigation report many called for prosecution. Amongst the deceased were five Australian citizens, two federal police officers, an AusAid head, a diplomat and a journalist from the *Australian Financial Review*. Another Australian, a reporter for the *Morning Herald*, was seriously injured, losing both her legs. They were on board the aircraft in connection with the then Foreign Minister Alexander Downer's visit to Indonesia. Political pressure was used by Downer himself as well as the Australian opposition leader saying that a basic national interest was at stake: they personally called the ambassador to Indonesia and the secretary-general of Indonesia's Foreign Affairs department respectively, making it absolutely clear that they insisted on prosecution. Downer stated 'I've asked our ambassador today [24 October] to make it absolutely clear to the Indonesians that we want people prosecuted for this accident. I want to see people who have negligently allowed Australians ... to be killed, I want to see those people brought to justice' (Barlow 2007).

The judicial authorities initiated the criminal investigation, obtained testimony from both pilots and requested data from the CVR and FDR. The response by the chairman of the National Transport Safety Committee (NTSC) reiterated ICAO Annex 13 (ICAO 2001), which provides that no information obtained from the technical report may be used in any subsequent criminal proceedings. He continued to state that the technical investigators are only permitted to provide testimony during a court hearing in their capacity as citizens of the nations and not as technical accident investigators (Forbes 2007).

On 4 February 2008 the captain was arrested and charged with manslaughter and the lesser offence of negligent flying causing death. He was released on bail on 15 February. As the Indonesian sentencing system does not provide for separate charges for each of the 21 deaths, the maximum sentence that the captain would serve is that of the seven-year penalty for criminal negligence causing death in an aviation matter. The captain's licence was suspended.

The captain is the first Indonesian to stand trial subsequent to an aviation accident. The judge stated that criminal prosecution and not civil proceedings was the correct forum in such circumstances by saying 'National law takes precedence over international convention, and the civil authority can only impose civil sanctions' (Fitzpatrick 2009). There were protests in Jakarta demanding his release and the Federation of Indonesian Pilots staged a rally at the House of Representatives. Two survivors of the accident also went to the House of Representatives to challenge those opposed to the prosecution of the pilot.

The trial lasted over a year and the captain wore his pilot's uniform and badges in every court appearance. On 6 April 2009 the Sleman District Court found the captain guilty of negligence and sentenced him to two years in jail. The captain immediately appealed and was released on bail, pending the appeal. Following the court's decision, faced with being fired, he chose to resign from the airline.

The pilot claimed that the accident occurred as a result of a mechanical malfunction in the aircraft and of a sudden downdraught as he came in to land. The court dismissed this because he did not alert the emergency services at the airport to the fact that he was making an emergency landing, which could have saved lives as the inability of fire services get to the burning wreckage played an important role in the number of deaths. The court stated that as a professional pilot he should have alerted emergency services (Fitzpatrick 2009).

The decision of the court sparked an outcry, not only amongst pilots worldwide, but also amongst the relatives of the deceased. The sister of one of the five Australians killed in the accident was adamant that justice had not been served and that the court should have imposed the maximum seven-year sentence allowed. The prosecution authorities had only requested a four-year imprisonment on conviction (*The Australian* 2009).

On the other hand pilots in Garuda Pilots' Association stated that the trial had set a dangerous precedent of criminalizing pilots. They claimed that this could actually disturb aviation safety as it would be hard for pilots to perform their duty with this pressure of criminalization, making them doubtful, which could lead to mistakes.

On 29 September 2009, the Yogyakarta High Court that heard the appeal, comprising of five judge panel, held that the captain's negligence was not legally proven and quashed the conviction. Again, there was much public outcry, particularly from the members of the Australian victims' families who felt that there had been no legal ramifications for the accident.

In January 2010 the prosecution lodged an appeal, trying to get the conviction reinstated by alleging that there was an error in the High Court's interpretation of the law.

Summary of Findings

In all of the case studies the official accident investigation was conducted by the relevant official accident investigation body/bureau in accordance with ICAO Annex 13 (ICAO 2001). Accidents that occurred within EU Member States from 1988 onwards were also conducted subject to European law (European Council Directive 94/56/EC) which establishes the fundamental principles governing the investigation of civil aviation accidents came into effect on 21 November 1994. The directive applies to investigations into civil accidents and incidents which occur in the territory of the European Community and accidents which occur outside the territory which involve aircraft registered in the EU when an investigation is not carried out by another State.

The specific words used in the official reports in relation to the probable cause(s) of the accident differ.

The technical investigations were conducted with the sole purpose of making safety recommendations to prevent the recurrence of similar accidents. This was clearly stated in the beginning of all the official technical accident investigations carried out. All the reports did include a number of safety recommendations which are not obligatory. Many of the safety recommendations were however implemented, thus enhancing aviation safety and fulfilling the aims and objectives of the technical investigation.

There are indications that limitations and inconsistencies exist in relation to the scope and level of investigations and the resources available.

In some cases, such as those of the Falcon 900-B, the Yak-42 and the ValueJet, the statements that were voluntarily made by the crew during the technical investigation were included in the final technical report. In the Linate case the ATCOs refused to provide statements to the technical investigators, pending the judicial investigation. In the Helios case all the statements made by the engineers to the technical and judicial investigators were made in the presence of their lawyers, in the UK.

The technical investigations of all the accidents were conducted amidst public outcry, great media attention and, often, political crises.

In the majority of the cases judicial investigations were conducted concurrently with the official technical investigation. In the Uberlingen mid-air collision and the Garuda case the criminal investigation began after the technical investigation.

As a result of the judicial inquiry criminal charges, varying in nature and seriousness and based on the breach of their legal duty and their inadvertent negligence, were filed against a number of aviation professionals, including pilots, ATCOs and engineers as well as middle and top managers.

The probable cause scenario or the causes stipulated to have contributed or to be factors in the accident were subsequently used by the courts.

The courts relied heavily on the accident investigation report and in the case of the Falcon the probable cause scenario was accepted and relied on in the court of first instance, but not in the Appeal Court. The court in the YAK-42 case makes continuous reference to the accident report to validate the judgment it delivered. In the A320 the court relied heavily on the accident report as well as aviation expert witnesses. The court in the MD-11 case (discussed on page 117) accepted the probable cause scenario and admitted the entire report into court.

Sensitive aviation data including transcripts of the CVR and FDR read-out were readily admissible in court and in nearly all cases provided damaging evidence against those accused.

There are a number of factors, such as the media, political pressure and financial interests, that may influence the prosecution of pilots and ATCOs.

Chapter 5
The Notion of Intermingling

Despite the accidents that occur, the aviation industry enjoys an admirable safety record which can be attributed largely to the manufacturers, airlines, service providers and aviation professionals' dedication to safety and the industry's ability to learn from past mistakes and failures which have been identified through scientific advancements in the investigation of aviation accidents and safety reporting programmes. The cornerstone of successful accident investigations and safety reporting programmes is the free exchange of information and admission of unintentional mistakes or omissions attributed to human factors which are now being threatened as a result of the increasing criminalization of aviation professionals.

Traditionally, aviation accidents were considered to be the result of human error and/or technological failures. Subsequent litigation has focused more on compensation and on the courts granting damages and thus criminal law applied only to a limited extent. As a result of changing perceptions of the aviation industry, attributed to the tremendous technological advancements and growth of the industry, society now considers aviation accidents as organizational or systemic failures and therefore demands accountability and blameworthiness. For many decades, the judicial authorities took a back step towards aviation accidents and the aviation industry in general, allowing this important industry to develop unhindered and to enhance aviation safety without the added pressure of facing criminal proceedings. This is not to say that there were no cases in which the judicial authorities took a harsh approach towards individuals following an aviation accident and prosecuted them.

As a result of the impact that an aviation accident has on society and the increased media attention given to an aviation accident stemming from the tremendous emotional pain and suffering of the victims as well as political, economic and industrial implications that may arise, the focus seems to have shifted to identifying those responsible for the accident. Consequently, the judicial authorities are more pressed to fulfil this social demand for justice and not surprisingly, they feel the need to more actively investigate aviation accidents in order to answer the increasing demands for accountability.

In Chapter 2 we examined negligence as the basis of criminal prosecutions subsequent to aviation accidents and in Chapter 3 we discussed the framework of the technical investigations, and then went on to present a number of aviation accidents, highlighting the subsequent criminal prosecution of aviation professionals involved in the accidents. In this chapter we will consider the approach of the judiciary in the investigation following an aviation accident and possible conflict with the technical investigation, considering the different aims and objectives of the two investigations. In addition, we will examine the methodology and approach of these investigations towards the analysis and use of evidence and data gathered during the investigation in fulfilling their respective but conflicting purposes, which, as will be illustrated, ultimately result in an intermingling of the two investigations.

The conflict stems from the fundamental differences in the aims and objectives of the two investigations. The judicial investigation, aimed at finding out the reasons for the death or injury of so many people, focuses on identifying those responsible and attributing blame, whereas the technical investigation aims at determining the reasons that led to the accident and at recommending corrective safety measures in order to eliminate the possibility of similar accidents and serious incidents from recurring, without apportioning blame or liability. There is thus a great divergence in the methodology and approach of these two separate but parallel investigations conducted in the aftermath of an aviation accident.

The approach taken by the legal system is to determine the fault and liability of a party and to then apportion blame. The criminal investigation is therefore punitive in nature. The judicial authorities focus on the most likely parties whose acts and omissions may have played a role in or contributed to the accident. They then gather facts and evidence to build their case to secure a conviction in a court of law. On the other hand, the technical investigation conducted is non-punitive and the accident scenario and sequence of events leading up to the accident are derived from the facts collected, the ultimate intention being the preservation of life and enhancing of aviation safety through safety recommendations.

The judicial investigators face a number of difficulties in their effort to conduct their investigation, the most obvious being the lack of knowledge and technical expertise when analysing and understanding the data collected from the aviation accident site, particularly the sensitive data obtained from the CVR and the FDR. The accident investigators are very knowledgeable about aviation-related issues and have vast experience in such investigations. The official investigators collect and analyse evidence by accurately recording all the relevant facts to determine the relationship between them and the accident and to identify the possible cause(s) in order that the relevant authorities bring about the necessary changes to prevent the recurrence of similar accidents.

As a consequence, where judicial and technical investigations are conducted in parallel, inevitably the judicial authorities rely on the findings of the technical investigation and where criminal prosecutions follow, the judicial authorities have often based the criminal charges on the probable causes of the accident identified in the technical report and have used the data from the CVR and FDR, the testimony obtained from the crew and even the final report in a court of law.

Technical investigators are empowered by local laws to carry out the investigation of the accident or serious incident and the investigator is authorized, and in co-operation with the judicial authorities where applicable, to have free access to the wreckage and all pertinent documents, information, recordings of the CVR and FDR and other related evidence and to conduct interviews, take statements and conduct any tests deemed necessary to achieve an efficient and expedient investigation.

Different countries have different laws and procedures that deal with each investigation. Common law countries like Australia, the UK and the USA have systems where the technical investigation is given preference unless a crime (such as a terrorist act) is suspected, whereas civil law countries which have adopted the Napoleonic Code give the judicial authorities greater powers than those afforded to the technical investigators in relation to access to the wreckage and to sensitive aviation data obtained from the CVR and FDR.

An analysis of the criminalization of aviation professionals in countries that have different legal systems and different approaches towards air accident investigation illustrates that there are great differences in the way that the investigations are dealt with by the judicial authorities from country to country. Judicial investigations differ depending on whether the country having jurisdiction to carry out the investigations has a common law legal system or one based on civil law or other legal system. The following provides an analysis of the powers that the judicial authorities have in relation to the investigation of aviation accidents differ in common law countries and countries that have a civil or other legal system.

Common Law Countries

In cases where the technical and judicial investigation run in parallel tension between the two may arise; however, in some countries, such as the UK, the two investigations have been conducted in parallel within a spirit of understanding and co-operation.

UK

The philosophy outlined in Chapter 5 of Annex 13 (ICAO 2001) stating that judicial or administrative proceedings to apportion blame should be separate from the technical investigation, whilst stressing the need for co-operation between the two investigations, is evident in the 2008 UK Memorandum of Understanding between the Crown Prosecution Service and the Air Accidents, Marine Accidents and Rail Accidents Investigation Branch. This is intended to ensure effective investigation whilst maintaining the independence of all parties (AAIB 2008). The memorandum stresses that the sole purpose of such an investigation is to prevent future accidents and not to apportion blame or liability. It also reinforces the basic principle that the ability of witnesses to talk freely and share information with the accident investigator is vital to the successful operation of the investigation.

The Crown Prosecution Service (CPS) HQ Special Crime Division is responsible for cases of corporate manslaughter and 'disaster' cases. As in most criminal cases, following the police investigation, the CPS will review the case to see if it passes an evidential test and a public interest test and then decide whether or not to continue with a prosecution. The evidential test is concerned with whether there is sufficient evidence to provide a realistic prospect of conviction; namely, whether a jury will more than likely convict the defendant of the charge(s) alleged. If the CPS is satisfied that there is sufficient evidence it will then consider the second test which is whether a prosecution is required in the public interest. Normally a prosecution will be brought unless there are public interest factors against continuing with the prosecution which outweigh the factors in favour thereof (AAIB 2008).

The legislative powers of the Air Accident Investigation Branch (AAIB) are defined by the Civil Aviation Act 1982 and the associated secondary legislation and in accordance with section 9 (para. 10) of AAIB (2008) have the powers to have:

> Free access to the accident site; the aircraft, its contents or its wreckage; witnesses; the contents of flight recorders; the results of examination of bodies; the results of examinations or tests made on samples from persons involved in the aircraft's operation and relevant information or records. They also have the power to control the removal of debris or components; examine all persons as they think fit; take statements; enter any place, building or aircraft; remove and test components as necessary and take measures for the preservation of evidence …

With regard to the sharing of evidence and information obtained during the course of the investigation it is clearly stressed that evidence is given to the investigator on a confidential basis and that such information will not be disclosed unless the investigator is required to do so in the public interest by the relevant court. Paragraph 18 states that:

> Confidential statements or declarations made by a witness cannot be disclosed by the AIB to any other party, including the police and the CPS. However, if a witness has provided a written statement or declaration, he or she will usually be given a copy of their statement or declaration and advised that he or she may share their statement or declaration with other investigators if they wish.

The Accident Investigation Branch (AIB) works on the principle of 'openly sharing factual technical evidence obtained during an investigation with other agencies involved in investigating the same event, unless precluded from doing so as a matter of law' (AAIB 2008, para. 19). It further provides that if the CPS has reviewed a case and decides to prosecute, the deputy chief inspector of the AIB should be informed and the basis of the prosecution should be described.

> The AIB will then review its evidence and, subject to the legislation, share that evidence which can be disclosed. If additional evidence or information is held,

which cannot be released without an order from the relevant court, the CPS will be advised whether it potentially undermines the prosecution case. If the AIB report is available, the CPS will be directed to the relevant section of the report. (para. 20)

A further interesting point is with regards to the destructive testing of evidence. An integral part of the investigation may be undertaking tests to further evidence that may entail modification or even destruction of the specimen. On the other hand, the criminal investigator has a duty to present to a court the best evidence available and this may be the physical evidence in the state in which it was recovered from the accident site. It is therefore provided that when the CPS notifies the AIB of its intention to possibly prosecute, the AIB will, before undertaking any destructive testing of evidence, consider the needs of the CPS.

It will give notice before commencing any destructive testing; consider any reasonable representations the CPS may make as to the impact such testing may have on their own investigation; permit the police (or other investigating authority, as appropriate) to be present during such testing and to take any reasonable records, photographs or video recordings that they require (or alternatively, on receipt of a request detailing the requirements, for the AIB's to make the records, photographs or video on the investigating authority's behalf); and make available to the CPS all factual records, and reports and analysis provided on the tests by independent technical experts. (para. 21)

When the CPS is considering or has decided to prosecute, the AIB is notified and the AIB then has to make available to the CPS a pre-publication copy of the finalized report at the earliest opportunity. This pre-publication copy of the finalized report given to the CPS is to be treated as confidential and not disclosed before the date of publication but the CPS may comment on the finalized report, specifically with regards to the timing of the publication vis-à-vis the timing of the criminal trial. If the report has not been published by the time of the trial, representations may be made by the CPS to the AIB (paras 27–8).

When it is suspected that the accident is a result of a criminal or terrorist act, the judicial authorities take over the investigation as was the case in the Pan Am 747 mid-air explosion over Lockerbie.

Pan-Am The investigations subsequent to the Pan-Am accident that occurred on 21 December 1988 provide an example of the excellent co-operation between the technical and criminal investigations. Flight PA103 had taken off from London Heathrow and was en route to JFK Airport in New York. The Boeing 747 airline owned and operated by Pan American World Airlines was cruising at flight level 31,000 feet for approximately seven minutes when at 19:03 GMT it exploded above the small Scottish town of Lockerbie. All 243 passengers and the 16 crew members were killed. In addition 11 residents of Lockerbie were killed from the debris from the explosion.

As in the aftermath of every aviation accident or serious incident, an official inquiry by the relevant aviation authority had to be conducted in terms of the Chicago Convention. In this case, the UK civil aviation authority's Air Accident Investigation Board conducted the investigation and in the official report it concluded that, 'The in-flight disintegration of the aircraft was caused by the detonation of an improvised explosive device located in a baggage container positioned on the left side of the forward cargo hold at aircraft station 700' (AAIB 1998). Soon it became evident that the aircraft was destroyed as a result of a bomb explosion and that the perpetrators of this act of terrorism had committed the murder of 270 people. The largest ever criminal investigation in Scotland began. The investigation was under the control of the local police force with the involvement of investigators and intelligence services from, inter alia, Britain, the United States and West Germany. Only after the technical investigation had identified the cause of the accident as an explosion that occurred in the forward cargo compartment did the judicial investigation take over (Michaelides 2001).

USA

In America, the investigation conducted by the NTSB normally takes the primary role unless it is suspected that a crime has been committed. However, in a number of aviation accidents, the judicial authorities commenced their own investigation.

Trans World Airlines B747 Flight 800 On 17 July 1996, a Boeing 747-131 operated by Trans World Airlines (TWA), Flight 800, scheduled to fly from New York to Paris, crashed in the Atlantic Ocean, just off the coast of Long Island, New York. All 230 people on board were killed, and the aircraft was destroyed. Visual meteorological conditions prevailed for the flight, which operated on an instrument flight rules flight plan. The four-year investigation ended with the adoption of the official report compiled by the NTSB in charge of the investigation. It determined that the probable cause of the accident was an explosion of the centre wing fuel tank resulting from ignition of the flammable fuel/air mixture in the tank, which was most likely ignited by a short circuit that allowed excessive voltage to enter the fuel tank through electrical wiring associated with the fuel quantity indication system (NTSB 2003c).

It was suspected, largely based on eyewitness accounts of a sudden explosion and trails of fire in the sky, that the accident was caused by a terrorist act or a test missile from a US warship. The Federal Bureau of Investigation (FBI) started a concurrent criminal investigation and took a leading role, applying their rules regarding the gathering of evidence and the release of information, which conflicted and hampered the technical investigations carried out by the NTSB. The secrecy surrounding the FBI investigation often resulted in the NTSB investigation being diverted and focusing on various theories, delaying the investigation and draining their resources (Fenwick and Huhn 2003). It is reported that 600 FBI agents were working on the case, that they interviewed over 40,000 people, including eyewitnesses and relatives of the deceased, and that they were present during the autopsies performed, trying to establish evidence to support their theory of criminal conduct that brought the plane down (Negroni 1997). At a Senate Judiciary sub-committee hearing reviewing the TWA investigation, NTSB investigators reported that the role of the FBI in the investigation was overpowering and at times unprofessional. The sub-committee chairman described the accident as a 'model of failure, not success'; and that the FBI's leadership in the case was 'a disaster that hindered the investigation' and 'risked public safety' (Walsh 1999).

Alaska Airlines MD-83 Flight 261   On 31 January 2000, MD-83 Alaska Airlines Inc. Flight 261, operating as a scheduled international passenger flight from Puerto Vallarta, Mexico, to Seattle with a stop at San Francisco, California, crashed into the Pacific Ocean. Both the pilots, three cabin crew members and all 83 passengers on board were killed. The aircraft was destroyed. Following the accident, the FBI initiated its own, separate, parallel criminal investigation into the accident amidst allegations of maintenance malpractices by the airline and an already ongoing criminal investigation by the FBI regarding falsifying maintenance records at the base of the crashed aircraft. The investigation, overseen by the chief federal prosecutor and comprising of three prosecutors, aimed at determining whether there was any criminally negligent or reckless behaviour that led to the crash. The criminal investigation was subsequently put on hold, pending the outcome of the NTSB report (Airline Industry Information 2003).

In December 2002, the NTSB attributed the probable cause of the accident to be the insufficient lubrication of the jackscrew which led to excessive wear on the nut threads, resulting in the stabilizer breaking off during flight (NTSB 2001a). The report found that the airline's maintenance practices as well as the FAA's failure to adequately oversee the carrier were contributing factors. The investigation focused on the damaged jackscrew and stabilizer and a number of maintenance issues, most of which were mentioned by the NTSB in their report.

Alaska Airlines had been criminally investigated since December 1998 for allegedly falsifying maintenance records on the MD-80 fleet. The FBI raided the Oakland, California, maintenance hangar as well as their Seattle headquarters where they seized maintenance logs and other records. An enquiry by the FAA revealed that during the period of 1998 to 1999, over 840 flights by the two MD-80 aircraft were in an unsatisfactory condition and that they were allowed to fly (White 2000). It is worth noting that an FAA investigator, present during an FBI meeting with the airline, stated that the airline was more concerned with the legal case against them than on focusing on safety issues (White 2000).

Even though no criminal charges were filed, the FBI investigation conflicted with the NTSB investigation in a number of ways, in particular with access to vital parts of the wreckage, maintenance records and other documentation and hardware confiscated by the FBI and interviews conducted with a number of professionals (Fenwick and Huhn 2003).

Emery DC-8 Cargo Flight　A further example of judicial authorities initiating criminal investigations subsequent to an aviation accident on the assumption that there was some criminal activity associated with the maintenance practices is the Emery DC-8 airliner accident in which the aircraft crashed two minutes after take-off on 16 February 2000, in Rancho Cordova, California, killing the three crew members on board the aircraft. The NTSB report compiled after conducting the technical investigation raised questions regarding the maintenance practices by the airline and its repair contractor, as well as the airline's oversight of contractor maintenance (NTSB 2003f).

USAir Boeing 737 Flight 5050　In 1989 Flight 5050, a USAir Boeing 737-400, ran off the runway at La Guardia airport and was submerged in water after the crew incorrectly trimmed the rudder for take-off. The take-off was aborted, the aircraft overran the runway and was partially submerged in water, resulting in the deaths of two of the 55 passengers.

The accident scene was declared a 'crime scene' and there was major conflict between the NTSB investigators and the judicial authorities, both of which claimed to have primary jurisdiction over the scene of the accident and the wreckage. After the investigation of the accident site, the judicial authorities withdrew and the NTSB continued the technical investigation of the accident. The NTSB investigation came under fire from the local police and port authority stating that the accident investigators were only concerned with the cause of the accident, that they ignored possible criminal violations on behalf of the crew and that they relied on unsworn statements made by the crew. The NTSB investigators defended their approach and criticized the actions by the judicial authorities which interfered with their investigation. They stated that this could result in crew remaining silent and withholding information pertinent to the investigation. The Queen's District Attorney (DA) convened a grand jury inquiry subsequent to the accident to determine if criminal charges of negligent homicide or reckless endangerment should be filed against the pilots. In the end it was decided not to press any charges but the judicial investigation severely hampered the technical investigation (McFadden 1989).

The NTSB determined that the probable cause of the accident was the captain's failure to exercise his command authority in a timely manner to reject the take-off or take sufficient control to continue the take-off, which was initiated with a mistrimmed rudder, as well as the captain's failure to detect the mistrimmed rudder before the take-off was attempted. The lack of teamwork among the crew as well as the airline's inadequate training and the crew combination of a relatively inexperienced captain with a brand-new co-pilot were criticized in the report. Based on the CVR transcript, the investigators stated that neither pilot knew what the other was doing during critical seconds as they 'were attempting to maintain directional control at one time and neither was steering' (NTSB 1990).

During the rescue operation, two police officers trained in detecting alcohol abuse spoke to the captain but did not detect any signs of intoxication. Rumours of substance abuse, however, were fuelled by the fact that the pilots disappeared for over 40 hours after the accident on the advice of their union representatives, after which blood samples were provided. At the time, it was not a FAA requirement to run post-accident toxicology tests of the flight crew. A statement was released by the NTSB stating that:

> The Safety Board is extremely concerned that no federal investigators were allowed to speak to the pilots of flight 5050 until almost 40 hours after the accident. Specific requests to USAir and ALPA to interview the pilots and to have them provide toxicological samples were made about ten hours and again about 20 hours after the accident. USAir representatives stated they did not know where the pilots were sequestered. The Air Line Pilots Association representatives initially stated that they also did not know where the pilots were, then later stated that their location was being withheld so they could not be found by the media. This complicated the investigative process to a great degree. The sequestering of the pilots for such an extended period of time in many respects borders on interference with a federal investigation and is inexcusable. (NTSB 1990)

In this case the technical investigators complained that the judicial investigation would result in the pilots withdrawing and remaining silent and that there was tension between the two investigations, particularly with regards to who had primary jurisdiction and control over the wreckage and the accident site (McCartney 2000). Once again, the judicial authorities intervened in the technical investigation and hampered the technical investigation.

Civil Law Countries

Countries such as France provide for concurrent technical and judicial investigation, whilst others have judicial, military or other inquiries which are not the norm (Fenwick and Huhn 2003). It appears that in countries that have the Napoleonic Code, the investigating magistrate has a stronger claim than the investigators in the technical investigation over the wreckage, records and the flight recorders.

It seems that in these countries prosecutors are increasingly attempting to take control of vital safety data and other evidence in an attempt to build their case against the increasing web of possible defendants.

As laws in both France and Italy allow the judicial investigation to take the primary role in investigating the accident and vital evidence, particularly from the

CVR and FDR have been withheld from the technical investigators conducting the official accident investigation in accordance with ICAO Annex 13.

Italy

BAC 1-11 An example of the conflict between the judicial and technical investigation resulting in the hindering of the technical investigation can be seen from the events following a UK BAC 1-11 accident near Milan, Italy, on 14 January 1969. The Italian judicial authorities, demonstrating their unwillingness to co-operate and their mistrust of a technical expert seized the FDR and refused to permit the UK accredited representative of the Italian Commission of Inquiry to obtain the FDR and take it to the UK for the read-out. The magistrate insisted that the read-out could take place in Italy and persistently refused the requests of the accredited representative who stated that as the read-out could be performed very close to Heathrow airport, it would be possible for the recordings to be back in the hands of the magistrate within a day. The Italian experts then declared that they were unable to read the recorded data. The UK accredited representative then raised his concerns of a further possible accident involving the same aircraft and eventually the magistrate agreed that the FDR be taken to London for the read-out, but insisted that he take it. The automatic print-out was made with ultraviolet light on photographic paper requiring exposure to strong light to fix it. In his haste to return to Italy, he took the recordings without allowing enough time for the necessary exposure with the result that on his return he had a blank sheet of photographic paper and no read-out and believed that he was tricked by the technical experts (Tench 1985).

Tunisair accident ATR-72 The ANSV official accident report (ANSV 2008) of the Tunisair accident ATR-72 accident which occurred on 6 August 2005 when the aircraft ditched into the Mediterranean Sea (see Chapter 4) discusses the relationship between the investigation conducted by the judicial authorities and the technical investigation. It outlines in paragraph 1.18 that it had, in accordance with the relevant legislation of 25 February 1999, arranged the necessary co-ordination with the appropriate judicial authority to ensure the prompt recovery of the required material to determine the cause of the accident (termed an 'occurrence' in the report). It then filed the necessary application to be given access to the documentation that the judicial authorities had in their possession, which was required for a proper technical investigation to be conducted.

Even though some of the documentation was given within a short time from the request, other documentation was released only after many repeated requests. In light of this, the ANSV made the following complaint with regards to the use of certain data, which the judicial authority, in accordance with applicable Italian law, was using for punitive measures, contrary to the provisions of ICAO Annex 13. The CVR and DFDR read-out were seized by the judicial authority and kept in their possession until it was ruled by the judicial authority on 30 August that they be taken to the ANSV headquarters, pending further orders from the judiciary. On 10 September, in the presence of the judicial authorities, the data in the CVR and FDR were extracted at the ANSV laboratories. The judicial authorities then sequestrated the data and the tapes removed and ANSV was not given a copy of the CVR data. A copy of the FDR raw data was made available to the ANSV for further decoding and analysis. A few days later, following a judicial authority decision, they were granted access to the CVR, but they were not permitted to supply the data from the CVR and FDR to the foreign accredited representatives who had a right to have access to that data. Nearly a year later, the ANSV was still requesting that the judicial authority lift the restriction they imposed to allow the ANSV to provide the data to the accredited representatives. The ANSV also complained that as a result of the restriction they were unable to conduct simulation which was necessary as part of the technical investigation.

On 9 November 2006, the judicial authorities allowed the data to be used unconditionally by the ANSV for their investigation and to be given to the accredited representatives. The report goes on to state that some of the accredited representatives' rights afforded to them by ICAO Annex 13, particularly in relation to expedient access to pertinent information which is vital to accident prevention, were limited as a result of the powers given to the judicial authorities in accordance with Italian law currently in force. A further point is made that on the same day that the judicial authorities made the content of the CVR read-out available to parties involved in the criminal investigation, the media also had possession of it and it was made public both in print and in the voice media (ANSV 2008).

Cessna 650 Citation III   On 7 February 2009 shortly after 06:00 local time, a privately owned Cessna 650 Citation III in air ambulance service encountered a bad thunderstorm and crashed in the Trigoria suburb, south-west of Rome. The aircraft had departed from Ciampino Airport for Bologna, where it was expected to pick up a medical team and transport them to Cagliari. Both pilots died in the accident. A judicial investigation was launched and the judicial authorities obtained the CVR and FDR. The official technical investigation was conducted by the Italian ANSV who reported that they were unable to conduct a complete investigation into the accident as the CVR and FDR had been seized by the judicial authorities. The judicial authorities also requested that the ANSV provide them with certain documentation which was vital to the investigation (Flight Safety Foundation 2009). ANSV complained about the effects of these potential conflicts between criminal and technical investigation and called for legislative amendment. In April the judicial authorities sent ANSV a copy of both transcripts, eventually providing them with access to the CVR and FDR transcripts of the accident.

Evidently the Italian legal system and its national laws giving the judicial authorities immediate access to the accident site and wreckage and affording them the powers to seize the CVR and FDR results in tremendous conflict between the legal and technical investigations, enhancing mistrust and unco-operativeness. In the examples above, there were strong presentations by the technical investigators that safety was jeopardized by the actions of the judicial authorities, leading to the ANSV calls for legislative reform.

France

Another country where the legal system provides that the wreckage and documents remain under the control of the judicial authority is France. It should be highlighted once again that France has notified ICAO and filed a difference between its national regulations and the ICAO Annex 13 International Standards and Recommended Practices as follows:

> In France, in accordance with Recommendation 5.4.1, an investigation separate from any investigation conducted under the provisions of this Annex is conducted when the judicial authority deems that there is a possible criminal offence. The law, in conformity with Standard 5.10, does establish the relationship between the two investigations and allows the investigator-in charge unhampered access to the wreckage and all relevant documents so as to be able to perform the necessary examinations and work without delay. However, it does not grant him/ her total control over the wreckage and documents, the latter of which generally remain under the control of the judicial authority. (ICAO 2003)

Concorde Flight 4590   On 25 July 2000, the departure of Flight 4590 from Charles de Gaulle Airport, Paris, was delayed by approximately one hour. The crew had requested a replacement of the thrust reverser pneumatic motor of the No. 2 engine and the rear bogie truck of the left-hand main undercarriage was replaced. When all 100 passengers had boarded the plane, the crew was cleared for take-off at 14:42:17 with one tonne over the maximum take-off weight. Shortly after take-off the left main landing gear was destroyed when it ran over a strip of metal lost by a Continental Airlines DC-10 aircraft which departed five minutes earlier. The tyre exploded and a piece of rubber was thrown against the underside of the left wing and ruptured a part of tank 5. A severe fire broke out under the left wing and engines 1 and 2 suffered a loss of thrust. The aircraft crashed into the Hotelissimo Hotel in Gonesse and burst into flames. All 109 people on board were killed and four people in the hotel were also killed.

Immediately after the accident, the French judiciary appointed a public prosecutor to head the judicial investigation. In applying the applicable provisions, the French judiciary initiated their own investigation into the accident. Soon after commencing their investigation the Deputy Public Prosecutor leading the inquiry contemplated laying charges for involuntary homicide against a number of aviation professionals. Throughout the investigation, the judicial authorities maintained control over the wreckage site, and seized maintenance records and other documents as well as the CVR and FDR.

Parallel to the judicial investigation, the official technical investigation into the Concorde accident was conducted by the Bureau d'Enquêtes et d'Analyses (BEA), the French accident investigation body. In accordance with ICAO Annex 13 (ICAO 2001) and European Council Directive 94/56 (European Council 1994), the United Kingdom, as the joint State of Design and Manufacture of the Concorde aircraft, had the right to participate in the investigation and as such an accredited representative and advisers from the AAIB were appointed. Technical advisers representing the organizations with design responsibility for airframe, engines and equipment were also appointed to assist in the investigation. As a result of the parallel investigations and the priority that the judicial investigations has over the wreckage and documents, the UK AAIB expressed major concern regarding the fact the judicial investigation withheld certain evidence and claimed their involvement hindered the investigation.

In the final report, comments made by the UK accredited representative expressing concern regarding the manner in which the French judicial authorities affected the technical investigation, were appended (BEA 2004). They state that the BEA and the AAIB co-operated during the investigation but make it clear that the French judicial authorities presented major obstacles to the AAIB's investigation. Specifically, the French judicial authorities did not allow the AAIB investigators to examine all the items of the wreckage or to participate in the component examinations of the strip of metal which burst the tyre and the part of tank 5's lower skin which was found on the runway, except very briefly, did not allow them to participate in the examination of most of the flight deck controls and instruments and did not allow them to be systematically involved in the examination of evidence (BEA 2004). In addition, the French judicial authorities did not allow the AAIB investigators full access to all relevant evidence as soon as possible and severely restricted their access to the site of the accident, withheld photographic evidence of the runway surface for six weeks which later proved valuable in understanding the events on the runway and hindered the prompt examination of evidence, which resulted in delaying significantly the implementation of safety actions. Access to a limited number of examinations was permitted on condition that a commitment to the judicial investigation, which restricted the use of the subsequent evidence, was signed, and this was not done. Participation in the examination of major components for which the United Kingdom had primary airworthiness responsibility, namely the engine bays, wing equipment bays and landing gear selector mechanism, was prohibited. These obstacles were in contravention with the State of Occurrence's obligations under the Chicago Convention and caused delays which subverted the directive requirement that 'air safety requires investigations to be carried out in the shortest possible time' (BEA 2004). The BEA in response reiterated the right of the French judicial authority to conduct a separate investigation and stated that this did not hinder the BEA's investigation in association with its foreign counterpart, but that it regretted the difficulties that the AAIB investigators and their advisers faced during their investigation.

The final report of the BEA attributed the accident to the high-speed passage of a tyre over a part lost by an aircraft that had taken off five minutes earlier and to the destruction of the tyre. The tyre debris then pierced the no. 5 fuel-tank within the left wing, the fuel stream caught fire and the debris and some unburned fuel entered the engine intakes resulting in loss of engine power.

Following the judicial inquiry into the accident, in March 2008 charges of manslaughter were filed against:

- Continental Airlines accused of negligently allowing its staff to use banned titanium strips for aircraft repairs
- a Continental mechanic, aged 41, who fitted the titanium strip which fell onto the runway before the doomed Concorde flight
- a Continental maintenance official, aged 70
- a former Concorde chief engineer of Aerospatiale from 1993 to 1995, aged 74, accused of not taking action to strengthen the fuel tanks
- the former head of the Concorde programme at Aerospatiale from 1970 to 1994, aged 74, accused of underestimating the gravity of previous tyre and fuel tank incidents and failing to demand design changes
- the former senior official at the French civil aviation directorate from 1970 to 1994, accused of underestimating the gravity of previous tyre and fuel tank incidents and failing to demand design changes.

In September 2006, the highest court in France rejected a request to dismiss the charges and decided that the trial would commence. The trial started in February 2010 in the Paris suburb of Pontoise.

This case clearly indicates the prevailing powers and rights of the judicial authorities over those of the technical investigators and the extent to which the French judicial authorities are prepared to go in order to fulfil their legal and social responsibilities in bringing those they consider to be responsible for a crime to justice in the aftermath of an aviation accident.

Habsheim   One of the most highly publicized aviation accidents in history was the A320 accident that occurred in Habsheim in June 1988 as part of an air show (see Chapter 4 for further discussion). There was a great dispute regarding the manner that the French law was applied to the investigation of this accident, raising doubts and developing a number of conspiracy theories regarding the CVR and FDR. As discussed in Chapter 4, in accordance with French law the FDR and CVR should have immediately been retrieved by the police after the accident for further examination by independent experts. The recorders should have been afforded the legal protection provided by the law. In this case, the black boxes were taken undamaged from the aircraft two hours after the accident but the recorders were taken by the civil aviation authorities and kept out of the control of the investigating court for ten days. What actually occurred however, was that the black boxes were in the possession of the Direction Generale de l'Aviation Civile (the director general of civil aviation), from 26 June to 6 July – that is for ten days after the accident – until the confiscation of the black boxes was ordered by the investigating magistrate. On 5 July the investigating magistrate at Mulhouse ordered the black boxes to be confiscated in Paris before 17:00 that day. The recorders were only taken the following day at 8 am. As a result, the investigating magistrate stated that this accident is 'also a legal crash' (Rogers 1998).

In this case, the technical investigation took control as the director of the French civil aviation had control of the black boxes for ten days. The black boxes that were used as evidence in the criminal proceedings against the captain were disputed as the captain continually argued that they had been tampered with (Rogers 1998). It is evident that there was great tension, an intermingling between the judicial and technical investigations and conflict between the two legal processes.

Greece

Another country with a history of criminalizing aviation accidents is Greece. In October 1979 just after 20:00, a Swiss DC-8-62 on route to Bombay landed on runway 15L of Athens Airport. After touchdown, the plane skidded over the last part of the runway. As the tail hit the edge of the slope the aircraft bent, cracked, immediately caught fire and was totally destroyed. None of the crew was injured. Fourteen passengers were killed and 11 were wounded. The accident was investigated by the accident investigation commission in accordance with the ICAO standards set up in Annex 13 of the Chicago Convention (ICAO 2001). A separate investigating commission was set up by the Greek prosecution authorities. After the initial inquiry by the local civil aviation authorities and the criminal authorities, the Greek police formally charged the captain with negligent manslaughter, negligent bodily injury and disrupting the safety of air services. Fifteen months later, the co-pilot was formally charged with the same charges as the captain. In the first instance trial both pilots were sentenced to five years' and two months' imprisonment. In the second instance trial the court unanimously sentenced the captain to four years' imprisonment and, by majority decision, the co-pilot to two years' imprisonment. Again, the pilots appealed and the court confirmed the captain's conviction but reduced his sentence slightly and acquitted the co-pilot (Taylor 1988).

In this case, the Greek judicial and technical investigations ran parallel. The judicial authorities, having minimum technical experience in air accident investigation, carried out their own tests and arrived at conclusions published in a judicial report which was later used as the basis for filing criminal charges against the pilots. The official technical report was compiled subsequent to the technical investigation by the Greek accident investigation body. It is important to point out that the judicial investigation report had a number of inaccuracies which were to the pilot's detriment and that the pilots may have been in a much better position had the court gathered the facts from the ICAO report (Dettling-Ott 1988). The Greek court correctly did not admit the technical report issued in accordance with ICAO procedures as evidence and relied only on the report written by the prosecutor.

The court did not go into technical details even though it could have made use of the experts at its disposal. It relied on generalities and placed a great emphasis on the fact that the aircraft failed to land safely on a runway on which other aircraft had successfully landed without incurring any major problems, practically at the same time. It is important to note that the question of whether other persons or entities such as the manufacturer, the operator of the aircraft, the airport authorities or the air traffic controllers might have been partly responsible for the accident was not considered.

The captain and co-pilot were both charged and tried with 14 counts of negligent manslaughter, 11 counts of negligent bodily injury, disrupting the safety of air services and interruption of air traffic in violation of the Rules of Air. On 26 April 1983 the trial at first instance began. For each count of manslaughter they were sentenced to ten months' imprisonment and to two months for each count of bodily injury; their total sentences were five years' and two months' imprisonment for each pilot. At the second instance trial, the captain was sentenced to four years' imprisonment by a unanimous decision and the co-pilot by a majority decision to two years imprisonment. The sentences were however converted into fines of approximately 20,000 Swiss francs. The decision of the court was based on the lack of care exercised by the pilots. The court held that touchdown occurred too late, the landing speed was too high and the braking measures were insufficient. It also criticized the violation of Swissair operational rules and the lack of diligent and reasonable judgment in light of the specific circumstances.

In 1986 the case was heard for a third time, referring the case back to the second instance with different judges sitting on the bench of the Court of Appeal. The captain's conviction was confirmed but his sentence was reduced to three years. The prison sentence was later converted into a fine and the co-pilot was acquitted based on a distinction between the different phases of the landing. The Athens Court of Appeal stated that the captain was criminally negligent for not employing all available braking measures in time although he knew that:

> Touchdown point was relatively long, speed on landing was high, runway length was shortened due to the displaced threshold, braking action was medium to poor and [that] rubber residues had been deposited [...] at the end of [the] runway and [that] this lowers the friction coefficient especially when the runway is wet. (Dettling-Ott 1988)

The manner in which the accident was investigated, the inaccuracies in the report compiled by the judicial authorities which formed the basis of charging the two pilots and the trial process ignited wide criticism from Swissair, IFALPA and other international organizations, resulting in IFALPA blacklisting Athens Airport for a number of years.

Learning from the above, the judicial authorities, subsequent to the investigation following the Olympic Airway Falcon 900-B accident (Bucharest, 1999; discussed in Chapter 4), employed a different tactic and appointed two independent safety experts as judicial investigators who were sworn in as part of the judicial investigating team. This move can be said to have implicitly given the judicial authorities the opportunity to benefit from their technical expertise and knowledge during the judicial investigation, overcoming problems in relation to the judiciary's inexperience in complex aviation accidents. It should be noted that in this case the two judicial technical aviation experts completely relied on the findings and probable cause theory of the official technical investigation. During the investigation of the Falcon accident, the two judicial investigators did not, at any stage of the investigation, request any further investigation to complement or enhance the official investigation conducted by the Romanian authorities. As a result, the final judicial report that was compiled by the two judicial aviation experts was almost identical to that of the official technical Romanian accident investigation report. It was this report that was used in a court of law to apportion blameworthiness and liability of the two Olympic Airways pilots and eight engineers. As a result, it can be argued that the official technical investigation report found its way into the courts, albeit in an indirect way through the adoption of the technical report by the two safety experts appointed by the judiciary.

In 2005 following the Helios B737-300 accident near Grammatikos, Athens, discussed in Chapter 4, the Greek judicial authorities initiated a parallel judicial investigation into the accident and appointed safety experts as sworn judicial investigators. The judicial investigating team was actively involved in the investigation. On 19 December 2005, a reconstruction flight was conducted by the technical investigators. The flight departed from Larnaca Airport at 09:07, three hours later than the accident flight had departed. This was done in order to attempt to achieve, as close as was possible, the same daylight and atmospheric conditions. Members of the Greek AAIASB and the Cyprus AAIIB as well as the Hellenic District Attorney in charge of the State Judiciary were on board the Olympic Airways B737-300 aircraft used for the reconstruction.

The presence of the Greek prosecutor in charge of the judicial authority on board the reconstruction flight clearly indicates the extent of the judicial involvement in air accident investigation and their determination to obtain undisputed evidence regarding the investigation as well as an intermingling of the two investigations. In contrast, an example of the tension between technical and judicial investigators regarding who would have control over the CVR and FDR can be seen by the events following the Turkish Airlines accident in Amsterdam.

The Netherlands

On 25 February 2009, a Boeing 737-800 Turkish Airlines Flight crashed short of landing at Amsterdam's Schiphol Airport, breaking into three pieces on impact and killing nine of the 128 passengers and three crew members and injuring more than 50 others.

The official accident investigation is, at the time of writing, being conducted by the Dutch Safety Board, the Onderzoekstraat voor Veiligheid (OVV) and a separate judicial investigation has also been launched. The cockpit voice recorder and the flight data recorder were recovered by the technical investigators shortly after the crash, after which they were transported to Paris to read out the data. The Dutch public prosecution initially asked the technical investigators to hand over the CVR an FDR, but they refused to do so (Haarlem District Prosecutor 2009). Unlike France, there is no legislation in the Netherlands allowing the judicial authorities control over the CVR and FDR and this resulted in a public confrontation between the public prosecutor and the head of the OVV.

The attempt by the Dutch prosecutor to gain immediate access to aviation safety data has been widely criticized and illustrates the eagerness of judicial authorities to obtain such data without considering the effect that this might have on aviation safety. In this case, the decision of the investigation not to provide the data was proven correct and enhanced aviation safety, avoiding a possible recurrence of the accident. Shortly after the accident, Boeing and Airbus issued an operating engineering bulletin notifying operators and flying crew of the possible consequences of the malfunctioning of the radio altimeter in flight and provided procedures on how to deal with such a malfunction. It can be argued that a delay in the investigation may have resulted in the recurrence of such an accident.

Russia

In Russia it is also routine practice to initiate a judicial investigation subsequent to aviation accidents as was the case following a Challenger 850 accident on 13 February 2007. The aircraft departing from Moscow-Vnukovo airport en route to Berlin with three crew members and no passengers on board crashed during the initial take-off, resulting in all three being injured. The prosecutor's general office commenced a criminal investigation following the accident (FlightAware 2007).

The above analysis illustrates the different approaches of the common law countries as opposed to jurisdictions that have a civil law and other legal systems, highlighting the inconsistencies in the powers given to the judicial authorities which lead to an intermingling of the two investigations.

Use of the Technical Accident Report in Subsequent Litigation

The legal framework surrounding the technical investigating of aviation accidents clearly shows that in each of the strata of legislation, it is specifically stated that the purpose of this investigation differs from that of a normal legal investigation, the purpose of which is to determine civil and/or criminal liability, and that it is not the purpose of an accident investigation to apportion blame or liability. This, however, does not ensure that in practice the evidence and the findings of the investigation are not used in subsequent legal consequences and litigation (Mateou and Michaelides 2005, pp. 77–84).

To what extent the findings of the accident investigations may be used in any subsequent criminal or civil proceedings depends on the national laws of each Member State. The official accident reports, and in particular, the probable cause scenario and the contributing factors, should normally not be admitted as evidence in a court of law to determine liability (Mateou and Michaelides 2005). The rationale for this is to exclude the court from a pre-determined decision regarding liability based on the reports determination of 'probable cause'. However, the content and the findings of the official accident investigation report and even the final report in its totality have been used in subsequent litigation against aviation professionals and this has been done in an inconsistent manner. As different legal systems have different approaches in adopting the official technical accident report or parts thereof in the subsequent criminal litigation against aviation professionals, this leads to inconsistency and contradictory approaches which results firstly, in a pilot possibly facing criminal charges in one country but not in another and, secondly, in that pilot being totally oblivious as to whether statements given during the technical investigation and the final accident report will be used against him in a court of law.

MD-11 Accident

The accident investigation conducted subsequent to the MD-11 accident in Japan (see Chapter 9 for a detailed discussion) included a probable cause scenario referring to the actions of the captain, stating that he omitted to disengage the autopilot and thus caused the oscillations which resulted in the death of the crew member. It is therefore evident that the probable cause scenario pointed to a particular person as being responsible for the accident and thus is connected with the search for blameworthiness. The judicial authorities investigated the accident and had direct accessibility to the findings and evidence of the technical investigation. Based on the findings of the official accident report, the prosecutors charged the captain that he had pulled the controls to reduce speed in turbulence without first disengaging the autopilot – a course of action which is prohibited by the aircraft's operational manual. The Nagoya District Public Prosecutors Office indicted the captain on a charge of professional negligence resulting in death. The trial lasted for a year and ten months and was concluded on 24 March 2004.

During the trial a legal point arose as to whether the accident investigation report should be admissible in the court. The prosecution argued that it should, as it provides evidence that the captain was responsible for initiating the oscillations which were the cause of the crew member's fatal injury. The defence raised the argument that in accordance with Annex 13 (ICAO 2001) the technical investigation has a totally different purpose and should not be used to apportion blame. The court, in an unprecedented move, ruled that not only were the findings of the report admissible, but that the entire report was admissible in court as it carried opinions by committee members who had expert knowledge and who could make fair judgment. At the end of the 18-month trial, the court ruled that the captain could be blamed for the abrupt movement of the flight controls but, as he could not foresee injuries, there was no proof of any criminal act on his part, and he was therefore found not guilty. This is a landmark case as it clearly indicates the intermingling between the accident investigation process, the judicial proceedings and the court outcome.

Falcon 900-B Accident

Based on the final accident investigation report conducted by the Romanian authorities, the Greek authorities charged both pilots with manslaughter as a result of their alleged criminal negligence which resulted in pilot-induced oscillations. The Greek court at first instance relied heavily on the findings of the prosecution report compiled by the appointed aviation experts and their testimony, thus allowing the official accident investigation report to enter the courtroom via the back door. The court proceedings were ultimately based on determining the credibility and the correctness of the findings of the official accident investigation report conducted by the Romanian authorities, as submitted by the prosecuting authorities, and the reasonable doubts that the defence raised as to the accuracy of the findings, the probable cause scenario and the conclusions therein. By a majority of two to one the court accepted the probable cause scenario, namely that the captain had induced the oscillation by interfering with the controls when the auto pilot was engaged. The court found the captain guilty, sentenced him to five years' imprisonment and acquitted the co-pilot and the engineers. Under Greek law the sentence can be converted to a fine. It can be concluded that based on the reliance placed by the Greek judicial authorities on the accident investigation report, there was an intermingling between the findings of the accident investigation and the court's decision in determining liability and apportioning blame on the captain (Mateou and Michaelides 2005).

Yak-42 Accident

In the litigation subsequent to the Aerosweet Yak-42 accident (Thessaloniki, 1997) in which two ATCOs were charged with manslaughter in the Thessaloniki courts, the criminal court relied heavily on the CVR transcripts. The following reports were submitted to the court and accepted as admissible evidence:

1. the official accident investigation report
2. the report compiled by the aviation accident review board.

In addition, the CVR transcripts were readily accepted by the court as evidence of the ATC and crew communication as well as the inter-crew communication in the cockpit. As stated above there were three transcripts of the CVR. The cockpit communication by a Ukrainian crew was in Russian and the first transcript of the CVR was recorded in Russian, and then translated by the Ukrainian authorities into English. A second transcript was produced by the Russian aviation authorities and then translated into English. Both transcripts were then translated into Greek and presented to the Thessaloniki court.

Throughout the lengthy judgment, the court continuously refers to parts of the official investigation report and the report of the aviation accident review board.

Once again, the great reliance that the court placed on the conflicting translation of the CVR transcripts is evident and it illustrates the effect that the evidence derived from the official accident investigation had when this court determined the liability of the ATCOs (Mateou and Michaelides 2005).

Super Caravelle Accident

In the trial following the SE-210 Super Caravelle of SATA accident in 1977 in Madeira, Portugal, in which 35 passengers and one crew member were killed, the Geneva court relied mainly on the findings of the accident investigation undertaken in accordance with the ICAO procedures. More importantly, statements made by the accused pilots were actually cited and used in the court proceedings. It cannot be conclusively decided whether in this particular case their statements, made during the accident investigation, were ultimately to their advantage or not.

As the CVR was never recovered and as the transcripts of the conversation between the cockpit and the tower were incomplete, it seems that the court relied heavily on the acts and omissions the accused admitted to in their statements. As the FDR was never found either, the only evidence at the trial was the witnesses, documents and a transcript of the conversation between the cockpit and the recorder. There was also a time span of three minutes in which the communication from the tower to the crew was contained, but not the reverse conversation from the crew to the tower. The statement made by a pilot is a crucial and determining factor in any criminal proceedings that may be initiated subsequent to an accident. It is therefore extremely important that a pilot be represented throughout the investigation of the accident. In addition pilots should have certain safeguards with regard to disciplinary consequences after an accident and be assured of a right of appeal (Dettling-Ott 1988).

In any criminal proceeding a crucial factor is the availability and admissibility of evidence. A difficult aspect of criminal proceedings against pilots is that the courts have to rely on technical issues and on experts interpreting the importance of such evidence. It is often this evidence that a court relies on to determine whether or not a pilot was at fault and, if so, blameworthy, as well as the extent of the blameworthiness to apportion to the pilot.

Summary of the Use of the Technical Accident Report

As illustrated above, a number of aviation accident investigation reports, particularly those which list probable causes for the accident (termed the 'probable cause scenario'), have become the basis for criminal action against aviation professionals. This emphasizes the degree to which the investigation and litigation process have become intermingled in a manner that could affect aviation safety, jeopardize the independence of the accident investigation and lead to injustice.

A further legal complication surrounding the technical investigation report was raised in the Comair case where the court had to decide whether the safety recommendations made by the NTSB were admissible in court as factual reports or inadmissible as conclusions and determinations of the board. The court stated that this matter is basically one of statutory interpretation. Previous cases held that they were conclusions and determinations and thus precluded by statute. The court held that the language of the statute indicates an intention to include more than just the probable cause determination and that as the statute precludes the admissibility of any part of a report related to an accident or the investigation of an accident, safety recommendations 'arise out of and are related to the investigation of one or more accidents and are therefore inadmissible in a court of law' (Dettling-Ott 1988).

The investigators involved in gathering the facts and data during the legal and technical investigation seek the same information and as has been pointed out this can, at times, lead to an intermingling of the two investigations resulting in legal complexities surrounding the collection and sharing of sensitive aviation data and other relevant data and evidence.

The Use of Data from the CVR and FDR in Subsequent Litigation

A particular point at the heart of conflict that arises between the two investigations is related to aviation sensitive data such as the data obtained from the CVR and information from the FDR. The success of the technical investigation process is in effectively identifying safety deficiencies by identifying mechanical defects that need to be corrected, operational procedures that need to be changed and human factor issues that need to be addressed. This is dependent upon investigators obtaining complete information from all parties directly involved in the conduct of the flight and making accurate analysis of the recorded data, such as the CVR and information from the FDR and electronically transmitted air safety reports. The information obtained, together with all other relevant data, is used by the accident investigation committee to determine the probable cause(s) of an aircraft accident. The findings as to what the probable causes(s) of the accident were are then recorded in the official accident report.

Investigators gain access to confidential information and it is imperative, not only to the actual investigation, but to aviation safety at large that such information is not misused. This issue is specifically dealt within Annex 13 (ICAO 2001), where Paragraph 5.12 which states:

Disclosure of Records

The State conducting the investigation of an accident or incident, wherever it occurred, shall not make the following records available for purposes other than accident or incident investigation, unless the appropriate authority for the administration of justice ... determines that their disclosure outweighs the adverse domestic and international impact such action may have on that or any future investigations. all statements taken from persons by the investigation authorities in the course of their investigation;

(a) all communications between persons having been involved in the operation of the aircraft

(b) medical or private information regarding persons involved in the accident or incident;

(c) cockpit voice recordings and transcripts from such recordings; and

(d) opinions expressed in the analysis of information, including flight data information.

These records shall be included in the final report or its appendices only when pertinent to the analysis of the accident or incident. Parts of the records not relevant to the analysis shall not be disclosed.

Paragraph 5.12 continues with a note. The note draws attention to the fact that the information contained in the records listed could be utilized inappropriately for subsequent disciplinary, civil, administrative and criminal proceedings. The note continues with something of a warning: 'If such information is distributed, it may, in the future, no longer be openly disclosed to investigators. Lack of access to such information would impede the investigative process and seriously affect flight safety.'

The evidence, data and other specific details gathered in the course of the investigation are also significant to the police authorities and the plaintiffs when establishing their claim. Annex 13, however, stipulates that the investigators shall not make the information available to those persons 'unless the appropriate authority for the administration of justice determines that their disclosure outweighs the adverse domestic and international impact such action may have on future investigations' (Chapter 5.2).

The success of the accident investigation process is in effectively identifying safety deficiencies which is largely dependent upon firstly complete and accurate information being obtained from all parties directly involved in the conduct of the flight and secondly accurate analysis of the recorded data, such as the CVR, the FDR and electronically transmitted air safety reports. This information collated with all other relevant data is instrumental in determining the facts and events that lead up to the accident or serious incident.

Both the FDR and the CVR are important tools in the investigation of an aviation accident, as much of the information provided by these recorders is often impossible to obtain by other means. Usually, the FDR is analysed first. All parameters are thoroughly checked in the time leading up to the crash, and any anomalies are noted. Very often, a simple analysis of the parameters will be inconclusive and therefore a computer-animated video reconstruction will also be produced. All aspects of pitch, yaw and roll can be determined from the FDR data and this then allows one to simulate the moments before the crash. The CVR records the communication between the flight crew, and between the flight crew and the ATC, the automated radio weather briefings, any conversation between the pilots and ground or cabin staff as well as any other sounds inside the cockpit. It consists of a 'cockpit area microphone', usually located on the overhead instrument panel between the two pilots, a data storage module and an underwater locator beacon (ULB). The microphone records all sounds in the cockpit, including engine noise, radio transmissions, explosions and voices. An investigator will listen for sounds such as engine noise, stall warnings, landing gear extension and retraction, and any other clicking or popping noises. From these sounds, parameters such as engine rpm, system failures, speed and the time at which certain events occur can often be determined.

The CVR recordings are treated differently to the other factual information obtained in an accident investigation. Due to the highly sensitive nature of the verbal communications inside the cockpit, a high degree of security is provided for the CVR tape and its transcript.[1] In addition, the content and timing of release of the written transcript are strictly regulated,[2] and the tape itself is rarely released to the public at trial. Security of this recorded information is highly sensitive and there needs to be a balance between individual privacy and the benefits that accrue to air safety from the monitoring of recorded information. A flight crew's individual right to privacy needs to be balanced with the advantages that an analysis and correct dissemination and use of such information can provide to aviation safety. Issues such as privacy, fairness and trust are raised when a crew member is faced with the use (or abuse) of a CVR against him or her. CVR information can be abused by the inappropriate release of the recorded information and the release of transcripts of non-pertinent conversation. On the other hand, similar future accidents may be prevented and safety may be enhanced by having access to such information. Protection against unauthorized or inappropriate use of recorded information is imperative but at the same time, it is necessary to afford

---

1   In the USA, Congress has required that the NTSB not release any part of a CVR tape recording. See http://www.ntsb.gov/aviation/CVR_FDR.htm [accessed: 1 June 2007].

2   Under federal law, transcripts of pertinent portions of CVRs are released at an NTSB public hearing on the accident or, if no hearing is held, when a majority of the factual reports are made public.

such privileged information with adequate protection in order that pilots continue to assist in enhancing aviation safety.

Ansett New Zealand DHC-8 (1995)

The debate about the use of information obtained from a CVR in a criminal investigation of an aircrafts operation was highlighted by an accident that occurred in New Zealand on 6 June 1995. Shortly after 8 am, the Ansett New Zealand DHC-8, Flight 703, scheduled to fly from Palmerston North, began a very high-frequency omnidirectional range (VOR) approach[3] to Runway 25. The aircraft experienced a landing gear problem while conducting the non-precision approach and the aircraft impacted a hill on the extended runway centreline. The weather was IMC,[4] but above the applicable landing minimum for the airport. The flight crew survived the accident but four passengers and the flight attendant lost their lives.

The New Zealand's Transport Accident Investigation Commission (TAIC) conducted a full investigation into the accident. As part of the investigation, the CVR and FDR were analysed. The technical aspects of the investigation did not create any problems; however, a number of important legal complexities arose subsequent to this accident. Concurrent to this investigation was the criminal investigation conducted by the police. As part of the criminal inquiry, the police requested that the TAIC provide them with actual CVR tape, not just a transcript of the recording, but the TAIC refused to do so. It must be noted that at the time of this accident New Zealand, like many other states covered by the Chicago Convention, had no legislation making it mandatory for an aircraft to use a CVR. The matter went to the High Court and then to the Court of Appeal of New Zealand. The court held that the police did have the right to obtain the actual CVR as the provisions of Annex 13 of ICAO did not make it clear that the CVR usage was protected, only that a court had to balance competing interests in allowing CVR information to be used. Another point made was that the provisions of Annex 13 were not automatically included in New Zealand law and that national law would be required to clarify the issue (Michaelides 2004). The police therefore executed a search warrant and took possession of the CVR tape. The first officer and Ansett New Zealand were not charged.

---

3   VOR approaches are approach procedures which use VORs as the primary navigational aid.

4   IMC conditions – meteorological conditions expressed in terms of visibility, distance from cloud and ceiling, less than a minimum specified for visual meteorological conditions.

American Airlines, Cali, Columbia B757

A further example is provided by the litigation subsequent to the 1995 accident in which an American Airlines Boeing 757 struck a mountainous terrain in Cali, Columbia. The plaintiffs' attorneys sought access to 23 documents compiled by American Airline's Safety Action Partnership which includes a data-gathering programme and a voluntary, confidential, pilot error-reporting system. The airline argued that the information was privileged and should not be disclosed. The court ruled in favour of the airline and denied the plaintiffs access to the documents in this particular case. Other cases, however, may be decided differently.

Annex 13 thus stipulates that accident reports and related material, specifically transcripts of interviews, communications with crew and CVR and FDR read-outs, must not be used for any purpose other than determining the cause of an accident or serious incident. Such data cannot be used to establish criminal or civil liability; however, a possible exception to this is where potential benefit would outweigh the negative effect on aviation investigations. Many countries do not have specific domestic laws dealing with the use of sensitive aviation data or have poorly drafted laws and this issue is therefore to be dealt with by the judicial authorities and the courts. It is therefore left up to the national courts to decide whether to invoke this exception and allow transcripts of interviews and CVR and FDR data may be admitted in a court against aviation professional being criminally prosecuted.

In re Air Crash at Lexington, Kentucky,

In the Comair case the plaintiffs moved for production of an unedited recording of the aeroplane's CVR, arguing that the written transcript that had initially been provided was incomplete, contained editorial inserts and did not reflect the 'changes in voice tone, tempo, volume and inflection' which the plaintiffs argued were relevant to the alleged pilot errors, and that 'the transcripts also did not contain a record of other sounds during the accident sequence that might be relevant to the plaintiffs' pain and suffering claims' (Green 2009). The District Court held that the unedited CVR recordings were admissible and ordered that they be produced to the plaintiffs stating that:

> [T]he recording of the cockpit conversations is one of the few neutral pieces of evidence available to plaintiffs. The court stated that the court encouraged 'the admissibility of the evidence in order not to deprive the plaintiffs of their legitimate right to place before the jury the circumstances and atmosphere of the entire cause of action which they have brought into the court, replacing it with a sterile or laboratory atmosphere.'[5]

---

5 *In re Air Crash at Lexington, Ky,* Aug. 27, 2006, 2007 WL 4321865 (E.D. Ky. Dec. 6, 2007) at p. 2.

An example of legislative provisions on recorded data that complies fully with the intent of ICAO Annex 13 is Section 28 of the Canadian Safety Board Act, which states that 'every on-board recording is privileged and, with very limited exception, no person shall knowingly communicate or be required to produce an on-board recording or give evidence relating to it in any legal, disciplinary or other proceedings'.

Investigators' Testimony in Subsequent Litigation

When building or defending a case, investigators and experts who have participated in an investigation are often requested to provide testimony. In addition, factual documents prepared for the investigation can be introduced into evidence in subsequent legal proceedings. It seems that prosecutors are increasingly attempting to take control of vital safety data and other evidence in an attempt to build their case against the increasing web of possible defendants, as is illustrated by the following cases.

Technical Investigation Report Not Admissible in Court – Winnipeg

After the 2002 accident in Winnipeg (see Chapter 4) the pilot was charged with criminal negligence causing death, criminal negligence causing bodily harm and dangerous operation of an aircraft. The Manitoba Queens Bench in *R v Tyfel* (2007) had to consider the prosecution's request that all relevant reports and conclusions of the official accident investigation conducted by the Transportation Safety Board of Canada (TSB) be produced to the court (Canadian Maritime Law Association 2008). The court re-affirmed the principle in accordance with Section 33 of the Canadian Transportation Accident Investigation and Safety Board Act which states: 'opinions inadmissible: 33. An opinion of a member or an investigator is not admissible in evidence in any legal, disciplinary or other proceedings'. A TSB investigator could not provide any opinion regarding the accident during the trial.

However, based on a further provision, Section 32, which states 'Appearance of investigator: 32. Except for proceedings before and investigations by a coroner, an investigator is not competent or compellable to appear as a witness in any proceedings unless the court or other person or body before whom the proceedings are conducted so order for special cause', the court had to decide whether there was 'special cause' in this case to grant the prosecution's request and allow such evidence to be admissible in the court. The court held that in circumstances where both the TSB investigators and the police were at the scene of the accident and where the police had the ability to conduct their own investigation and where the prosecution had sufficient evidence to prove its case against the defendant, there was no special cause and denied the request. It should be mentioned that the court noted that 'there will be a chilling effect on the effectiveness of the TSB in fulfilling its mandate if TSB personnel were required to testify in court proceedings where the outcome is directed at the finding of civil fault or criminal guilt'.

In another recent decision in *White Estate v E&B Helicopters Ltd* (2008) the Supreme Court, in deciding on a similar request in a civil trial, held that in this case the evidence which the investigator was able to produce could not be obtained from another source and that the plaintiffs had done everything reasonable to obtain the evidence from other sources. The court therefore granted the order that the TSB investigator be determined a competent and compellable witness at the trial (Canadian Maritime Law Association 2008). The court stated that 'while investigative integrity and administrative convenience were laudable objectives, they cannot be preserved to the point where the likely result is injustice, whether to the plaintiff or the defendant.'

An example of parallel technical and judicial investigations conducted is that of the Garuda B737 accident in Indonesia. In this case, the official technical investigators were only permitted to give evidence in a court of law as an expert witness and not as the official technical investigator.

Garuda B737

Following the 2007 Garuda B737 accident at Yogyakarta Airport, Indonesia (discussed in Chapter 4) the technical investigation was conducted by the National Transportation Safety Committee of Indonesia (NTSC). The committee found that the accident in which the aircraft overran the runway on a landing, caught fire, killing 20 passengers and a crew member was caused by, inter alia, the captain trying to land at twice the proper speed, his failure to react to the 15 GPWS warnings and the first officer's two calls to initiate a go-around. A parallel investigation was carried out by the police and at the end of their investigation a 200-page report was handed over to the prosecutors.

As outlined, in accordance with international aviation accident investigation recommended practices (Annex 13; ICAO 2001) the findings of a technical investigation report are not admissible in a criminal prosecution. The judicial investigation should be conducted independently. It was clearly stated subsequent to the accident that the technical investigators from the NTSC could not speak to the police but that the only permitted action under the legislation was to testify, as an expert witness, at a court hearing, once the trial had begun. This would ensure that the two investigations run parallel, but separately. A member of the committee called to give evidence would do so merely as an expert witness as the report itself could not be used in a court of law. The chairman of the NTSC stressed that no information from the report could be used in any criminal or civil liability investigations as the objective of the report was to enhance safety and not to establish blameworthiness. He said that the report had data obtained from the CVR and FDR, according to international regulations such information would not be given to the police for liability purposes (Fitzpatrick 2008).

Conclusions

Evidently, the wording of Annex 13, aiming at awarding protection for CVR information, is not conclusive enough to ensure that its purported aim is achieved. Secondly, few countries have effective domestic legislation that regulates the disclosure and admissibility of accident investigation information. Domestic legislation addressing this issue offers different degrees of the protection envisaged by ICAO Annex 13 (Michaelides 2004). The international framework (created by Chapter 5.12 of ICAO Annex 13), is that the public interest in air safety is enhanced by limiting the disclosure and use of official accident records. Unfortunately, as a result of the inconsistencies in the way that this protection is applied by the various contracting states, a crew member often does not enjoy this protection (Michaelides 2004).

The legal framework surrounding the technical investigating of aviation accidents clearly shows that in each of the strata of legislation, it is specifically stated that the purpose of this investigation differs from that of a normal legal investigation, the purpose of which is to determine civil and/or criminal liability, and that it is not the purpose of an accident investigation to apportion blame or liability. This, however, does not ensure that in practice, the evidence and the findings of the investigation are not used in subsequent legal consequences and litigation (Mateou and Michaelides 2005).

As each investigation has a different basis, purpose and approach which often results in conflict, aviation professionals such as pilots and ATCOs are found in a predicament between supplying information pertinent to the investigation of an aviation accident in order to enhance safety, and the fear that doing so may incriminate them.

There is evidently a tension between the two investigations that are conducted subsequent to an aviation accident. The technical and judicial investigation processes have a different basis, purpose and approach. It is also evident that different states have different legal systems and that as a result of the different legal approaches, this leads to inconsistencies.

As a result of this, pilots, ATCOs, engineers and other aviation professionals found at the centre of both these investigations are not only overwhelmed by them but also face the difficulty of how to effectively participate in the technical investigation by providing relevant facts that may enhance safety without self-incrimination and possibly criminal prosecution.

Consistent and clearly worded legislative enactments and amendments where necessary, are essential steps to be taken in effectively ensuring that aviation sensitive data is afforded legal protection whilst enhancing aviation safety, thus ensuring that a balance is achieved between enhancing safety and protecting individuals rights.

Chapter 6
The State of Play

In this chapter the main issues emanating from our research are discussed in relation to the technical investigation of aviation accidents, the 'probable cause', as well as a number of limitations and external pressures that are exerted on the technical investigations. As a result, the idea of establishing a European accident investigation branch is offered. The use of CVR and FDR data and the testimony provided by parties involved in an aviation accident in addition to the inconsistencies regarding the criminalization of aviation professionals, the criminal charges filed and the consequences to defendants, a European aviation tribunal or aviation court is proposed as a way of ensuring that consistent and uniform application of legal principles are applied to aviation professionals who are prosecuted subsequently to an aviation accident.

Accident Investigation and Limitations

It is undisputed that technical investigations play a catalytical role in aviation safety as important findings and recommendations from them have resulted in necessary changes with regards to the manufacturing of aircraft, advancement in technology, training of pilots and cabin crew and improvement in practices, designs and other procedures. However, as illustrated, in most cases, the parallel judicial investigation has had a negative effect on the technical investigation and often hindered it, resulting in delays and disputes, and may have thus affected aviation safety. As Williams Voss, president of the Flight Safety Organization, so aptly comments, 'We cannot allow the safety of the aviation system to be jeopardized by prosecutorial overreach' (Voss 2009).

All the case studies examined were investigated in accordance with ICAO Annex 13 (ICAO 2001) and the relevant domestic legislation. Recent accidents within the European Union were investigated in accordance with Annex 13 as well as EU Directive 94/56/ (European Council 1994) adopted by Member States by means of national legislative enactments and which is applicable to all 27 European Union Member States, encompassing the philosophy of ICAO Annex 13 as well as providing more explicit guidelines on conducting the technical investigation. Recognizing the possibility of conflicting interests that may arise when an accident investigation board is a governmental body, the directive requires all Member States to establish an independent accident investigation board, thus attempting to safeguard the impartiality of the board. In other parts of the world, a number of accidents have been investigated by technical investigation bodies that were not independent from government departments, civil aviation authorities and the military, as in the case of the 2006 mid-air collision between the Gol Boeing 737 and the Embraer in Brazil, raising doubts regarding the impartiality and the outcome of the investigations.

The EU directive does not directly address the problems arising from the parallel technical and judicial investigations, which, as has been shown in the previous chapter, is a major issue among many EU countries, particularly those with the Napoleonic Code, often resulting in tension between the two investigating teams. France has filed a difference with ICAO permitting the judicial authorities to maintain control over the accident wreckage, documentation and data recovered from the accident site. Italy has not filed a difference but the handling of the Linate and Tuninter accidents demonstrates that the judicial authorities did not conform to the provisions of Annex 13. In the Tuninter case the judiciary exercised full control over the CVR and FDR, and they did not allow the accredited representative from Tunisia, the State of the Operator, to take part in the investigation or have access to the original findings. This clearly shows that even though the accident investigations are conducted largely in accordance with Annex 13 and the EU directive, often, the philosophy and safeguards proposed by Annex 13 are not strictly adhered to and this may have an adverse affect on aviation safety. On the other hand, in Holland, following the Turkish Airline accident in Amsterdam in 2009, the technical investigators refused to hand over the CVR and FDR to the Dutch public prosecution as there is no legislation in Holland allowing the judicial authorities to have control over such sensitive aviation data. Evidently, there are many inconsistencies in the way that ICAO Annex 13 and the EU Directive are implemented in practice. Even though Directive 94/56 attempts to provide a common legal framework for investigating aviation accidents, it does not adequately deal with the conflict and tensions that arise between the technical and judicial investigations which hinder the technical investigation and amelioration of aviation safety.

The official accident investigation reports use different terms to refer to the factors that have led to the accident. Some of the more widely used terms used by investigators to denote this concept of 'causes' are 'causal factors' (Doe 1997), 'determining factors' (Kjellen and Larsson 1981), 'contributing factors' (Hopkins 2000), 'safety problems' (Hendrick and Benner 1986) and 'active failures and latent conditions' (Reason 1997). A critical analysis of the wording of the earlier official accident investigation reports indicates that the relevant section(s) outlining the possible cause(s) of the accident, often termed 'causal factors' or 'probable causes', refers to acts and or omissions of the parties who are later investigated by the judicial authorities. From a legal point of view, these acts and omissions have been tied up with the legal duty of care expected of each individual, the breach of which has led to legal liability and criminal prosecution. In an attempt to ensure that the final technical investigation report does not direct blame or liability to specific individuals and to ensure organizational and human factors issues are identified, significant changes to ICAO Annex 13 were introduced in

1994. In the *Human Factors Training Manual* (ICAO 1998b) and the Human Factors Digest No. 7 (ICAO 1993), ICAO provides guidelines on using the Reason Model (organization accident model) when investigating an aviation accident. Evidently, many accident investigating bodies have now adopted a systems safety approach to the investigation. The more recent accident reports, such as the final report of the Uberlingen accident in 2002, identified systemic failures; the Helios accident report published in November 2006 did not state the 'probable cause(s)' of the accident, but the 'direct and latent causes' of the accident. The report of the Tunisian Tuninter ATR 72 accident in 2005 uses the Reason Model and outlines a number of errors and omissions on the part of the pilots and mechanic, the active, organizational and latent failures, which caused the accident. In those cases where the organizational model was used and the systemic failures were identified, the web of defendants was expanded as top managers and post-holders were held accountable in addition to the pilots and ATCOs and were criminally charged subsequent to the aviation accidents.

As has been highlighted the technical investigation has a number of limitations as there are no specific guidelines regarding the scope and extent of the investigation and this is therefore left up to the chief investigator to determine. In the Helios case, it became evident during the testimony given by the BEA expert during the trial, that only parts of the FDR and the CVR were analysed as the chief investigator of the Greek AAIASB had requested the analysis of specific parts only. The chief investigator, in exercising his discretion, considered that the full analysis of the FDR and CVR was not necessary in order to complete the technical investigation. His experience and professional judgment as well as factors such as the cost and time involved may have affected his decision. However, when questions regarding the unanalysed read-outs or additional data are posed in a court of law, the lack of this evidence creates a lacuna and this may have a detrimental effect on the defendants. In the Falcon case, the technical investigation had to determine the exact time and reason for the autopilot disengagement in order to determine whether the aircraft's oscillations, which caused the fatal injuries of seven passengers, could be attributed to a technical malfunction of the autopilot or to pilot error. As the CVR was not available and the FDR data could not provide conclusive answers, the Romanian chief accident investigator used data obtained from the non-volatile random access memory (NAVIRAM) memory of the Flight Guidance Computers FGC 1 and 2 which were sent to the manufacturer of the autopilot. Astonishingly, critical data was lost during the downloading process due to an error of the manufacturer's technician. The manufacturer, using the remaining data, simulations and mathematical calculations, provided the Romanian accident investigation board with a probable cause theory: autopilot disengagement which was attributed to the captain's interference with the control column of the aircraft when the autopilot was engaged. The manufacturer of the autopilot thus cleared both the autopilot and the aircraft from any malfunction, and attributed the accident to pilot error. The chief accident investigator did not consider taking any additional action to independently evaluate this probable cause scenario such as, for example, test flying the aircraft, as it was not possible to reconstruct the accident in a Falcon 900B simulator. It can be argued that this was due to technical, financial, practical constraints or other factors. The final report included the probable cause scenario and other comments and findings that pointed to the blameworthiness of the pilots.

The Greek judicial authorities conducted their own investigation and appointed two safety experts who adopted the exact probable cause scenario and findings of the Romanian accident investigation board. Thus they endorsed the probable cause theory put forward by the manufacturer of the autopilot, exculpating them from any blame. It could be argued that since the extent of the technical investigation is not clearly defined in Annex 13, but is left up to the individual investigator's discretion, the judicial authorities should have more astutely questioned the probable cause scenario submitted by the manufacturer. In the first instance trial, the court accepted the probable cause scenario submitted in the report of the judicial authorities and found the captain guilty of criminal negligence and sentenced him to five years' imprisonment. The Appeal Court did not accept the probable cause theory and cleared the captain of the charge of unlawfully interfering with the control column when the autopilot was engaged as stipulated in the probable cause scenario but did hold him liable for not switching the seat belt sign on, on top of descent, as required by the aircraft's flight manual. The court reduced his sentence to 35 months' imprisonment, suspended for three years. It should be noted that the captain did not switch the seat belt sign on in compliance with the policy of Olympic Airways, approved by the Greek civil aviation authority, which required the seat belt sign to be switched on five minutes prior to landing. Even though the technical investigation raises the issue of the seat belts in the final report, it does not satisfactorily address this point.

When the technical investigation requires in-depth scientific analysis and explanations regarding aircraft components, systems and computer performance and the read-out and analysis of data, the manufacturer of the relevant aircraft, part, system or computer assists the official investigating board by performing this function. Such analysis is done in the presence of the technical accident investigators and/or accredited representatives. However, there are cases where the findings, explanations and probable cause theories developed based on this analysis have been disputed by those facing criminal charges – such as in the Habsheim, Falcon, Japan MD-11 and Helios cases – questioning the practices used and the impartiality of the analysis done by those who may have a vested interest in the outcome of the investigation.

It is important to note that those on trial, normally the pilots, ATCOs and engineers, are in the impossible position of not being able to dispute such findings due to being under tremendous financial constraints and having limited or no access to independent laboratories that can perform specialized analysis of aircraft components, systems computer performance and the relevant data. This is of significant importance, as illustrated by the Falcon 900B accident in Romania, the

A320 accident in France, the B737 crash in Indonesia and in the MD-11 accident in Japan, since courts are all too ready to accept the probable cause scenario and the findings of the technical accident investigation – in the case of the MD-11 accident, the entire accident report was accepted in court. The result is that the court becomes a battlefield where the defence team tries to discredit and dispute the findings of the technical investigation.

Financial, technical and human resources as well as the limitation of the technical investigation may pose constraints which can adversely affect the outcome of the technical investigation. This may be more evident in smaller countries with limited resources and reduced technical and financial ability to undertake a large-scale, complex air accident investigation. This difficulty is evident within the EU where small EU Member States, with limited experience in aviation accidents and limited technical, financial and human resources to conduct a major accident investigation, have collaboration agreements with other accident investigation branches in the form of memoranda of co-operation for mutual assistance in order to overcome some of the difficulties. Cyprus, for example has a memorandum of co-operation with the UK air accident investigation branch. As a result, the majority of the larger and more complicated accident investigations are conducted in one way or another with the participation of at least one of the accident investigation boards of larger Member States.

Apart from the internal limitations of the technical investigations and the limitations of some countries to carry out complex air accident investigations, it is important to consider other factors such as external pressures including the media, public demand for justice, financial interests and political pressure which may be exerted in some form or another in the technical investigations.

External Pressures Exerted on Technical Investigations

Perhaps one of the most highly publicized aviation accidents is that of the A320 accident in Habsheim, France, in 1988, discussed in Chapter 4. As the aircraft was a new fly-by-wire aircraft, the success of which would have a great impact on the future of Airbus Industrie, the investigation of the accident was conducted amidst great media and political attention, with financial and technological issues at stake. The possibility that the aircraft had a serious technical malfunction may have led to the collapse of Airbus which was a State-owned consortium with the governments of France, Germany, Britain and Spain being major shareholders. The ramifications – the loss of thousands of jobs and the investments made by the governments – may have been one of the reasons that led to the announcement by the French government, Airbus and Air France, prior to any findings from the technical investigations, that there was nothing wrong with the aircraft. The accident attracted world media attention for months regarding the new technology and the safety of the aircraft. The technical investigation was carried out parallel to a judicial investigation that exerted its own pressure and added to the complexities of the technical investigation. The technical investigation was under tremendous pressure as its findings would have had a tremendous impact on the future of the A320 aircraft and could have damaged national interests.

The mid-air collision of Gol Flight 1907 and the Embraer Legacy jet in Brazil is a further example illustrating the role of the media and the public pressure exercised following the death of 154 people. The devastation and personal loss renewed worldwide criticism of aviation safety in Brazil, particularly regarding its air traffic services which were under the control of the Brazilian air force. The detention of the pilots by the Brazilian judicial authorities almost led to a diplomatic incident between the United States of America and Brazil and drew protests from pilot unions and other safety organizations internationally. In addition to the alleged blameworthiness of the pilots, the question of the responsibility and possible liability of the ATCOs on duty soon arose. Shortly after the accident the ATCOs, reacting to the accusations, initiated a number of protests and strikes, bringing chaos to the Brazilian aviation system. Amidst this chaos the technical investigation was conducted by the Brazilian accident investigation board, CENIPA. The US NTSB also conducted their investigation into the accident. In Brazil the air accident investigation board is a governmental body and the technical investigation was conducted by members of the air force who controlled the air traffic system and who had to critically evaluate and investigate their own system. Amidst media and public pressure, both the NTSB and CENIPA had to balance a number of conflicting interests and pressures and unsurprisingly the US NTSB disagreed with the interpretations and conclusions of the CENIPA report. Criticism of the aviation system was heightened by another aviation accident in Brazil in 2007 and on the same day of the accident the president fired the defence minister who was responsible for the country's aviation system. This accident attracted world media attention which questioned aviation safety in Brazil, particularly its air traffic control system. This could have been perceived by the government as a severe threat to the national and economic interest of the country, as any questioning of a country or its airline directs the travelling public away and it takes years to rebuild the public's confidence in the country. It can be argued that directing blameworthiness to individuals – the pilots and ATCOs – prior to the conclusion of the technical investigation, aimed at directing public and media attention away from the systemic failures of the country's ATC system, maintaining trust in the aviation safety and minimizing the political impact on the government as well as serving the demands of accountability and justice from the deceased's relatives.

The world media very closely followed the technical investigations conducted into the ground collision in thick fog at Linate, Italy, and the mid-air collisions over Uberlingen, Germany, demanding explanations and questioning European aviation safety, particularly its ATC system. In both the Linate and the Tuninter cases the technical investigation was affected by the judicial investigation. In particular, the technical investigation of the Tuninter accident attracted local and international media attention and criticism from pilots and ATCOs unions as well as from aviation safety organizations when the CVR was broadcasted by the media. In the Garuda case the technical investigation was conducted in circumstances in which the Indonesian aviation safety standards were being questioned and resulted in the banning of all Indonesian carriers from flying into Europe.

Research conducted by the Eurocontrol society and economic research workshop on air traffic management (ATM) safety in European press reports that French, Swiss and German media mainly focus on the technical investigation reports while local press following the Linate mid-air collision covered the legal proceedings conducted by the Milan public prosecutor's office in more detail than the technical investigation. The report also concludes that the continuous media coverage contributed to the court handing down such severe sentences (Mahaud 2006).

The great majority of the pilots and ATCOs who participated in our research felt that external factors adversely affected the official accident investigation and the outcome of the final report. The following factors were highlighted as external pressures: media; politics, government pressure and corruption; pressure from the manufacturer and the industry; judicial inquiry; financial interest and conflicts of interest. All the respondents concurred that the influence of the media, political influences and pressure as well as financial stakes (manufacturers' or airlines') were the factors having the most influence on the technical investigation (Michaelides-Mateou and Mateou 2007). One of the interviewees was quite adamant and vociferous in his opinion. He stated:

> There are without doubt external pressures exerted on those investigating an accident and this can affect the outcome. In small countries, where everybody knows one another and where politics plays a big role in every aspect of our daily lives, it is well known that you cannot progress or advance unless you have great financial backup or backup from some politician or political party. It is not what you know but who you know that matters. If you want to influence someone or make something go a certain way, it can happen and I believe it has happened in the past ... why should it be any different for the investigation of an aviation accident where so many interests, often conflicting interests are at stake. (Interviewee X)

Another was of the opinion that, 'people will do anything to protect themselves and use whatever means available to do so. Money is power and having power allows you to do almost anything you want and to manipulate people and circumstances' (Interviewee Y).

The limitations of the technical investigation highlights the limited resources that investigation bodies may be faced with, as well as external factors that may have an influence on the technical investigation, and this calls for a discussion of a Central European accident investigation branch (EAIB).

A European Accident Investigation Branch

With the implementation of a common regulatory framework within the EU (EU Ops-1), the establishment of the European Aviation Safety Agency (EASA), which oversees the harmonization and implementation of these regulations, and EU Directive 2003/42 on Occurrence Reporting in Civil Aviation (European Council 2003), the next step would be the establishment of a European Accident Investigation Branch (EAIB) which would investigate major aviation accidents and serious incidents within the EU. The EAIB would ensure the uniform application of procedures and methodologies from an organization and possess technical, financial and human resources to advance the investigation of accidents within the EU. This independent centralized investigation body would be detached from local media and political influences and conduct the investigation without being influenced by external factors and interferences. It would also be better able to absorb the pressures exercised by manufacturers and other bodies that may attempt influencing the investigation. The EAIB would be able to create highly sophisticated laboratories and testing facilities equipped to perform technical analyses, without relying on the manufacturers for such analyses.

There is no doubt that a meticulous and detailed investigation enhances aviation safety by identifying active and latent failures, human errors, human factors, design defects, operational and other procedures and making appropriate recommendations for corrective measures. A European accident investigation branch in which all interested parties would have an open and co-operative role in the investigation process and contribute their individual expertise and knowledge. It would create a transparent framework allowing for independent, objective investigation into the causes of the accident.

The EAIB should have the primary responsibility, like the NTSB, to obtain the CVR and FDR from the accident scene and decode and analyse the data at its own central facilities and laboratories in a timely manner. This will eliminate the current threat to aviation safety arising from the delay in analysing the data because the judicial authorities seize the CVR and FDR, as was illustrated in a number of recent cases. Further, it would ensure the proper implementation of ICAO Annex 13, particularly regarding the protection given to the use of sensitive aviation data, avoiding the improper use of such data. In addition such a centralized body should have the responsibility to provide the judicial authorities with certain data when requested, within the provisions of Annex 13.

Our research found that pilots and ATCOs supported, by a small majority, the establishment of central European accident investigation branch which would mitigate negative factors by providing a centralized, common and impartial body to conduct the investigation. Respondents from larger Member States like the UK, France and Germany, seem to be satisfied with their national accident investigation bodies, largely because the AAIB is greatly respected and has been effectively and efficiently conducting investigations over many decades (Michaelides-Mateou and Mateou 2007). The interviewees provided the following remarks. One of the interviewees felt that 'a central accident investigation branch may result in minimizing the external factors like politics and other factors that are dominant in a country and provide a more just and balanced forum.' Another stated that 'a central accident investigation branch may be better but I am not sure. This may help the smaller countries that have limited resources, however I think that it will become very bureaucratic and as a result, ineffective.' Disagreeing with the establishment of an EAIB, an interviewee stated that, 'I do not think that Europe or many Europeans are ready for a central accident investigation branch yet'(Michaelides-Mateou and Mateou 2007).

The establishment of an EAIB may be faced with some opposition especially from the larger Member States which have well-established accident investigation bodies who may not agree to relinquish their powers. On the other hand, it may be welcomed by smaller Member States that are struggling with resources and experience difficulties in handling large-scale complex aviation accidents. In order for an EAIB to be established, support from the European Member States and European institutions is necessary to overcome the political and legal complexities involved.

Use of CVR and FDR

In order to completely understand the accident and to make suitable safety recommendations, the investigators have to obtain all the relevant information and evidence from all party(s) involved in some way with the accident. This includes sensitive aviation data such as that obtained from the CVR and the FDR. In March 2006 the ICAO Council adopted legal guidance for the protection of information from safety data collection and processing systems. Attachment E to Annex 13 (applicable 23 November 2006) which covers both general principles and more specific guidance states that safety information should be protected from inappropriate use which refers to the use of safety information for purposes different from that for which it was collected, namely, use of the information for disciplinary, civil, administrative and criminal proceedings against operational personnel, and/or disclosure of the information to the public (ICAO 2001, Attachment E Annex 13).

As has been extensively analysed in the previous chapters, data from the CVR and FDR have been extensively used during the criminal prosecution against pilots, ATCOs, engineers and other aviation professionals. It can be argued that the admissibility of the CVR and the fact that the audio recording of the conversations in the cockpit, which were very detrimental to the pilots and ATCOs, played a significant role in the court's decision. Notable examples are the Tuninter accident and the Yak-42 accidents discussed. In the case of the Tuninter the persuasive arguments by the prosecution that the pilot had panicked and did not discharge his legal duties to complete the emergency check list was given weight the moment the CVR transcript was heard in court and the captain was heard praying. In the case of the Yak-42 the court relied completely on the CVR recordings in order to interpret the state of mind of the deceased pilots and give legal weight to the instructions provided by the two ATCOs on trial. The two A320s, the Falcon and Boeing 737 Garuda criminal proceedings, are cases in which the FDR data was extensively used in court. The FDR data was at the centre of the criminal trials as it was disputed by the defendant's lawyers and expert witnesses. In a number of cases, the courts relied on the analysis of the data provided in the technical report and the way that the data was interpreted by the prosecution and were reluctant to accept any contrary statements provided by the defendants' technical experts.

There is no common legal protection given to sensitive aviation data and this data is often used in criminal proceedings against aviation professionals prosecuted subsequent to aviation accidents. As it is up to the national laws of each country to determine whether local law affords protection to sensitive aviation data and the extent thereof, pilots and ATCOs do not enjoy the same protection in all countries. This has a greater impact on pilots who fly across borders and are therefore at the mercy of dissimilar foreign laws that may afford little or no protection.

A significant development regarding the evidence used in a court is the decision of the courts in Japan in the criminal proceedings against the captains of the Japan Airlines MD-11 accident, allowing the technical investigation report as a whole to be admitted for the first time as expert evidence. Equally important to note is the approach taken by the judiciary in the Linate and the Falcon cases in which the judicial investigation appointed safety experts to compile the judicial investigation report which was almost identical to the final technical report, and which was used in the criminal proceedings.

Surprisingly, over half of the respondents in our research were not aware of what evidence and data are used in a court of law in criminal proceedings or that sensitive aviation data such as FDR read-outs and CVR transcripts and other evidence obtained during a technical investigation have been used in a court of law (Michaelides-Mateou and Mateou 2007).

Testimony Provided

Testimony obtained from the individuals involved in an accident provides crucial information that undoubtedly assists in gaining a better understanding of the circumstances that have led to the accident. Such testimony should be given freely, voluntarily and truthfully as its purpose is to enhance safety.

It has clearly been shown that testimony given by pilots and ATCOs in the course of the official accident investigation, which was self-incriminating or incriminating of colleagues, has been used in subsequent criminal proceedings against the pilots and ATCOs. Pilots and ATCOs are faced with a predicament between supplying information and assisting in the technical investigation of an aviation accident and the fear of incriminating themselves. Both have serious consequences to pilots, ATCOs and other aviation professionals. On the one hand, not supplying information which is aimed at enhancing safety and preventing future accidents may impede safety; on the other hand, supplying such information may possibly result in it being used against the reporter in subsequent criminal prosecution, affecting reputation and even liberty. In the Falcon case the statements of both pilots were included in the official accident investigation which was later admitted in the courts. These statements, which were taken shortly after the accident at a time when both pilots were suffering from post-traumatic stress as was diagnosed by the psychiatric report,[1] were used during the trial by the prosecution to incriminate the pilots.

In the Helios case the two mechanics who had vital information pertinent to the investigation of the accident provided statements to the Greek accident investigation and safety board during the technical investigation and to the Greek judicial authorities in the presence of their lawyers. This clearly shows that when they participated in the technical investigation and gave their statements they did so in a manner aimed not to incriminate themselves in the subsequent judicial investigation. The official accident investigation report makes specific reference to the statements of the mechanics in which they state the position at which they left the pressurization after they had performed the pressurization test prior to accident. This information is crucial in understanding the sequence of events that led to the accident. The following extract is taken from the official AAIASB accident report (p. 4):

> According to a written statement by the Ground Engineer (number one), written immediately after the accident at the Technical Manager's instruction, the Captain reported that *'the ventilation cooling fan lights were off.'* Due to the lack of clarity in the message, the Ground Engineer asked him to repeat. Then, the Captain replied *'where are the cooling fan circuit breakers?'* The Ground Engineer replied *'behind the Captain's seat.'* According to another statement given by the Ground Engineer to the Cyprus Police on 19 August 2005, the Captain reported *'both my equipment cooling lights are off.'* The Ground Engineer replied *'this is normal'* and asked the Captain to confirm the problem *'because it did not make sense, as the lights are normally off when the system is serviceable'* [that is operating properly]. The Captain replied *'they are not switched off.'* Since the message from the Captain did not make any sense to the Ground Engineer and *'given the close proximity of the pressure control panel and the fact that he* [the Ground Engineer] *had used the pressure panel prior to the flight and the pressure panel 5 has four lights'*, the Ground Engineer asked the Captain to *'confirm that the pressurization panel was selected to AUTO.'* The Captain replied *'where are my equipment cooling circuit breakers?'* The Ground Engineer replied *'behind the Captain's seat'.*

---

1   Unpublished human factors report on Falcon 900-B, March 2000.

Figure 6.1   Helios B737-300 pressurization panel

Figure 6.2   Helios B737 air conditioning control panel

Evidently, the fear of self-incrimination and prosecution and the presence of their lawyers resulted in the engineers' statements being made in a way that minimized the possibility of them being criminally prosecuted. Undisputedly, this provides documented evidence that if this practice is used in the process of the technical investigation, aviation safety may be affected, as vital information may be withheld from the accident investigation board for fear of prosecution.

To this day the exact events that led to an aircraft flying for hours over the Aegean Sea with both pilots incapacitated have not been clearly established. The statements by the engineers indicate that the flying crew, for some unknown reason, selected the pressurization system to manual. The Greek accident investigation board indicate that the switch was wrongly left to manual by the engineers and this was not discovered during the subsequent checks by the flying crew, resulting in the aircraft climbing unpressurized and causing the deaths of the passengers and crew. As both crew members died in the accident, their side of the story will remain untold. The reality, however, is that the engineers, fearing criminalization and subsequent prosecution, may have kept vital information from the investigation which could pose a risk to aviation safety today.

It is important to note that, in a different twist, the Linate mid-air collisions, the ATCOs refused to provide testimony to the technical investigators, protecting themselves from self-incrimination, pending the judicial investigation. They did, however, provide testimony to the judicial authorities and in remarkable shift the technical investigators obtained those statements to assist them in their technical investigation.

The use of sensitive aviation data, testimonies provided and the final report being used in a court of law undermines the accident investigation process and aviation safety, as aviation professionals increasingly fear that their testimonies and other information provided during the technical investigation will find a way to the judicial authorities and into the court room. Even though every accident investigation report specifically states that it is not its purpose to apportion blame and liability, it can be seen that in practice, this is not always the case, as aviation professionals have been prosecuted based on findings and evidence obtained from the technical investigation. The fear of self-incrimination undermines the trust that aviation professionals have in technical investigations which have for so many years contributed to the advancement of aviation safety. As illustrated, pilots, engineers and ATCOs are refusing to provide testimony or are providing testimony in the presence of their lawyers, or after obtaining legal advice, shifting the perception that aviation professionals have, that the technical investigation is purely safety oriented. It should be noted that a number of professional organizations and unions now provide guidelines to their members when they are facing an investigation.

Inconsistencies

Nowadays, modern aircrafts are capable of crossing half the globe, flying non-stop from Singapore to New York and from London to Sydney. During the flight the aircraft will traverse countries with different legal systems and aviation legislation. As was illustrated, following an aviation accident countries apply Annex 13 in different ways and have different approaches regarding judicial investigations in the aftermath of an aviation accident. Emanating from the study of aviation accidents around the world are the apparent inconsistencies in the approaches towards aviation accidents and the steps taken by the judiciary.

The approach taken by various jurisdictions regarding the criminalization of aviation professionals varies. Very rarely, some countries relinquish their jurisdiction to prosecute as in the case of the SE Super Caravelle accident in Madeira, Portugal, in December 1977, in which 35 passengers and one crew member died. In this case, the Portuguese authorities waived their jurisdiction and both pilots were prosecuted in Switzerland by the Geneva courts. Even though the sentences were never served, both pilots were left with a criminal record. Both were found guilty but no sentences were served as the statute of limitations ran out.

On the other hand, some countries prosecute readily and in one case have even charged pilots who had died in the accident. One such case is in the ATR-42 accident that occurred in October 1987, in Italy, when the aircraft took off from Milan for a flight to Köln in icy conditions. The crash killed all 34 passengers and the three crew members. Despite the fact that both pilots died in the accident, they were posthumously charged with murder and convicted. The co-pilot's conviction was later overturned on appeal. The designers of the aircraft were also convicted of homicide.

Aviation professionals who have been criminally prosecuted subsequent to an aviation accident were charged with a variety of criminal offences. Despite the differences in the legal systems and the penal codes of each country, the common elements of the charges are based on breach of duty, negligence and manslaughter. The charges filed are, inter alia, manslaughter and causing death through a reckless, careless and dangerous act in the Helios case; criminal negligence causing death, criminal negligence causing bodily harm and dangerous operation of an aircraft in the Winnipeg case; manslaughter and negligent flying causing death in the Garuda case and negligent homicide and negligently disturbing public transport in the Uberlingen mid-air collision.

The sentences imposed on those who have been found guilty also vary. In the Korean Airlines DC-10 accident in Tripoli in 1989, in which four crew members, 68 passengers and six persons on the ground were killed, the pilots who were arrested by the Libyan authorities were sentenced to life imprisonment and extradited to Korea. Other sentences range from a number of years' imprisonment, as in the Yak-42 accident in Thessaloniki where the ATCOs were sentenced to five years, to probation, as in the Falcon 900B accident in Romania. Following the mid-air collision in Zagreb in 1976 in which all 176 people on board both flights were killed, the upper-sector assistant ATCO who was on duty at the time of the accident was found guilty and actually served 27 months in prison before being released. In the Tuninter ATR 72 accident the Italian courts sentenced the captains to ten years' imprisonment and in the accident that occurred at Linate the courts imposed sentences ranging from six to eight years.

In the majority of the cases, the trial resulted in a conviction, not necessarily of all the accused parties, which was then appealed. In some cases, such as the Garuda and the MD-11, the court reversed the conviction and in others, such as the Linate and the Falcon, the sentences were reduced. In some cases the court upheld and even increased the sentence imposed as in the A320 Habsheim case. In the Linate case, some defendants were acquitted on appeal, then the prosecution appealed and they had their initial convictions reinstated. Similarly, in the Garuda case the prosecuting authorities are appealing to have the sentence and conviction of the pilot reinstated.

A very important factor is the time taken for a case to reach the trial courts and ultimately the appeal courts. The trial of the ATCOs after the Zagreb mid-air collision commenced seven months after the accident. In France, the case of the A320 accident in Habsheim took nine years to go to court and ten years to go to the Appeal Court, the Concorde case took ten years and the Air Inter 14 years. In the case of the Falcon 900-B accident ten years later it is still to be heard in the Supreme Court of Greece. The trial following the MD-11 accident in Japan took seven years; the trial following the Linate accident three years and the trial after Uberlingen four. Undoubtedly, the length of time that it takes for the completion of the judicial investigation, the laying of charges and the commencement of the court proceedings increases the financial and emotional burden on the accused and cause additional damage to their reputation.

Consequences to Defendants

An aviation accident is, by its very nature, a tragedy affecting many people and a very costly one at that. Costly not only in the sense of the financial repercussions to airlines – many becoming bankrupt following the accident – but costly in ways that cannot be quantified in monetary terms to those who have lost their lives and to the friends and relatives who have lost their loved ones.

On 1 January 1953, an Aer Lingus Dakota DC3, the Saint Kieran, was on a scheduled flight from Dublin to Birmingham when both engines cut out while the aircraft was descending for approach at Birmingham. The captain performed a forced landing in a farm. The co-pilot was injured, the crew members and the 22 passengers were unhurt. An investigation, carried out by the UK Ministry of Civil Aviation, concluded that the aircraft's engines had cut out because both engines were being fed by fuel from the same tank which had run dry. This conclusion was not accepted by the captain who requested that the UK hold a public inquiry. The UK minister refused this request but the Irish Minister for Industry and Commerce agreed to hold a public inquiry. The court was convened under The Air Navigation (Investigation of Accidents) Regulations, 1928. The inquiry lasted several days in June 1953 and had great media coverage in the local press.

The court decided that the primary cause of the accident was the loss of engine power due to fuel starvation, caused by selecting the port engine to the right main tank to which the starboard engine was also selected, which could have been avoided had the crew diagnosed the cause of the trouble and changed the fuel feed to another tank. The then Minister for Industry and Commerce, on the sole recommendation of the Secretary and against the views of the chief aeronautical officer, decided that the captain should never again fly passenger aircraft. The captain was accused of criminal negligence, suspended from flying for life and moved to Hawaii to work as a flight dispatcher (Keane 2002). At the time of the accident, the captain, who was also president of the Irish Airline Pilots' Association, was in conflict with the airline, Aer Lingus, regarding safety issues.

There was no right to appeal the decision. The family sought the quashing of the original verdict. The family had insisted that the accident was caused by water contamination to the aircraft's fuel and that a report of a second crash landing by an Aer Lingus pilot at Glasgow airport six years after the accident in question, also caused by water contamination of the fuel, supported the initial defence they had put forward (O'Kelly 2001).

In 2002 the minister decided to appoint a senior counsel to carry out a review of the 1953 inquiry. The review decided that it was reasonable for the inquiry in 1953, based on the evidence, to conclude as a matter of probability that fuel mismanagement had been the cause of the accident and that there was no additional evidence that would have led the inquiry to come to a different conclusion (Department of Public Enterprise Report 2002).

The captain and his family had insisted for 49 years that he was not to blame for the accident.

The burden of being blamed for an aviation accident is a heavy one to be borne; the accused may suffer emotional distress and financial burdens, lose their licence, suffer damage to their reputation, often face many years of litigation and, in some cases, lose their liberty.

The ATCO found guilty in the Yak-42 accident suffered severe mental distress and one of the air force members accused in the LAPA accident in 1999 in Argentina was found dead in 2005 and it is suspected that he committed suicide. In another case, that of the British Airways B747 incident at London Heathrow Airport in 1989, the pilot resigned from British Airways after losing his licence and then committed suicide on 30 November 1992. In the Uberlingen case, nearly two years after the accident, the air traffic controller on duty at the time of the collision was stabbed to death at his home by a man who had lost his wife and two children in the accident. This man was subsequently convicted in 2005, released in 2007 and hailed a hero on his return home to North Ossetia.

There are many discrepancies that exist in the various jurisdictions with regards to court procedures, admissibility of evidence, time factor and sentences imposed, which ultimately result in injustice. The uncertainty and unpredictability surrounding the criminalization of pilots takes away one of the fundamental rules of any legal system, namely that of predictability and certainty of the law

Figure 6.3   Relatives attack defendants in the Helios case on their way to trial

and of being aware of the legal ramifications when violating the law. A further complication may arise where for example a pilot who is in foreign airspace and is faced with passenger injuries due to turbulence, may decide not to divert to the nearest airport if he is aware that the judicial practices of that country involve ready prosecution or the imposition of higher sentences. By not diverting the pilot may inadvertently endanger the lives of the passengers.

The cases examined indicate that some countries have prosecuted aviation professionals on a number of occasions. Countries that have a civil legal system seem to more readily prosecute aviation professionals, whereas countries that have a common law legal system seem more reluctant to prosecute them for their unintentional negligent acts or omissions. Italy, Greece and France for example have a well-established policy of criminalizing pilots and ATCOs, whereas in the USA, Canada and the UK it is very rare for a pilot to be prosecuted for unintentional errors.

Individuals Prosecuted

From our analysis of the cases, it became evident that the extent of persons charged and/or prosecuted has now widened. Whereas in the past the authorities charged and prosecuted mainly those individuals at the sharp end (pilots, ATCOs, engineers) who allegedly had a role to play in the accident or serious incident, the trend now is to investigate the role of middle and senior managers and even the corporation as well. In the case of the ValueJet and Helios accident the corporation as a legal entity was criminally prosecuted. The UK has enacted legislation aiming to prosecute companies, corporate bodies and other bodies that employ people in relation to deaths at work. The Corporate Manslaughter and Corporate Homicide Act 2007 came into force on 6 April 2008. Under this statute an organization is guilty of corporate manslaughter if the way in which its activities are managed or organized causes a death, and amounts to a gross breach of a duty of care to the person who died and a substantial part of the breach must have been in the way activities were organized by senior management. This development undoubtedly increases the possibility that aviation corporations, service providers and airlines may be more readily prosecuted following an aviation accident or serious incident. It will be interesting to see if other countries will follow with similar legislation.

In the Airbus A320 Air Inter accident in Strasbourg, the French judicial authorities prosecuted the manager of Airbus who was responsible for the design of a system which allegedly played an important role in the accident. This prosecution indicates that the judicial authorities no longer take technological advancement or an aircraft system as a given, but now are able to judge and determine whether the technological advancement or an aircraft system was correctly designed. In some cases, such as the Linate and the TAM A320 runway overrun at Sao Paolo accident in Brazil, senior civil aviation authority officials were also charged for their alleged inadequate supervision of the airport and air traffic control service provider.

In many of the cases, including the A320 Habsheim, A320 Air Inter, Crossair, Concorde, Linate, Uberlingen, Helios and TAM A320, the judicial authorities prosecuted senior and middle managers such as, inter alia, CEOs, accountable managers, airport managers, post-holders, safety managers, training managers and supervisors. The duties and responsibilities of managers and post-holders and the way that they discharge their responsibilities is increasingly becoming the focus of the judicial investigation. In a number of cases, such as the LAPA, Helios and Crossair, the management was prosecuted for having pilots operating an aircraft as they knew or should have known that, based on their performance records, they were allegedly below the required standard. With the implementation of quality and safety management systems aiming to proactively assess and manage the safety risks of every aviation organization, it can be argued that any lapses or failure of the quality and safety management systems could result in more criminal prosecutions. This argument will be tested in the near future with the implementation of the Safety Management Systems SMS which is now an ICAO and European Aviation Safety Agency EASA legal requirement.

In almost all of the cases, the parties involved at the sharp end of the accident or serious incident were prosecuted for their alleged acts, omissions and violations that were found to have resulted in or contributed to the accident, the loss of life, injury and/or damages suffered. In the case of ATCOs the acting ATCO on duty at the time and the supervisor have been prosecuted. Flight engineers, ground engineers and supervising engineers have also been prosecuted.

In the case of pilots, both the PIC and the co-pilot have been prosecuted in a number of cases such as the A320 Habsheim, Falcon 900 B, Swiss Air DC 8 Athens and Tuninter. In some cases the courts differentiate between the legal status and responsibilities of the PIC and the co-pilot. In the trial following the Funchal accident the court held that the PIC had totally disregarded the Portuguese law, the SATA regulations and his superior instructions when he delegated the landing to the pilot under check, and that by so doing he undertook a certain risk. In addition, he also neglected his duties as assisting pilot in that he did not set the altimeter correctly after having received the correct information enabling him to do so, nor did he pay attention to the radio messages for which he was responsible. The court held that these factors alone constituted severe negligence, which resulted in the plane flying at a much lower altitude than the pilots believed. The court stated that even though the PIC lost sight of the approach lights over a long period of time, instead of calling off the approach, he expressly ordered the flying pilot to continue. The court concluded that 'the absence of the view of the runway lights, alarming in itself, called necessarily for immediate reaction that is calling off the approach, a lifesaving reaction, which can be expected from a professional pilot in charge of human lives' (translation; Dettling-Ott 1988). The court added that during the crucial manoeuvres, the PIC was preoccupied with trivial details such as adjusting his seat and his shoulder harness. The court held that the accident was caused by these consecutive negligent acts and omissions and sentenced the PIC to two years' imprisonment and the co-pilot to one and a half years.

At the trial following the accident in Athens in 1979, the decision of the court was based on the lack of care exercised by the pilots. The court held that touchdown occurred too late, the landing speed was too high and the braking measures were insufficient. It also criticized the violation of Swissair operational rules and the lack of diligent and reasonable judgment in light of the specific circumstances. The court stated:

> They proceeded to land without having succeeded in [having the aircraft] stabilized, that is, without having achieved the desired speed to angle of descent ratio, as provided in the Swissair manual. … [They] should have made full correct use of the reverse thrust systems of the engines and ground braking as such use is provided [...] in the Swissair manual and dictated by the rules of diligent and reasonable judgment, in view of those specific circumstances. (Dettling-Ott 1988)

When the pilots appealed the Supreme Court of Appeals referred the case back to the second instance. The case was reopened for the third time and the court confirmed the captain's convictions based on the same grounds as before but slightly reduced his sentence. The co-pilot was acquitted based on a distinction between the different phases of the landing. The court held that the excessive speed and late touchdown performed by the co-pilot as flying pilot was not the sole cause of the accident. As it was the captain who had the responsibility for braking, the court had no grounds on which to convict the co-pilot.

In the Falcon 900-B accident by a majority of two to one the court found the captain guilty, sentenced him to five years' imprisonment and acquitted the co-pilot and the engineers. In the MD-11 accident in Nagoya, Japan, it was just the captain who was charged. In the Garuda case despite the fact that the technical investigation criticized the co-pilot for not initiating a go-around, only the captain was prosecuted. However in the Tuninter accident both the pilot and the co-pilot were prosecuted and sentenced to the same term of ten years' imprisonment.

The inconsistencies in the manner that various countries around the world approach the issue of criminalization of pilots, ATCOs and other aviation professionals raises serious doubts as to whether justice is being provided equally. It is almost certain that a pilot having an accident in Greece will be prosecuted for his acts or omissions leading up to the accident, whereas a pilot who performs the same actions/omissions in another EU Member State may not be faced with prosecution. This point highlights the need for the establishment of a European aviation tribunal to review the evidence and decide whether there has been wilful misconduct or wilful negligence. If so, the prosecution should proceed in the relevant national courts. However, if this independent judicial review decides that there is no evidence to support wilful misconduct then no prosecution should take place. This will ensure that aviation professionals who engage in wilful misconduct or wilful negligence will be prosecuted and that those who lack the *mens rea* required for a crime may freely and truthfully provide pertinent information without the fear of prosecution, thus enhancing safety.

To ensure that all aviation professionals are treated equally, a European tribunal that would review the evidence gathered from the technical and judicial investigation in order to decide whether to initiate criminal prosecutions in the relevant national courts, may provide the necessary forum to achieve this objective. This tribunal should be comprised of judges with experience and expertise in aviation and should have the characteristics of openness, fairness and impartiality. This tribunal could be formed as an extension of the European aviation safety agency. Difficulties in relation with whether national courts will relinquish their jurisdiction will need to be addressed.

The idea of a permanent European tribunal or similar body with the authority to review the circumstances and the evidence provided by national judicial authorities in order to determine whether or not the prosecution of pilots, ATCOs or other aviation professionals should commence, was greatly supported by the findings from the survey. This proposition is offered as an alternative that would allow the national courts to maintain their independence and sovereignty, guaranteeing equality and greatly limiting the external factors that have been identified as having such an adverse affect on the investigation of an accident and the final outcome.

European Aviation Court

An alternative to the Aviation tribunal is the establishment of a European aviation court that would deal with the prosecution of pilots, ATCOs and other aviation professionals. This would result in a uniform set of rules creating uniformity, certainty and predictability. This European aviation court could be a central forum in which the criminal prosecution of aviation professionals would take place. Specific rules of procedure and rules of evidence would be established and function similarly to those of the European Court of Human Rights.

The establishment of a European aviation court was overwhelmingly supported by the respondents as it was thought that this would provide a court with a common legal basis to commence a criminal prosecution, dealing specifically with aviation matters and having the specialized knowledge and experience in such matters.

A large majority of pilots and ATCOs supported the establishment of a European aviation court or tribunal which would be impartial, independent, professional and experienced; would have experts in the specific field; would be based on a just culture; would ensure common standards and would be more fair and just. Those who disagreed with the idea of a European aviation court or tribunal provided the following reasons: Europe contains too many different cultures, understanding and procedures; the court would undermine the protection given in the home country and the existing system is sufficient as it is (Michaelides-Mateou and Mateou 2007).

Three quarters (75 per cent) of the pilots and ATCOs supported the establishment of a permanent European tribunal or similar body with the authority to review the circumstances and the evidence provided by national judicial authorities to decide whether or not to commence prosecution of pilots, ATCOs and other aviation professionals (Michaelides-Mateou and Mateou 2007). The following extracts illustrate some of the views of the respondents in relation to the establishment of an Aviation tribunal or court.

Respondent A

[Such a body would be] more professional and more experienced and will have experts in specific fields and if based on a just culture it will ensure common standards and will be more fair and just.

Respondent B

Most of the legal world is not aware of the real nature of aviation. Of course law is law and should be applied everywhere but what about the special circumstances that both ATCOs and pilots undergo? A court of law with judges and lawyers that are experts would offer a better trial.

Respondent C

There are parts of the world community that always look for someone to blame and that often 'get' the wrong person. It depends what 'culture' the tribunal has. In my country it take a long time before the voluntary and non-blame culture becomes the point of view by everybody. It can be hard to just overnight deal with problems with this fundamental base. People should have a fair trial.

Respondent D

International Standard should be applied to the aviation industry because aviation safety affects not only one country but also the international society.

Respondent E

National courts are not capable of solving these kinds of cases because there is a lack of knowledge in aviation related questions.

Respondent F

Being European it should be composed of relevant members who are used to the European aviation scenario and thus be accustomed to the good and bad practices that have being going around in the industry during the recent years. ATCOs in Europe are different from the rest of the world and therefore it requires a separate court or tribunal.

A European Accident Investigation Branch

In considering the feasibility of establishing the suite of three European inter-related organizations, viz., the European accident investigation branch, the European aviation tribunal and a permanent European aviation court, it is accepted that there are many problems to overcome and that their creation is a formidable task. We shall look first at the central European accident investigation branch.

A major problem that will need to be addressed is the readiness of well-established national accident investigation bodies to relinquish their authority as an independent body to a centralized European body. Most accident investigation bodies of larger Member States are reputable longstanding bodies with many years of experience and are equipped with the necessary resources and expertise to cope with any major accident.

1. Location – The location of European institutions involves decisions by Member States each of which has its own self interests. This may

lead to the location of an institution where the logical infrastructural, financial and intellectual arguments are not readily understandable. For instance, why is the European Court of Human Rights in The Hague and not in Brussels, London or Berlin? The resulting political struggle is unpredictable and far from simple. The additional complexity of reputation and prestige mean that the selection of the location can take an inordinate length of time for instance, as with the European Bank of Reconstruction.

2. Cost – One of the disadvantages includes the initial cost of establishing such an institution. However the size of this fixed cost and the subsequent ongoing cost of staff depend on the selected location. Moreover, the location can be appealing to the experts required or less so, depending on the cost of living and the form of payment to the employees. For instance, the average salary in Euros compares badly with that of the UK.

3. Time – A tremendous amount of bureaucracy has to be dealt with before this body will be up and running and there may be a danger that it will end up as just another expensive administrative body. Due to the political, economic and location issues the time taken post policy decision to set up these entities is difficult to estimate.

4. Staffing – The issue of staffing is a complex one and may be dependent on the location and remuneration packages offered.

5. Politics – The design of these central European entities may have a direct influence on the policy outcomes arising out of a collective decision-making process. It is recognized that they may also be faced with policy considerations, political and other pressures. The overriding problem with the establishment of the central European accident investigation branch may prove to be political as it requires the solving of a number of major issues such as governance, management, resources, locations and staffing.

Alternatives to the European Accident Investigation Branch

As alternatives to the establishment of a central European accident investigation branch the following alternatives have been considered at a theoretical level only and are offered more as suggestions than formal recommendations.

1. Smaller Member States may choose to collaborate closely with the accident investigation body of a larger Member State. This will be different to the memoranda of understandings that accident investigation bodies have with other bodies which call for assistance in the investigation of a serious accident or incident. Small Member States will partner up with the accident investigation body of a larger Member State that will provide training, equipment, resources and participation in accident investigation. The advantages of this compared to the original proposal is that it

needs no centralized authority and it is cheaper and quicker to organize; however, it lacks an organic element which will give voice to the smaller organization.

2. As another option to having a central European accident investigation branch, it may be more feasible to have a number of regional accident investigation bodies comprised of a number of neighbouring states. This may still remain dominated by the big northern European countries and thus have the same problems for developing small country capability as discussed above.

3. A third and midway option is for small countries to have a more proactive sustainable and efficient accident investigation body. This would lead to a collaboration of equals in setting up an agency which would have sufficient membership and resources to effectively investigate Member State accidents and would not require dependence upon large country investigation bodies. Mutual benefit will thus accrue to these countries whilst they retain a degree of autonomy over their national aviation domains. This suggestion potentially overcomes mega European political issues of location and so on, as it would not compete with but complement the existing arrangements.

4. A further option may be establishing a European accident investigation branch which will not fall within the structure of the European Union, like to the European Space Agency (ESA). Membership of this body may be optional for European Member States but may include non-EU Member States such as Switzerland. This will ensure that all states will maintain their national accident investigation bodies whilst being able to provide support and expertise. This will ensure close ties between the European accident investigation bodies.

The new proposed legal infrastructure would meet with the same political and ideological issues that we have mentioned with regard to the European accident investigation branch. However, given the existing pan-European structures such as the European Court of Justice (ECJ) and the European Court of Human Rights, we believe these proposals may be grafted on these existing institutions. It may be feasible to explore the possibility of establishing the European aviation court (EAC) under the umbrella of the ECJ in a similar manner to the Court of Auditors. Similarly, members of the EAC could be members appointed by the European Commission with relevant aviation and legal expertise. This will not overcome all of the potential barriers but may ameliorate some of the main issues. Moreover, we feel building a legal structure would support any of the above options we propose.

Chapter 7

The Effect of Criminalization on Aviation Safety

The majority of pilots and ATCOs who participated in the survey conducted were very much aware of the criminalization of aviation professionals from high-profile criminal investigations and prosecutions following accidents which received world media attention and the reaction of international professionals bodies such as the International Federation Association of Air Line Pilots (IFALPA), International Federation of Air Traffic Controllers (IFATCA), Professional Aviation Maintenance Association (PAMA), Flight Safety Foundation (FSF) Eurocontrol and the International Society of Air Safety Investigators (ISASI) (Michaelides-Mateou and Mateou 2007).

Even though pilots and ATCOs are aware of the possibility that they may face criminal charges after an aviation accident or serious incident, there seems to be a general lack of awareness among them of the law and of the legal process subsequent to an aviation accident (Michaelides-Mateou and Mateou 2007). Specifically, they have little knowledge regarding the law of negligence and how this is applied to their profession; nor do they realize that CVR transcripts and FDR read-outs and statements made by aviation professionals have been admitted in subsequent criminal proceedings. Both pilots and ATCOs felt that the fear of prosecution would prevent the voluntary and truthful reporting of incidents and stated that they would be very reluctant to provide relevant information during an investigation for fear of incriminating either themselves or their colleagues. This fear will consequently encourage the hiding of certain errors or mishaps and the opportunity to extract safety lessons may be missed, therefore impeding safety. Pilots and ATCOs who are already working under great pressure to maintain a high safety level and achieve high productivity targets due to the economic pressures of the industry, are alarmed that the additional fear of prosecution due to an error will increase their stress and this will have a negative effect on their concentration, decision-making and ultimately on their performance (Michaelides-Mateou and Mateou 2007).

The following extracts from some of the respondents are worthy of quoting as they clearly provide a deeper and more comprehensive reasoning for their answer.

Respondent H

The judicial authorities and airline investigators have differing priorities when investigating the causes of an accident. The judicial authorities will only be looking for such evidence that will show whether somebody is to blame and therefore can be successfully prosecuted. Inevitably the search for such evidence concentrates on pilots, ATCOs, aircraft mechanics, and so on. The deeper and more complicated potential institutional, structural and managerial causes of the accident, which are the province of the accident investigator tend to be ignored (and in certain countries actively suppressed because the Government is directly involved with the running of the aviation industry). Therefore, there can be an element of scapegoating with criminal prosecutions, which does not further the improvement of flight safety

Respondent I

ATCOs and pilots are not going to their work having in mind to produce an incident or an accident. They represent the sharp end of organizations and thus they are more visible in the case of an accident/incident than the blunt end of their organization. It is very common for the accident/incident reports to stop the chain of events leading to a disaster or a near miss whenever an ATC or pilot action is 'identified' as the root, proximate or contributory cause to the case. Consequently ATCOs and pilots' actions represent a convenient stopping point in an event-chain model of accidents because of the following reasons: ATCOs and pilots actions are reported and criticized only when they have a negative impact on safety and not when they have prevented/ averted disasters; it is unrealistically assumed that ATCOs and pilots can deal effectively with any kind of conceivable emergency situation they may face; ATCOs and pilots are normally intervening in many cases where management inefficiencies, system design problems and political imposed constraints (representing in general the blunt end) are hindering the normal flow of their everyday tasks.

Respondent J

The Accident Investigation conducted by the accident investigation authority and the Criminal Investigation conducted by the Police must be separated. And the Accident Investigation Report should be protected by the law from not being used in the criminal court. If the Accident Report could not be used for the document of the evidence in the criminal court, the prosecution of pilots or ATCOs would be very difficult. Basically a pilot or ATCO does not make the mistake intentionally. There are some background reasons that they happen to make mistakes. Searching the cause of the accident technically would contribute for improving the flight safety. To enable the searching causes of the accident technically, the honest concerned person's testimonies are very vital. But if the witness feels the testimonies affect the criminal investigation, all persons will not speak the word to help flight safety. The witness speaks only a little word and the important points will be hidden by the non-intentional behaviour. Thus, the important thing is the protection of the Accident Report.

All interviewees, except one, were adamant that the criminalization of pilots and ATCOs had no positive effect, but that it in fact impedes safety. One of the pilots interviewed stated that 'People cannot work with the fear of being prosecuted haunting them. Blaming and punishing someone will not help aviation safety. How can safety lessons be learnt if everyone is too scared to report an error or mishap?' An ATCO concurred with the above statement by saying that 'creating a blame culture will be counter-productive. It cannot be said that countries that have prosecuted pilots and ATCOs have a higher safety record. Having a healthy safety culture allows mistakes to be picked up and learnt from. Prosecuting people discourages others from reporting their mistakes.' On the other hand, a pilot dissented completely by saying:

> People should not feel that they can get away with anything. We have a very responsible job and have peoples' lives in our hands. Prosecuting those who do something wrong will only help others to be more careful and responsible. Prosecuting aviation personnel will ensure that aviation is conducted strictly within the laws and regulations of aviation.

A very small number of respondents felt that the criminalization of aviation professionals does have a positive effect on safety. They believed that:

- others in the profession should be aware that in case of wilful or particularly egregious reckless conduct, one can be sentenced;
- it makes others in the profession aware of their responsibilities to comply with regulations and be more careful;
- someone has to pay if someone does something wrong and people get injured or die and there is no management or technical explanation;
- aviation safety should be handled within aviation laws and regulations;
- criminal or multiple gross negligence should be prosecuted to clearly demonstrate that the aviation community does not tolerate this;
- those (pilots) who carry out illegal acts may be made more aware of possible prosecution and think twice. (Michaelides-Mateou and Mateou 2007)

Analysis of Pilots and Air Traffic Controllers Survey Results

Aviation safety reporting systems have played a catalytic role in the improvement and advancement of aviation safety during the last decades. The role in and contribution of the technical investigation to aviation safety is well recognized. The safety recommendations made following the technical aviation accident investigation are a reactive approach to aviation safety. In the modern era of proactive aviation safety management systems, the technical investigation focuses on investigating serious incidents and other occurrences which provide the opportunity to identify latent and active failures within the system, which if corrected, will eliminate risks and minimize accidents. Most accident investigation bodies now adopt this approach to investigating occurrences and the participation of and information provided by all parties involved in the occurrence plays a crucial role in the outcome of the investigation. Fearing the repercussions of openly sharing information with the investigations will undoubtedly jeopardize the aims and objectives of the technical investigations, and have a negative impact on aviation safety.

This danger was supported by a large majority of aviation professionals who indicated their reluctance and concerns over participating in the investigation subsequent to an aviation accident or serious incident because they feared the legal consequences and punitive measures following the outcome of the investigation. A number of pilots and ATCOs unions provide their members with guidelines to follow in the event of having to provide statements to either the technical investigators or the judicial authorities. An increasing number of pilots, ATCOs and engineers are participating in an investigation in the presence of their union representative or after they have sought legal advice.

This development clearly highlights apprehension amongst aviation professionals who participate in technical investigations, which undermines the notion that the technical investigation is not to be used to apportion blame and liability.

The fear of criminalization is slowly but surely eroding the safety reporting system which has been trusted for many years by frontline aviation professionals. Its non-punitive culture allowed the mandatory and voluntary safety reporting programmes to provide valuable information from the reporting of unintentional errors and mishaps.

The Danish example of establishing a compulsory, non-punitive and strictly confidential system for the reporting of aviation incidents ensures strict immunity against any punishment and disclosure and makes it a punishable offence for non-disclosure. It is a strictly confidential reporting system as the reporter's identity may not be revealed outside the agency dealing with occurrence reports. Immunity is guaranteed if the report is made within 72 hours of its occurrence and if the incident does not involve an accident or deliberate negligence due to substance abuse. During the first year of implementing the system Navair received 40–50 reports of loss of separation between aircraft compared to the 15 reports of the previous year (Nørbjerg 2003). The strength of this reporting system was tested by the courts in 2002 when a general aviation pilot was criminally prosecuted for flying in a dangerous manner when he took off with an insufficient amount of fuel and had to land in a cornfield. The trial commenced from the incident report that the pilot had submitted. The court held that the pilot's report could not be used as a basis for the trial and the prosecuting authorities had to base their case on other facts and evidence. The pilot was found guilty and had to pay a fine (Nørbjerg 2003).

In recent years mandatory and voluntary safety reporting programmes became the centre of a legal battle following aviation accidents when plaintiffs' lawyers, in their effort to obtain evidence to strengthen their case against airlines, have requested data from the airlines' air safety reporting system. This is well illustrated by the case of Comair Flight 5191.

Comair

Comair Flight 5191, a scheduled domestic flight from Lexington, Kentucky, to Georgia, crashed while attempting an early morning departure. The aircraft was assigned the airport Runway 22 for the take-off, but used Runway 26 instead, which was too short for a safe take-off. The aircraft overran the end of the runway before it could become airborne. It crashed just past the end of the runway, killing all 47 passengers and two of the three crew members. The flight's first officer was the only survivor. He suffered serious injuries and had his left leg amputated. As a result of his injuries he has no memory of the accident (Serrano 2006). He later filed a lawsuit against the airport and the company that designed the runway and taxi lights (Ortiz 2007).

The pilots had many cues that they were on the wrong runway, including the fact that the lights on Runway 26 were not lit. The NTSB (2007) found pilot error was the probable cause of the accident in that the flight crew members failed to use available cues and aids to identify the aeroplane's location on the airport surface during taxi and failed to cross-check and verify that the aeroplane was on the correct runway before take-off. Contributing factors were determined as the flight crew's non-pertinent conversations during taxi, resulting in a loss of positional awareness, and the FAA's failure to require that all runway crossings be authorized only by specific ATC clearances. In the subsequent civil litigation the plaintiffs (the relatives of the deceased who were claiming civil compensation) filed a motion that Comair disclose 'all ASAP reports [aviation safety reports filed in accordance with the Aviation Safety Action Programme] involving runway incursions; attempted take-off from a runway other than the runway for which the aircraft had been cleared for take-off; any confusion at Blue Grass Airport regarding runway and/or taxiway configurations; and any reports wherein a flight crew violated air traffic control instructions during ground operations.' In its response, Comair argued that compelling disclosure of the ASAP reports would contradict the intent of Congress and the goals of the FAA and it sought protection from producing the ASAP reports on the basis that they were within the protection of the self-critical analysis privilege, and/or a limited common-law privilege created specifically for ASAP reports (*Aviation and Space Law* 2009). The court rejected that the qualified judicial privilege recognized in *Re Air Crash near Cali, Colombia* in 1995, had been followed by later courts and was not applicable to the case at hand.[1] The magistrate and the District Court rejected the arguments submitted by Comair and ordered it to produce the requested ASAP reports for the plaintiffs (Re Air Crash at Lexington, US District Court 2008).

The above court decisions may have serious implications. Aviation professionals in Europe now have a legal responsibility to file an occurrence report in accordance with EU Directive 2003/42/EC (European Council 2003). In other parts of the world there are similar programmes in place. Considering the possibility that the airline may be asked to provide its air safety reporting database to lawyers or to the judicial authorities, the reporter may not provide a complete and detailed report and may also provide minimum information to the technical investigators. In addition, this may result in a poor safety culture where management, fearing liability, may develop a 'hiding' culture.

Worse still will be the development whereby management will concentrate on protecting itself from the legal consequences instead of focusing on maximizing safety. Considering the actions taken by the judicial authorities following the recent accidents of Uberlingen, Tuninter, Helios, TAM, Concorde, Crossair and LAPA, in which the management, post-holders, safety and quality managers, head of manufacturers, designers, managers and civil aviation professionals were criminally charged subsequent to an aviation accident, a great concern is the possibility that a legally defensive safety management (LDSM) approach will develop which will neither save lives nor improve aviation safety, nor will it serve the purpose of justice. Adopting the LDSM approach will ensure that management will take a defensive approach towards safety management in order to protect themselves and the organization from criminal liability instead of aiming to continuously monitor and improve safety.

Aviation professionals are being criminally prosecuted for the part that their acts and omissions have played in aviation accidents. An accident is by definition something that occurs without it being intended or having been foreseen. It follows that strictly speaking, an accident cannot be a crime as one of the necessary elements required for there to be a crime – namely, the *mens rea* or the intention/foresight required for the commission of a crime – is missing. An accident is normally the unforeseen consequence of human error and it is therefore vital to make the distinction between an inadvertent error which is made while trying to comply with the law and wilful misconduct, egregious reckless conduct or intentional acts such as terrorism or even sabotage which should be investigated and prosecuted.

---

1   *In Re Air Crash Near Cali, Colombia* on 20 December 1995, 959 F. Supp. 1529 (S.D. Fla. 1977).

Imposing blanket immunity on aviation professionals will not serve the interests of justice. Intentional acts that are committed, knowingly violating the law and regulations, and some unintentional errors or mistakes should be punished. Many aviation professionals, including IFALPA, have reacted to the conviction of the pilot who was sentenced to two years' conditional sentence after the aircraft that he was flying ran out of fuel in Winnipeg, by saying that it was an appropriate outcome as the pilot had made a conscious decision not to take sufficient fuel (McCarthy 2009). Clearly, anyone who wilfully contravenes a law, breaches his legal duties and responsibilities and engages in egregious reckless behaviour should be held accountable. Wilful misconduct which exceeds the limit of acceptable conduct, gross negligence and substance abuse should be prosecuted and punished. However, the line between acceptable and unacceptable behaviour is difficult to draw.

Many airlines and organizations are implementing a positive safety culture where reporting is encouraged and even rewarded, thus recognizing the important contribution of air safety reporting systems. On the other hand intentional violations, omissions and wilful negligence cannot be tolerated in such a high-risk industry such as that of aviation. A just culture therefore is necessary where violations, omissions and wilful acts of negligence will not be tolerated.

The main purpose of criminalizing someone's acts or omissions is to punish the wrongdoer and to deter others from doing the same thing. Punishing pilots and ATCOs for making an inadvertent error whilst trying to perform their duties will not have the desired effect of deterrence. Moreover, it seems to have a negative effect on safety. On the other hand, identifying inadvertent errors and then formulating and implementing necessary changes to ensure lessons will be learnt, will result in a safer environment and will therefore enhance safety.

Aviation safety is enhanced by identifying and rectifying mistakes and this will not be possible if aviation professionals work in an atmosphere of fear. It is vital that both latent failures are identified when investigating an aviation accident in order to learn the safety lessons, but this will only be achieved if there is a move from a blaming and punishing culture to a learning and safety culture.

The criminalization of pilots and ATCOs and other aviation professionals is not only on the increase but it seems that more countries around the world are criminally prosecuting pilots and ATCOs and that the category of defendants who are being criminally charged subsequent to aviation accidents is expanding to include middle and top managers and post holders.

We have pointed out most of the pilots and ATCOs were not aware of the fact that the official technical accident investigation report or parts thereof or that sensitive aviation data obtained from the CVR and FDR have been used in criminal proceedings. In the previous chapters the cases have shown that testimony given by aviation professional during the technical investigation was admissible in a court of law, thus illustrating the intermingling of the technical and judicial investigations. Notably in the Linate case, the ATCOs, being aware of the practice of intermingling of the two investigations in Italy, refused to provide statements to the technical investigation and provided testimony only to the judicial investigators. Similarly, the engineers in the Helios case only provided statements during both the technical and judicial investigation in the presence of their lawyers.

The fear of criminalization and the inadequate protection of aviation safety data will lead to a change in attitude towards the technical investigation as aviation professionals will lose their trust in its purpose and surrounding philosophy since it has, in practice, albeit indirectly, been used to apportion blame and liability contrary to Annex 13 and not solely for the enhancement of aviation safety. In addition, there are increasing conflicts between the judicial authorities and the technical investigators who are being hindered by the judiciary's involvement in aviation accident investigations. This was evident in the Concorde and Tuninter crashes and the Canadian jet accident at Vnukovo.

The aviation industry faces many economic, environmental and technological challenges which put pressure on aviation professionals. However, the increasing cases of criminalization and the expanding of the web of defendants is a factor which, as has been illustrated throughout the book, will affect the industry's most valuable achievement, its safety record. Holding aviation professionals accountable for their inadvertent acts and omissions has no positive effect on aviation safety and does not minimize the risk or reduce aviation accidents. On the contrary, there are strong indications emanating from our study that this may possibly develop into a Legally Defensive Safety Management (LDSM) approach which may protect aviation professionals, but will not enhance aviation safety.

Chapter 8
The Way Forward

The book has examined documented cases of criminalization following aviation accidents which is a high-profile area of enormous importance. The book explored the interaction between the intermingling of the technical and judicial investigations and the effect of criminalization on aviation safety but it has the limitation that the methodology does not permit statistical extrapolation. At the case level it confirms current practices of criminalization and identifies enormous conflicts in the methods, practices and objectives of the technical and the judicial investigations that are conducted, which hinder the technical investigation and possibly its outcome. This demonstrates the need for further work on the issue of criminalization. The book has discussed the problems of managing complex aviation accident investigations and the court proceedings that follow criminally charging aviation professionals for being responsible for the accidental death of passengers and crew. It clearly demonstrates the need to develop uniform procedures to deal with the issue of criminalization and more importantly, the impediments to aviation safety stemming from the increasing fear of prosecution.

It can be argued that criminal law expresses the moral and practical judgment of what society considers criminal activity. The significant shift in the public's perception towards professional negligence is evident in the increasing criminal prosecution of doctors, lawyers, architects, drivers, estate agents and accountants. Pilots, air traffic controllers and other aviation professionals are also being held accountable for their professional negligence and face criminal charges for unintentional errors and mistakes in performing their daily duties and responsibilities.

The comprehensive collection of cases that we have included shows that there were 27 cases of aviation accidents which were criminally investigated from 1956–99 and 28 cases from 2000–2009. We note that this may not be an exhaustive list of cases and that there may be additional cases of which we are unaware. However, this does not minimize the fact that there were 27 cases spanning 43 years and over 28 cases in the last decade. Our research into cases where aviation professionals have faced criminal charges subsequent to an aviation accident has led us to believe that there will be a significant increase in cases where aviation accidents will be followed by criminal prosecutions. This will be in line with the evidential shift of the public's perception towards aviation accidents and society's demand for accountability in aviation and other forms of transportation. This demand is based on the public's expectation that criminal prosecutions will ensure aviation safety and perhaps judicial authorities believe that prosecution will be the only way to increase safety and protect the public. There is no evidence, however, that prosecuting aviation professionals for their unintentional acts and omissions which have resulted in the death of passengers improves safety. On the contrary, criminally prosecuting aviation professionals impedes safety. Our research clearly indicates that aviation professionals fear prosecution and that this is perceived as having an adverse effect on aviation safety through the hindrance of the free, voluntary and truthful sharing of safety information. This is a cornerstone in aviation safety resulting in many safety lessons being learnt and aviation safety is advanced from the free communication and voluntary, truthful reporting of mishaps and errors. Pilots and ATCOs tend to feel that the fear of being prosecuted has the effect of making them more wary and cautious and even hesitant to report any mishaps and errors. Consequently, this results in less safety lessons being learnt and therefore this has a negative effect on safety.

One of the most important issues highlighted is the notion of the intermingling between the technical and the judicial investigations. Clearly, evidence such as the final technical investigation report, the CVR and FDR, testimonies and other evidence obtained by the technical investigation has been used in criminal proceedings against aviation professionals prosecuted. This does not only undermine the technical investigation, the integrity and the non-blameworthy philosophy governing accident investigations, but also establishes a climate of mistrust and suspicion surrounding the investigation process.

There is growing concern in the aviation industry regarding the criminalization of aviation professionals and the negative effect that this has on aviation safety. In January this year, ISASI endorsed the joint resolution regarding the criminalization of aviation accidents which was signed by safety agencies and organizations in 2006. The president of ISASI stated, 'The Executive, International Council and membership of ISASI believe that the current trend of criminalizing aviation accidents has a deleterious effect on the appropriate investigation of said occurrences, the finding of contributing factors and probable causation and the formulation of recommendations to prevent recurrence.' In addition there are a number of international and European initiatives being taken by ICAO and the EU Commission to improve co-ordination, encourage interaction and establish effective lines of communication with a view to optimizing co-operation and understanding between judicial and technical investigations. However, whilst this is a step in the right direction, it is unlikely to have the desired impact to resolve matters.

Recent litigation such as that in the Air France A340 accident that occurred on 2 August 2005 in Toronto Pearson International Airport when the aircraft overran out of the runway, pitched into a ravine and burst into flames, supports the notion of the intermingling of the two investigations. In the civil suit of *Société Air France et al v Greater Toronto Airport Authority* (2009), Air France and its insurers are claiming damages of over $200 million against NAV Canada (the entity responsible for air traffic control), a number of NAV employees, the Greater Toronto Airport Authority (GTAA) and the Attorney General of Canada. NAV requested that the CVR be released to parties alleging that the CVR contained vital information that the parties and the court should have the benefit of hearing this information in order to have a fair trial. The court acknowledged that the use of CVR data in a court of law is inconsistent and outlined that in order to reach the decision it had to listen to the recordings of the CVR and hear submissions of the parties to determine whether in the circumstances the public interest and the proper administration of justice outweighed the privileged attached to the recording by Canadian national law. The court considered that the CVR contained no communication of an irrelevant personal nature that would be embarrassing to either of the pilots nor were there any utterances made anticipating the impeding impact. Since the content was highly relevant, probative and reliable, the court decided to release the CVR transcript. This case applied the test of balancing the public interest in the administration of justice and decided that without the CVR evidence there was a risk that the parties and the court would not have the most reliable evidence concerning the main issues of the case. The court also determined that in this case the release of the CVR under appropriate restrictions would not interfere with aviation safety, damage the relationship between the pilots and their employers or impede aviation accidents.

The legal arguments raised in this case go to the heart of the philosophy of the technical investigation which is that the sole objective of the technical investigation should be the prevention of accidents and incidents and not the apportioning of blame or liability. Section 5.12 (ICAO 2001) dealing with the non-disclosure of records clearly provides protection to the extent that the judicial authorities decide that in the interest of justice such records should be disclosed. The increasing confrontation between the technical and judicial investigations regarding the control of the wreckage, the CVR, FDR, documents and evidence as well as demands for accountability results in an over-excessive involvement by the judiciary, thereby impeding the technical investigation process.

We have also highlighted that there are a number of factors that influence the investigation of an aviation accident and the ones identified in the case studies as supported by the respondents are media, political and governmental pressure, financial and other economic interests. Drawing on the above, we suggest that a European aviation accident investigation branch which would ensure impartial, effective and independent technical investigations of aviation accidents should be established.

There is no doubt that the criminalization of aviation professionals will inevitably follow an aviation accident. Despite the fact that aviation accidents are decreasing, criminalization is on the increase and the web of defendants is widening. Even though it is increasingly becoming accepted that human error is one of the factors leading to an accident and is a system of the failures of an organization, society still pushes for punishment, accountability and justice. This is fuelled by the media and often leads to scapegoating. This view undoubtedly results in the fear of prosecution which impedes safety and casts doubts upon the integrity of the technical investigation.

The increasing number of aviation managers and post-holders who have been criminally prosecuted in the last decade leads us to believe that we will see the development of what we term 'a legal defensive safety management approach' whereby aviation managers try to protect themselves and the organization from criminal prosecution instead of taking actions to improve aviation safety.

Taking the above into account in addition to the readiness of some jurisdictions to prosecute and the inconsistencies in the criminal proceedings the way to ensure that justice is being applied and that this is done consistently is to establish a European aviation tribunal to review requests from national judicial authorities considering the prosecution of pilots, ATCOs and other aviation professionals before they commence the litigation in the national courts. An alternative to the Aviation tribunal is the establishment of a European aviation court to hear cases of aviation professionals who are criminally prosecuted which will provide a uniform set of rules, providing uniformity, certainty and predictability. ICAO, the EU Commission, judicial authorities and other relevant bodies should consider the setting up of an Aviation tribunal or court to ensure the equitable and consistent implementation of legal principles to the criminalization of aviation professionals.

Chapter 9

Cases of Prosecution of Aviation Professionals

A chronological overview of cases in which pilots, ATCOs, engineers and other aviation professionals were either criminally charged or convicted subsequent to an aviation accident is presented in the following comprehensive collection of cases.

Air France Transports Aériens Intercontinentaux DC-6, Cairo, Egypt (1956)

On 20 February 1956 a DC-6 Air France aircraft operated by Transports Aériens Intercontinentaux (TAI) scheduled to fly from Saigon to Paris, France, left Karachi for Cairo. The captain, who was a check pilot, occupied the right-hand seat during the flight leg between Karachi and Cairo, and the co-pilot, who was being checked as a trainee captain, was in the left-hand seat. When the crew reported that they had Cairo Airport in sight, at an altitude of 4,500 feet, both pilots were under the impression that they were going to overshoot so they lowered the undercarriage and the flaps to increase the rate of descent while maintaining the same speed. The aeroplane descended to an altitude 1,500 feet below the minimum safe flight altitude for the sector. They continued to descend until the aircraft impacted the ground, killing 49 passengers and three crew. The Air France captain was convicted of involuntary manslaughter.

Civil Air Transport Company, B727, Taipei, China (1968)

On 16 February 1968, a Boeing 727 flight by Civil Air Transport Company ('CAT') from Hong Kong to Taipei crashed in marginal weather during an ILS approach into Taipei's main airport. The director of flying for CAT, an American captain, was in the left seat and the Taiwanese co-pilot was in the right seat. Another American captain was riding the jump seat opposite the flight engineer. Twelve passengers (including the wife of the captain in the left seat and three flight attendants) were killed and both captains were badly injured. They were both charged with manslaughter and the second American captain was additionally charged with professional negligence. Both had their licences revoked and were not allowed to leave Taiwan. As a result, the captain was unable to attend his wife's funeral in the USA. The co-pilot and flight engineer were not charged. Both pilots were eventually acquitted in January 1969 by the Taipei Criminal District Court.

Lufthansa B747, Nairobi, Kenya (1974)

On 20 November 1974, a Lufthansa B747, Flight LH 540 on a scheduled flight from Frankfurt, Germany, to Johannesburg, South Africa, with an intermediate stop at Nairobi, crashed when the aircraft lost altitude and the rear fuselage made contact with the ground approximately 1,120 metres beyond the departure end of Runway 24. Of the 157 people on aboard, 59 were killed. This was the first accident of a Boeing 747.The official report was released in 1979 stating that the accident was caused by the crew initiating a take-off with the leading edge flaps retracted, because the pneumatic system which operates them had not been switched on. The flight engineer was charged with negligent homicide but was later acquitted.

Zagreb Mid-air Collision, Trident 3B and DC-9, Croatia (Yugoslavia) (1976)

On 10 September 1976, the world's deadliest mid-air collision with the highest death toll at the time occurred when a British Airways Flight 476 Trident 3B with nine crew members and 54 passengers en route from London to Istanbul collided in mid-air over Zagreb with an Inex-Adria Aviopromet Flight 550, a DC-9 with five crew and 108 passengers scheduled to fly from Yugoslavia to West Germany, at 11:15 local time. All 176 people on board both flights were killed. Charges were filed for endangering railway, sea or air traffic and threatening the lives of men or property. On 11 April 1977 the court found the upper-sector assistant controller at the time of the accident guilty and sentenced him to seven years' imprisonment. After a petition and complaints that he was used as a scapegoat, he was released on 29 November 1978 after serving 27 months in prison.

SE-210 Super Caravelle of SATA, Madeira, Portugal (1977)

On 18 December 1977, just after 20:00, in good weather conditions, a SE-210 Super Caravelle of SATA crashed in Madeira, Portugal, killing 35 passengers and one crew member. The aircraft crashed into the water about 4 km short of the runway of the Funchal Airport, broke apart and then sank. Two captains flew the aircraft. The one pilot who was also the head of operations of the SATA Company declared that the flight was to be a route check. He was assigned to act as PIC and he instructed the pilot under check to take the left-hand seat and to fly the plane during the approach. The check pilot was the route check pilot, PIC and co-pilot simultaneously.

As the Portuguese authorities waived their jurisdiction, it was the courts in Geneva that prosecuted both the pilots. The first instance trial took place seven and a half years after the accident had occurred. The court held that the accident was caused by a number of consecutive negligent acts and omissions of the PIC and sentenced him to two years' imprisonment. The pilot under check was found guilty and received a prison sentence of one and a half years. This was a slightly lighter sentence because he was under the command of the PIC who was his superior as head of operations and he was on a route check. Both pilots appealed. The appeal was never heard as three weeks after their convictions the statute of limitations ran out. Even though the sentences were never served, both pilots have been left with a criminal record.

Swiss Air DC-8, Athens Airport, Greece (1979)

On 8 October 1979 a Swiss Air DC-8 ran off the end of Runway 15 left following a landing at Athens Airport. Fourteen of the 142 passengers were killed and another 11 were wounded. Greek prosecutors brought negligent manslaughter, negligent bodily injury and disrupting the safety of air services charges against the captain and co-pilot. On 26 April 1983 a Greek court sentenced the PIC and the co-pilot to five years' and two months' imprisonment. In a further appeal, the co-pilot was acquitted and the PIC's sentence was reduced to three years. The prison sentence was later converted into a fine.

JAL DC-8, Tokyo, Japan (1982)

On 9 February 1982, a Japan Airlines DC-8 on a domestic scheduled passenger flight from Fukuoka, Japan, to Tokyo, crashed on approach to Tokyo Haneda Airport. The accident was caused by the captain's deliberate reversal of two of the aircrafts engines in flight. Despite the efforts of the co-pilot and the flight engineer, they could not regain complete control of the aircraft and it touched down in shallow water 300m short of the runway. Of the 166 passengers and eight crew on board, 24 passengers were killed. It was later discovered that the captain was known to be mentally ill and that he had suffered from a psychosomatic illness prior to the incident. The captain was charged but based on the psychiatric tests conducted on him, the charges were later dropped. A criminal investigation was then opened against the doctors who had examined him before the flight and against his supervisory pilots.

THY B727-200, Ankara, Turkey (1983)

In January 1983, a THY Boeing 727-200 crashed about 500 feet (150m) short of the runway during poor visibility (fog and snow) and possibly wind shear in

Ankara, Turkey. Out of the 60 passengers, 47 died. The captain and first officer were tried and convicted.

Avensa DC-9, Barquisimeto, Venezuela (1983)

On 11 November 1983, an Avensa DC-9 crashed at Barquisimeto, Venezuela. The aircraft lost directional control after touchdown, broke up and burned. One of the five crew members and 21 of the 44 passengers were killed. It was determined that the accident was caused by technical factors. Both pilots were prosecuted and convicted to eight years' imprisonment. They were both eventually pardoned by the president.

JAL B747-SR, Tokyo, Japan (1985)

On 12 August 1985, a Japan Air Lines Boeing 747-SR on a domestic flight crashed into Mount Otsuka, 70 miles northwest of Tokyo. In the world's worst single-aircraft disaster, 520 of the 524 people on board the aircraft were killed. A flawed splice made by Boeing seven years earlier was identified as the probable cause. The manufacturer was charged with professional negligence but there were no convictions.

TU-134A, Kuybyshev Airport, Russia (1986)

On 20 October 1986, a TU-134A on a scheduled flight to Kuybyshev Airport, Russia, crashed whilst executing a low visibility approach, killing four of the seven crew (including the co-pilot) and 66 of the 85 passengers on board the aircraft. The captain and flight engineer were subsequently criminally prosecuted and convicted to long terms of imprisonment.

Aero Traporti Italiani ATR 42, Milan, Italy (1987)

On 15 October 1987 an Aero Traporti Italiani ATR 42 took off from Milan for a flight to Köln. Icy conditions existed at the time of departure. About 15 minutes after take-off, the crew progressively lost control of the aircraft and crashed nose down into a 2300 foot (700m) mountain, Mt Crezzoin, in Italy, following an uncontrolled descent. All 34 passengers and three crew members were killed. Despite the fact that both pilots died in the accident, they were charged with murder and convicted. The co-pilot's conviction was later overturned on appeal. The designers of the aircraft were also convicted of homicide.

Air France A320, Habsheim, France (1988)

On 26 June 1988 Air France Flight 296, a chartered flight of the new fly-by-wire Airbus A320, was scheduled to fly over Mulhouse-Habsheim Airport as part of an air show. The aircraft was to fly at a low speed with the landing gear down at an altitude of 100 feet but slowly descended to 30 feet before crashing into the tops of trees beyond the runway, killing three passengers. The captain and first officer, two Air France officials and the president of the flying club sponsoring the air show were charged with manslaughter. All five were found guilty. The captain was sentenced to six months in prison, plus 12 months' probation, and the other accused were sentenced to probation.

Korean Airlines DC10-30, Tripoli, Libya (1989)

On 27 July 1989, a Korean Airlines DC10-30 from Jeddah to Tripoli, Libya, crashed about one mile short of the airport during a daylight landing attempt in thick fog. Weather was poor and fuel in the aircraft was critically low. In addition, airport navigational equipment for an instrument landing on the intended runway was apparently not working at the time of the event. By final approach the aircraft had no fuel left and crashed short of the runway, striking four houses and multiple cars. Four of the 18 crew members and 68 of the 181 passengers were killed. Six persons on the ground were also killed. The pilots were arrested by the Libyan authorities, sentenced to life imprisonment and extradited to Korea.

USAir Boeing 737, New York, USA (1989)

On 20 September 1989 a USAir Boeing 737-400 ran off the runway at La Guardia Airport and was submerged in water after the crew incorrectly trimmed the rudder for take-off. The take-off was aborted, and the aircraft overran the runway and was partially submerged in water, resulting in the death of two of the 55 passengers. A grand jury inquiry was subsequently convened to determine if criminal charges of negligent homicide or reckless endangerment should be filed against the pilots but it later decided not to press any charges.

British Airways B747, London Heathrow, UK (1989)

On 21 November 1989, the pilot of a British Airways B747 did a go-around during a Cat. II Runway 27R ILS approach at London Heathrow Airport after he had difficulty in getting the autopilot to lock on to the ILS. The aircraft deviated to the right off the Runway 27R centreline. The aircraft cleared a hotel alongside a major road by just about 12 feet (3.5m). The captain lost his licence and resigned from British Airways. In May 1991 he was convicted of negligently endangering his aircraft and passengers and was fined £2,000. On 30 November 1992, he committed suicide.

Air Inter A320, Strasbourg, France (1992)

On 20 January 1992, an Air Inter A320 domestic flight that departed from Lyon, France and scheduled to land at Strasbourg, crashed into the mountains whilst on approach for landing on a VOR/DME[1] approach to Runway 5. The aircraft had 90 passengers and six crew members on board. The accident resulted in 87 fatalities. Criminal charges were subsequently brought against six aviation professionals. It took 14 years for the case to go court and in May 2006 the nine-week trial began in the Colmar correctional court. The six defendants were eventually cleared of all criminal charges but Airbus and Air France (Air Inter was the domestic subsidiary of Air France and has since been absorbed into the parent airline) were held liable to pay damages.

Contactair DHC Dash 8, Paris, France (1993)

On 6 January 1993 a Contactair DHC Dash 8 crashed on landing in Paris, France, killing four persons. The crew was subsequently convicted but it is believed that no time was actually served.

Korean Air A300-600, Cheju, Korea – 1994

On 10 August 1994, a Korean Air A300-600 skidded into a safety barricade on a wet runway on the southern resort island of Cheju, Korea. The aircraft crashed and burst into flames after landing. There were no fatalities amongst the 160 people on board and eight people sustained minor injuries. The Canadian captain was tried in absentia and the co-pilot was also criminally charged.

New Zealand Ansett DHC-8, Palmerston North, New Zealand (1995)

On 9 June 1995 Flight 703, an Ansett DHC-8 scheduled to fly from Auckland Airport to Palmerston North, crashed west of the Tararua Ranges and 16 km east of Palmerston North Airport, during an instrument approach in bad weather. There were 18 passengers and three crew members on board the aircraft. One crew

---

1 VOR/DME – very high frequency omnidirectional range/distance measuring equipment.

member and three passengers lost their lives and the other two crew members and 12 passengers were seriously injured. The captain was charged with four counts of manslaughter.

As part of the criminal inquiry, the police requested that the Accident Investigation Commission provide them with actual CVR tape, not just a transcript of the recording, but the commission refused to do so. It must be noted that at the time of this accident, New Zealand, like many other states covered by the Chicago Convention, had no legislation making it mandatory for an aircraft to use a CVR. The matter went to the High Court and then to the Court of Appeal of New Zealand. The court held that the police did have the right to obtain the actual CVR, as the provisions of Annex 13 of ICAO did not make it clear that the CVR usage was protected, only that a court had to balance competing interests in allowing CVR information to be used. Another point made was that the provisions of Annex 13 were not automatically included in New Zealand law and that national law would be required to clarify the issue. The police therefore executed a search warrant and took possession of the CVR tape. In September 1999 legislation was passed prohibiting the use of flight recorders in criminal or civil proceedings against pilots. The Crown Court ruled that the CVR was inadmissible in court. The Court of Appeal later overturned this ruling. The captain was eventually acquitted.

Inter Austral Airlines, Argentina (1995)

On 19 August 1995 a cabin crew member of an Inter Austral Airlines flight died when she fell from the aircraft after opening the door. Three engineers and a maintenance technician of the company were subsequently charged with 'negligent aircraft accident with aggravation of death as accessories'.

ValuJet DC-9-32, Florida, USA (1996)

On 11 May 1996 a MD DC-9-32, ValuJet Flight 592, a scheduled flight from Miami, Florida, to Atlanta, Georgia, crashed in the Florida Everglades shortly after take-off from Miami International Airport. All the 105 passengers, the pilot, the co-pilot and three flights attendants died. The US Federal and Florida State Prosecutors brought criminal charges, 110 counts of manslaughter and 110 counts of third degree murder, against ValuJet's maintenance contractor, SabreTech, SabreTech's maintenance supervisors and two mechanics who worked on the plane. In addition, SabreTech was charged with violation of hazardous material regulations, failing to train its employees on proper handling of hazardous materials, placing a destructive device on board an aircraft, conspiracy to falsify records and making false statements. SabreTech's maintenance supervisor and two mechanics who worked on the plane were charged with conspiracy and making false statements. ValuJet was never prosecuted but SabreTech was the first American aviation company to be criminally prosecuted for its role in an American aviation accident.

SabreTech settled the state charges. The company was found guilty on the mishandling hazardous materials and improper training charges. SabreTech's maintenance supervisor and the one mechanic were acquitted on all charges. The second mechanic failed to appear in court and is still currently missing. SabreTech was fined $2 million and ordered to pay $9 million in restitution. In 2001 the appeal acquitted SabreTech of the federal charges based on its wilful mishandling of the oxygen generators. The conviction for improper training was upheld and the company was sentenced to a $500,000 fine, three years' probation and no restitution.

Japan Airlines MacDonnell Douglas MD-11, Nagoya International Airport, Japan (1997)

On 8 June 1997 a JAL MacDonnell Douglas MD-11, Flight 706 from Hong Kong to Nagoya, with 179 passengers and crew members on board, experienced abrupt and abnormal altitude changes for about 15 seconds. The crew managed to re-establish the normal descent altitude and landed at Nagoya International Airport. The aircraft was not damaged but 13 persons were injured (ALPA Japan Technical Support Team and Japan Airlines Captain Association. n.d.). A cabin crew member died 20 months later as a result of the injuries sustained. The captain was prosecuted for professional negligence but was eventually acquitted by the Nagoya High Court on 9 January 2007.

Ukrainian Yakovlev-42, Thessaloniki, Greece (1997)

On 17 December 1997 a Ukrainian Yakovlev-42 aircraft, leased to the Ukrainian airline Aerosweet, crashed in northern Greece, southwest of its destination at Thessaloniki's Macedonia Airport, killing the 64 passengers and eight crew members. The aircraft crashed 37 nautical miles west of Thessaloniki, during a missed approach procedure. Based on the findings of the official accident report, legal action was taken against two ATCOs by the Greek prosecution authorities. Both controllers were found guilty of manslaughter as a result of their criminal negligence and sentenced to five years' imprisonment. Both controllers appealed. The appeal commenced in November 2002 and the appellate court confirmed their conviction and sentence.

Delta Airlines B767-300, Schiphol Airport, Amsterdam, Netherlands (1998)

On 10 December 1998 a Delta Air Lines Boeing 767-300 had been cleared for take-off at Runway 24 at Amsterdam Schiphol Airport. Almost at the same time a

KLM Boeing 747, being towed and accompanied by a yellow van, was cleared to cross Runway 24 at the position of Exit 2. The take-off of the Delta Airlines was aborted. Low visibility conditions made visual control from the tower impossible. None of the 126 passengers and 12 crew members was injured (Dutch Transport Safety Board 2001). In 2000 three ATCOs were prosecuted and two of the Controllers were found guilty and fined.

LAPA Boeing 737-204C, Buenos Aires, Argentina (1999)

On 31 August 1999, LAPA Flight 3142 was a flight from Buenos Aires to Córdoba, Argentina, operated by the Argentinean airline LAPA. The plane crashed at the Aeroparque Jorge Newbery in Buenos Aires on 31 August 1999 at 20:54 local time, shortly after take-off. The crash resulted in 65 fatalities, 17 people severely injured and several people with minor injuries, making it one of the deadliest accidents in the history of Argentinean aviation.

On 5 July 2005 the judge formed a tribunal to try nine accused. They were six LAPA officials, the ex-president of LAPA, the director general, two operations managers, the head of the B-737 line at LAPA, the human resources manager of LAPA and three members of the Argentinian air force, the ex-commander of Aerial Regions, the ex-director of Aeronautical *Habilitacion* and the ex-director of the National Institute of Aeronautical and Aerospace Medicine. On 23 July 2005, one of the three air force members accused is reported to have committed suicide. On 28 February 2006, the request by the two former members of the air force that the tribunal dismiss the charges against them because of the statute of limitations, was accepted, since the crime for which they had been accused had a maximum sentence of two years and four years had already lapsed since the first accusations and the end of the trial. In July 2010 the court acquitted the six former officials and LAPA employees. One of the former operations managers and the head of the B737 line were found guilty and received suspended sentences of three years.

Dassault Falcon 900B, Bucharest's Otopeni Airport, Romania (1999)

On 14 September 1999 a Dassault-Falcon 900B operated by Olympic Airways for the Greek government made an emergency landing at Bucharest's Otopeni Airport. Twenty minutes prior to landing during the descent, at 15 000 feet, the pilots lost control. The aircraft shook violently and the pilots regained control at about 2,000 feet. As a result, a Greek government minister, his only son and five other individuals lost their lives and three other passengers were seriously injured. None of the passengers killed were wearing their seatbelts. The pilot and co-pilot were not seriously hurt and were able to safely land the plane without any external structural damage. Both pilots immediately submitted to medical examinations and blood tests.

The Greek prosecuting authorities charged the PIC and the co-pilot (who was also a captain) with manslaughter and causing bodily injury. Additionally, eight Olympic Airways ground engineers were charged for omitting to rectify the pitch feel malfunction. The trial court found the captain guilty, sentenced him to five years' imprisonment and acquitted the co-pilot and the engineers. On appeal, the court rejected the probable cause scenario and reduced the sentence to 36 months. The captain has now appealed to the Supreme Court.

British Airways, Girona Airport, Spain (1999)

On 14 September 1999 a Britannia Airways Flight BY226A, a holiday charter flight from Cardiff, Wales, crashed on landing at Girona Airport, Spain. The aircraft, a charter flight from Cardiff, Wales, carrying 236 passengers and nine crew members was attempting to land in thunderstorms and heavy rain. The aircraft broke apart resulting in the death of one passenger who succumbed to his injuries some days after the accident. The pilots were criminally charged with negligence but were not convicted.

Alaska Airlines MD-83, California, USA (2000)

On 31 January 2000 a MD-83 Alaska Airlines operating as a scheduled international passenger flight from Puerto Vallarta, Mexico, to Seattle with a stop at San Francisco, California, crashed into the Pacific Ocean. Both the pilots, three cabin crew members and all 83 passengers on board were killed. Alaska Airlines had been under criminal investigation since December 1998 for allegedly falsifying maintenance records on the MD-80 fleet. The FBI raided the Oakland, California, maintenance hangar as well as their Seattle headquarters where they seized maintenance logs and other records. An enquiry by the FAA revealed that during the period of 1998 to 1999, over 840 flights by the two MD-80 aircraft were in an unsatisfactory condition and that they were allowed to fly. No charges were filed.

Emery DC-8, California, USA (2000)

On 16 February 2000 an Emery DC-8 cargo flight crashed in Rancho Cordova, California, killing the three crew members on board the aircraft. The NTSB report compiled after conducting the technical investigation raised questions regarding the maintenance practices by the airline and its repair contractor, as well as the airline's overseeing of contractor maintenance.

Hapag Lloyd A310, Vienna, Austria (2000)

In July 2000 a Hapag Lloyd commercial airlines A310, Flight 3378, carrying 142 passengers and eight crew members from Khania (Crete), Greece, to Hanover, Germany, was forced to make a crash landing in Vienna after it ran out of fuel. Twenty-six passengers were injured during the evacuation with the emergency slides. Shortly after take-off from Crete the pilot was unable to retract the landing gear and decided to divert the flight to Munich. The captain received a six-month suspended prison sentence from the Hanover court in Germany for endangering lives.

Alliance B737-200, Patna Airport, India (2000)

On 17 July 2000, an Alliance Air Boeing 737-200 en route from Calcutta to New Delhi with scheduled stops in Patna crashed at Patna Airport as it attempted to land. In addition to the 55 passengers and crew who lost their lives, five people on the ground were killed. Immediately after the accident, the government asked the Patna High Court to nominate a sitting judge to conduct the inquiry. However, the court was not able to do so because of a shortage of judges. As a result, the government appointed a court of inquiry headed by an air marshal who was the programme director (test flight) for the development of the light combat aircraft in Bangalore and a test pilot, and two assessors, a retired director-AIB safety, Air-India and a general manager, engineering. The deputy director of airworthiness, DGCA, was the secretary of the court of inquiry. The inquiry stated that the accident was caused by loss of control due to pilot error. In July, the Patna police registered a first information report against the two deceased Alliance Air pilots in accordance with various sections of the Indian Penal Code and the 1982 Aviation Act. The charges (causing death by rash and negligence act, loss of government property and unlawful interpretation of the Civil Aviation Operation Act, 1982) were eventually dropped. (Rediff.com 2000)

Concorde 203, Air France, Paris (2000)

On 25 July 2000, the first fatal accident involving Concorde occurred. Less than two minutes after take-off, Concorde 203, F-BTSC departing from Paris and scheduled to fly to New York, suffered a tyre blow-out causing a fuel tank to rupture. A fire broke out, two engines failed and the aircraft then crashed onto a hotel in Gonesse. All 100 passengers and nine crew on board were killed. In addition, four people in the hotel were also killed. The former head of the Concorde division at Aerospatiale and the Concorde chief engineer were charged with negligence. A Continental mechanic, a manager of Aerospatiale and a former employee of the French airline regulator were charged with manslaughter and a Continental maintenance manager was charged with manslaughter and involuntary causing injury.

In September 2006, the highest court in France rejected a request to dismiss the charges and decided that the trial would commence. The trial commenced in February 2010, in the Paris suburb of Pontoise and is ongoing at the time of writing.

Air Glaciers Travel, Buson, Switzerland (2000)

In September 2000 an Air Glaciers Travel helicopter crashed in Buson, Switzerland. The pilot was charged with negligent homicide and sentenced to five months and the co-pilot to four months. Both sentences were suspended.

Singapore Airlines B747, Taiwan (2000)

On 31 October 2000, three pilots were taken into custody by police after a Singapore Airlines Boeing 747 crashed at the International Airport in Taoyuan, Taiwan, after it had commenced take-off in strong winds and heavy rain and struck construction equipment on the runway. Eighty three of the 179 persons on board the aircraft were killed and a further 39 were seriously injured. The pilots were subsequently released and were only permitted to leave Taiwan in late December. They returned, voluntarily, to Taiwan for questioning in 2002. The captain and co-pilot were charged with negligent killing but their indictments were suspended for three years. They were not permitted to fly an aircraft to Taiwan for a year.

Japan Airlines B747 and McDonnell Douglas DC-10, Tokyo, Japan (2001)

On 31 January 2001, a near mid-air collision between a JAL B-747 and a JAL McDonnell Douglas DC-10 occurred just before the B747 landed at Tokyo, Haneda Airport. Forty-two of those on board the Boeing were injured during the evasive actions taken by the crew but no-one on board the DC-10 was injured. Three police officers entered the cockpit shortly after landing to interview the crew.

Two Japanese ATCOs and a JAL captain were criminally prosecuted and faced possible imprisonment. In this case the pilots became confused by contradicting commands from the ATC control tower and the TCAS alert system on board the aircraft. They were eventually acquitted by a District Court in 2006. On 11 April 2008 the Appeal Court overturned the earlier decision and found both ATCOs guilty, sentencing the one ATCO to one year's imprisonment and the second to one year and six months. Both were placed on probation and the sentences were suspended for three years.

SAS MD-87 and Cessna, Milan, Italy (2001)

On 8 October 2001 an SAS MD-87 aircraft and Cessna jet collided in heavy fog on a runway at Linate Airport in Milan, Italy. All 110 persons on board the MD-87, the four persons on board the Cessna and another four persons on the ground were killed.

The authorities found that an inoperative ground radar system contributed to the accident. Eleven defendants were charged in two separate trials. In the first trial, on 16 April 2004 the Linate ATC (ENAV), the former director of ENAV, the former managing director of Linate Airport (ENAC) and the former manager responsible for Linate and Malpensa Airport from ENAC were sentenced to jail terms ranging from six and a half to eight years. The former director of the Linate Airport was sentenced to eight years' imprisonment. The former CEO of Italy's air traffic control agency ENAV and the person who oversees Milan's two airports was sentenced to six and a half years' imprisonment each. The air traffic controller who was on duty at the time was sentenced to eight years imprisonment.

In the second trial the general manager of ENAC, the manager of Linate Flight Assistance Centre and his local supervisor, the central safety supervisor of Linate Airport, an official from ENAV and the two managers from the airport management company (SEA) were tried. The general manager of ENAC was convicted and given a sentence of four years and four months, the manager of Linate Flight Assistance Centre and his local supervisor a sentence of three years and ten months and the central safety supervisor of Linate Airport and the official from ENAV to three years and four months. The two managers from the airport management company (SEA) were found not guilty and acquitted. The prosecution then appealed their acquittal and in 2006 the Appeal Court convicted them and sentenced them each to three years' imprisonment.

The Supreme Court, in February 2008, upheld the convictions of the general manager, the ATCO and the former director of Linate Airport and overturned the acquittals of the former director of Linate Airport and the manager overseeing Milan's two airports on behalf of ENAC. The court acquitted the two SEA managers.

Crossair Avro RJ100, Zurich, Switzerland (2001)

On 24 November 2001 a Crossair Avro RJ100, Flight 3597 from Berlin, crashed on its approach at Zurich Airport in rain and snow. Twenty-four of the 33 persons on board (28 passengers and five crew) were killed and nine were injured. The Swiss aircraft investigation bureau concluded the accident was the result of pilot error. Swiss investigators reported that the accident was caused by an overtired pilot who descended below the minimum descent altitude without having the required visual contact to the approach lights or the runway. Six former managers of Crossair, including the operations chief, the chief trainer, the former chief executive officer of Swiss International Airlines and the former chairman of Crossair, were prosecuted. On 16 May 2008 the court found the accused not guilty and acquitted the former CEO, the chairman and the four Crossair middle managers. The court awarded damages to the six defendants totalling about SFr850,000 ($814,000).

Air China CA129, Pusan, China (2002)

On 15 April 2002, an Air China plane CA129 carrying 166 passengers and 11 crew from Beijing crashed into Tottaesan Mountain in Kimhae after circling to land at Kimhae International Airport, Pusan. The accident claimed 129 lives and injured 37 people. The plane was completely burnt and destroyed after crashing into the mountain. The Korea aviation accident investigation board, after a three-year investigation, attributed the accident to pilot error. The pilot was held under 'house arrest' from April until December and was ultimately released without charges.

Piper, Winnipeg, Canada (2002)

On 11 June, 2002 a Piper aircraft with six passengers on board was damaged when taking off from a private airstrip near Pennsylvania, Winnipeg. Several passengers were injured and one of the passengers died from his injuries after the accident. The pilot was charged with one count of criminal negligence causing death, four counts of criminal negligence causing bodily harm and one count of dangerous operation of an aircraft. The pilot was found guilty of all charges but in December 2009 the Court of Appeal overturned the convictions of criminal negligence causing death and four counts of criminal negligence causing bodily harm and upheld the conviction of dangerous operation of an aircraft.

DHL B757 Collision with a Bashkrian Airlines Tu 154, Uberlingen, Germany (2002)

On 1 July 2002, a DHL B757 cargo plane collided with a Bashkirian Airlines Tu-154 over Überlingen in southern Germany over the Swiss–German border. In a tragic twist, the ATCO on duty that day was stabbed two years later by a man who had lost his wife and children in the accident. In August 2006 Swiss prosecutors laid 71 charges of negligent homicide and negligently disturbing public transport against eight Swiss Skyguide ATCOs, namely three ATC managers, the ATSEP project leader for maintenance work at the airport at the time of the accident, an ATSEP employee, the ATCO on duty at the time of the accident, the ATCO supervisor and a technical systems manager. In 2007 the court found the three ATCO managers guilty of the offences charged with and sentenced them to one-year prison sentences, suspended for two years, plus court costs. The TSEP project leader was also found guilty and imposed a fine suspended for two years and court costs. The other four Skyguide employees were found not guilty and cleared of any wrongdoing. The four Skyguide employees who were found guilty decided not to appeal their sentences.

Boeing 737-700 Flash Airlines, Sharm el-Sheikh International Airport, Egypt (2004)

On 3 January 2004, a Boeing 737-700 crashed into the Red Sea shortly after take-off from Sharm el-Sheik International Airport. None of the 134 passengers and six crew members survived. Even though the accident occurred in Egypt and involved an Egyptian-registered aircraft, the French judicial authorities conducted their own criminal investigation. Flash Airlines, the airline; its insurer; Boeing, the manufacturer of the aircraft; IFLC, the owner of the aircraft and Honeywell Aerospace (provider of aircraft engines, avionics and other systems in the aerospace industry) were prosecuted.

Helvetic Airways DC-9-83, Pristina Airport, Kosovo (2004)

On 21 October 2004, a Helvetic Airways DC-9-83 crashed on approach into Pristina Airport, Kosovo, in heavy fog with 165 passengers on board. The co-pilot had control of the aircraft and the captain delayed in taking control. There were no fatalities. The two Swiss pilots were charged with endangering the lives of the passengers and crew .The Federal Criminal Court in Bellinzona fined the pilots equivalent to 90 and 60 days worth of pay, or SFr15,750 ($14,414) and SFr12,000, respectively. The judge suspended the sentences but ordered them to pay court costs totalling SFr18,148.

Challenger CL-600, Teterboro, New Jersey, USA (2005)

On 2 February 2005 a Bombardier Challenger CL-600-1A11 ran off the departure end of Runway 6 at Teterboro Airport, New Jersey, at a ground speed of about 110 knots, through an airport perimeter fence, across a six-lane highway striking a vehicle and then into a parking lot before impacting a building. The two pilots and the two people in the car were seriously injured. The cabin aide, eight passengers and a person in the building received minor injuries. The NTSB determined that 'the probable cause of the accident was the pilots' failure to ensure the airplane was loaded within weight-and-balance limits and their attempt to take off with the center of gravity well forward of the forward takeoff limit, which prevented the airplane from rotating at the intended rotation speed'. In addition to the pilot, who was charged with conspiracy and lying to federal investigators, the two co-founders, manager, director of charters, maintenance director and pilot were charged with conspiracy, fraud and endangering the safety of aircraft, falsifying flight logs and overloading the plane with fuel.

Tuninter ATR 72, Italy (2005)

On 6 August 2005 a Tunisian Tuninter ATR 72 flight from Bari, Italy, scheduled to fly to Djerba, Tunisia, ran out of fuel and after gliding for approximately 16 minutes, ditched in the ocean off the Sicilian coast resulting in the death of 14 passengers, the airline engineer and the senior flight attendant. Nine people were charged with multiple manslaughter charges and with causing a disaster. The captain and co-pilot were sentenced to ten years' imprisonment. The director general and the technical chief were sentenced to nine years while the airline's head of maintenance, the chief mechanic and the maintenance squad leader received eight-year sentences. Two members of the airline maintenance crew were acquitted.

Helios B737, Athens, Greece (2005)

On 14 August 2005 and Helios Airways Boeing 737, on its way to Prague, via Athens, crashed into the mountain side of Grammatiko, north of Athens, killing all 121 passengers and crew on board the aircraft. The official accident investigation was conducted by the Greek air accident investigation and aviation safety board (AAIAB). One hundred and nineteen charges of manslaughter and causing death through a reckless, careless and dangerous act were filed in the Nicosia District Criminal Court against the chairman of the Board of Directors and CEO of Helios, the chief pilot, the general manager of Helios, the operations manager and the airline, Helios Airlines. The company, 'Helios Airways' was renamed 'Ajet' and the Cyprus government detained Ajet's aircraft and froze the company's bank accounts.

In February 2010 the Greek judicial authorities, despite the fact that four individuals as well as Helios Airlines as a legal entity were already on trial at the Nicosia Criminal Court, proceeded with charges against the same individuals but included the two engineers. It is the first case in which criminal trials in two jurisdictions were initiated against aviation professionals subsequent to an air accident.

Gol Airlines B737 Collision with an Embraer Legacy in Brazil (2006)

On 26 September 2006, a collision took place over the Amazon jungle between an American registered executive jet and a Gol Airlines 737. The deaths of all 154 passengers and crew on board the 737 aircraft made this the worst aviation disaster in South America. The jet, an Embraer Legacy, was damaged but landed safely at a remote air force base.

The two American pilots were detained in their hotel for 71 days, had their passports revoked by a magistrate and were threatened with charges of involuntary manslaughter. The pilots were finally allowed to leave on 15 December, after being formally charged with the offence of 'endangering air safety'. The transcript of the CVR prepared by the NTSB and obtained by a Brazilian newspaper indicated that there were communication and language problems between the pilots and the ATCOs, leading to speculation that this may have contributed to the accident. The investigation was led by the Brazilian air force. Both pilots and four ATCOs were formally charged. Brazilian authorities stated that the controllers faced charges as they had failed to divert the Boeing 737 after the Embraer Legacy jet disappeared from their radar screens. The pilots and three ATCOs faced charges similar to involuntary manslaughter and up to one to three years' imprisonment. The fourth controller was charged with the more serious crime of knowingly exposing an aircraft to danger, a charge which carries a prison sentence of eight to 24 years.

In a press release issued on 4 June 2007, IFALPA stated that the judge's decision to indict the pilots and the ATCOs is a 'crime' against air safety and that the decision is flawed for the following reasons. Firstly, it is contrary to the principles of just culture laid down in Attachment E to Annex 13 that states that there should be no criminal liability without intent to do harm and secondly, permitting a police investigation to pre-empt the findings of the official technical investigation will not assist in establishing the sequence of events leading up to the mid-air collision and hence will not improve air safety.

In mid-July 2007 the Brazilian Congress concluded in an inquiry conducted by the lower house that the American pilots flying the Embraer Legacy were partially to blame for the accident. The inquiry concluded that the pilots and two of the ATCOs should be charged with involuntary manslaughter and a third ATCO with voluntary manslaughter. If found guilty, the pilots and ATCOs could receive a 12-year prison sentence and the ATCO facing the charge of voluntary manslaughter a 20-year sentence. In 2007, the two pilots were initially charged with unintentionally committing a crime against the safety of the national air transport system. However, in 2009 the Federal Public Prosecutor's Office filed new charges against the pilots alleging a crime intentionally committed against the safety of the national air transportation system.

Canadian Jet, Vnukovo Airport, Russia (2007)

On 13 February 2007, Russian prosecutors opened a criminal investigation subsequent to the accident of a Canadian built corporate jet which crashed after one of its two engines caught fire during take-off in a heavy snowstorm from Vnukovo Airport, Moscow. One of the three crew members was left in a coma, another was in intensive care and the third had suffered lesser injuries and was hospitalized. The prosecutor's office said that it was routine practice to initiate a criminal investigation in Russia after a major transportation accident.

Garuda B737-400, Indonesia (2007)

On 7 March 2007, a B737-400 Garuda Indonesia Flight 200 scheduled to fly from Jakarta to Yogyakarta overran the runway upon landing at Yogyakarta Airport, Indonesia. One flight attendant and 20 passengers were killed and a flight attendant and 11 passengers were injured. On 4 February 2008 the captain was arrested and charged with manslaughter and the lesser offence of negligent flying causing death. In April 2009 the captain was found guilty of negligence and sentenced to two years' imprisonment. The captain immediately appealed and was released on bail, pending the appeal. In 2009 the High Court quashed the conviction, but in January 2010 the prosecution lodged an appeal trying to get the conviction reinstated.

TAM Linhas Aéreas Airlines A320, Brazil (2007)

On 17 July 2007 a TAM Linhas Aéreas Airlines A320 Flight 3054, a scheduled domestic passenger flight, departed from Porto Alegre at 17:19 local time destined for Sao Paulo Congonhas Airport. The approach to Runway 35L of Congonhas occurred uneventfully. The aircraft was operating with the number 2 engine reverser de-activated. The runway was wet and slippery, according to information provided by the tower to the crew. After the touch-down, which occurred at night, 18:54 local time, the aircraft did not slow down as expected. The aircraft veered to the left, overran the runway, crossed over and hit a fuel service station and the airlines air cargo service building. All 181 passengers, six crew members and a further 12 people on the ground were killed.

During an extensive criminal investigation that lasted 16 months, charges of involuntary manslaughter and breach of air transport safety, which could result in imprisonment of up to 12 years, were investigated against ten government and TAM officials. They were the president and director of Brazil's civil aviation agency (ANAC) at the time of the accident, the former president of Brazil's airport authority, Infraero, two heads of TAM's flight safety and flight operations division, three ANAC officials who managed the airport's infrastructure and safety operations and two Infraero employees based at the Congonhas Airport .

Boeing A75, Wisconsin, USA (2008)

In February 2008, the first domestic pilot in the USA was convicted of negligently operating a motor vehicle and disorderly conduct subsequent to an accident that occurred in 2004 during a charity event. The pilot performed aerobatic manoeuvres with the Boeing A75 when the aircraft hit power lines before crashing into a river, killing the passenger. The pilot was cited by the FAA for 'careless and reckless' flying, defining the river as a 'congested area', and for violating minimum safe altitude rules which could amount to felony conviction with a maximum sentence of ten years' imprisonment. After pleading guilty to two misdemeanours, negligent operation of a motor vehicle and disorderly conduct, the pilot was sentenced to 30 days in jail, 60 days of work release and 1,000 hours of community service in addition to fines, court costs, counselling fees and two years' probation during which he was not permitted to fly.

Spanair MD-82, Madrid, Spain (2008)

On 20 August 2008, a Spanair flight departing from Madrid Barajas Airport destined for Gran Canaria Airport, Spain, crashed just after take-off from Runway 36L, killing 154 people. The cause of the accident was determined to be the crew's failure to set the flaps and slats to their take-off setting; they were not warned because the configuration of the warning did not sound when they applied power to accelerate after take-off. Two maintenance engineers and their supervisors were charged with manslaughter. It is alleged that their actions to correct a problem the pilots had reported may have had a connection to the failure of the take-off configuration warning system to operate.

Itek Air B737-200, Tehran, Iran (2008)

On 24 August 2008, a Boeing 737-200, Itek Air Flight 6895, scheduled to fly from Bishkek, Kyrgyzstan, to Tehran, crashed soon after it had departed from Bishkek. The aircraft attempted to return to the airport after encountering a technical problem. The aircraft failed to maintain height while attempting to stabilize the approach and crashed, killing 64 of the 90 people on board. The captain was sentenced to five years' and two months' imprisonment and the co-pilot to five years.

Airbus A320 Leased by XL Airways Germany A320, Perpignan, France (2008)

On 27 November 2008 an Airbus A320 leased by XL Airways Germany was undergoing a test flight at Perpignan before it was to be returned to its owner, Air New Zealand. A captain and a co-pilot from the airline XL Airways Germany, a pilot and three engineers from Air New Zealand and a representative of the New Zealand Civil Aviation authority were on board the aircraft. The aircraft crashed into the Mediterranean Sea off the coast near Perpignan, France approximately 7 km before Saint-Cyprien, killing all seven people. In an ongoing investigation at the time of writing, the French judicial authorities are investigating the accident in order to determine whether criminal charges will be filed.

Air One Executive Cessna 650 Citation III, Rome, Italy (2009)

On 7 February 2009 a privately owned Cessna 650 Citation III operated by Air One Executive in air ambulance service crashed in the Trigoria suburb to the south-west of Rome, causing the deaths of the two pilots. The aircraft had departed from Ciampino Airport for Bologna, where it was expected to embark a medical team and to carry it to Cagliari. At the time of writing the judicial authorities are investigating the accident in order to determine if any criminal charges should be filed.

References

AAIASB. 2006. *Aircraft Accident Report, Helios Airways Flight HCY522, Boeing 737-31S, at Grammatiko, Hellas, on 14 August 2005.* Hellenic Republic Ministry of Transport and Communications and the Air Accident Investigation and Aviation Safety Board. Available at: http://www.pio.gov.cy/MOI/pio/pio.nsf/all/F15FBD7320037284C2257204002B6243/$file/FINAL%20REPORT%205B-DBY.pdf [accessed: 30 November 2006].

AAIB. 1998. *Report on the Accident to Boeing 747-121, N739PA at Lockerbie, Dumfriesshire, Scotland on 21 December 1988.* Aircraft Accident Report. No 2/90. EW/C1094.

AAIB. 2008. 'Memorandum of understanding between the Crown Prosecution Service and the Air Accidents, Marine Accidents and Rail Accidents Investigation Branch.' Available at: http://www.aaib.gov.uk/cms_resources.cfm?file=/MOU%20AIB-CPS.pdf [accessed: 3 November 2009].

Aero-News.net. 2007. 'Brazil supreme court: US pilots cannot be compelled to travel to Brazil.' Available at: http://aero-news.net/news/commair.cfm?ContentBlockID=5ADF7F19-5827-4F74-A01C-43469241D7D2&Dynamic=1 [accessed: 11 October 2009].

Air Accident Digest Independence of Boards. 2007. Available at: http://www.aaib.gov.uk/cms_resources.cfm?file=/MOU%20AIB-CPS.pdf [accessed: 6 July 2005].

AirDisaster.Com. 2000. Photograph of Hapag-Lloyd Flight 3378. July. Available at: http://www.airdisaster.com/photos/hf3378/photo.shtml [accessed: 12 November 2006].

Air Industry Information. 2004. 'Crossair crash blamed on "overtired" pilot.' 3 February. Available at: http://www.findarticles.com/p/articles/mi_m0CWU/is_2004_Feb_3/ai_112868643 [accessed: 8 June 2009].

Air Safe. 2005. 'Fatal plane crashes and significant events for the DC10.' Available at: http://www.airsafe.com/events/models/dc10.htm [accessed: 11 July 2008].

Air Safety Week. 2000. 'Reversal of "no prosecution" tradition could undermine air safety, Experts Fear.' 31 July. Available at: http://www.findarticles.com/p/articles/mi_m0UBT/is_31_14/ai_63805243 [accessed: 14 October 2007].

Airline Industry Information. 2003. 'Federal prosecutors reopen criminal investigation into 2000 Alaska Airlines crash.' Available at: http://www.allbusiness.com/operations/shipping-air-freight/480054-1.html [accessed: 2 March 2002].

ALPA Japan Technical Support Team and Japan Airlines Captain Association. n.d. Japan Airlines 706 Accident Investigation Report. Japan Airlines McDonnell Douglas MD-11 JA8580 Over Shima Peninsula, Mie Prefecture, Japan, 8 June

1997. Available at: http://www.jalcrew.jp/jca/old/706/706%20Accident%20 Investigation%20Report%20TST%28Body%29.pdf [accessed: 2 May 2005].

ANSV. 2004. *Final Report: Accident Involved Aircraft Boeing MD-87, Registration SE-DMA, and Cessna 525-A, Registration D-IEVX, Milano Linate Airport October 8, 2001*. N.A/1/04. Para 1.1.6 Test and Research, 20/01/04. Newsletter published by the International Association of Defense Counsel, Aviation and Spae Law Committee. Available at: http://www.ansv.it/cgi-bin/eng/ FINAL%20REPORT%20A-1-04.pdf [accessed: 6 December 2009].

ANSV. 2007. *Final Report: Accident Involving ATR-72, Reg. TSLBB*. Available at: http://www.ansv.it/cgi-bin/eng/FINAL%20REPORT%20ATR%2072.pdf [accessed: 4 July 2008].

ANSV. 2008. *Final Report: Accident Involving ATR-72 Aircraft Registration Marks TS-LBB Ditching Off the Coast of Capo Gallo (Palermo – Sicily), August 6, 2005*. Available at: http://www.ansv.it/cgi-bin/eng/FINAL%20REP ORT%20ATR%2072.pdf [accessed: 29 September 2009].

Aviation and Space Law. 2009. 'Discovery of ASAP Reports.' IADC Committee Newsletter. February. Available at: http://www.tklaw.com/resources/documents/ Aviation_SpaceLaw_February2009[1].pdf [accessed: 25 September 2008].

Aviation Human Factors Industry News. 2009. Volume V, Issue 03, April. Available at: http://www.airsafety.org/Human_Factors_Industry_News_-_2009-03.pdf [accessed: 4 July 2008].

Aviation Safety Network. 1994. Available at: http://aviation-safety.net/database/ [accessed: 12 June 2009].

Aviation Safety Network. 1999. 'Accident description: Dassault Falcon 900B, 14 September 1999.' Available at: http://aviation-safety.net/database/record. php?id=19990914-2 [accessed: 9 December 2002].

Aviation Safety Network. 2009. 'Accident description: Cessna 650 Citation III, 7 February 2009.' Available at: http://aviation-safety.net/database/record. php?id=20090207-0 [accessed: 6 August 2009].

Barlow, K. 2007. *The World Today. Downer seeks prosecution of Indonesian plane crash case 23 October 2007*. Available at: http://www.abc.net.au/worldtoday/ content/2007/s2067651.htm [accessed 7 January 2008].

Barra, B. 2009. 'The Blame Culture in Italy: Two accidents and subsequent convictions illustrate severe shortcomings.' *The Controller*. December. Available at: http://www.aerohabitat.eu/uploads/media/The_Controller_-_Journal_of_ ATC_-_Dec_2009_-_Special_Safety.pdf [accessed: 20 January 2010].

Bartsch, R. 1996. 'Reliance a key factor in establishing duty of care,' *Aviation Law in Australia LBC Information Services*. Sydney: Airline Operations Management Course, UNSW.

Batista, P. n.d. 'Federal public prosecutors in Brazil file new charges against pilots of the Legacy jetliner.' Available at: http://www.associacaovoo1907.com/img/ doc_sli/1244393574.doc [accessed: 9 September 2009].

BBC News. 1987. Zeebrugge disaster was no accident. BBC On this Day: 8 October. Available at: http://news.bbc.co.uk/onthisday/hi/dates/stories/october/8/newsid_2626000/2626265.stm [accessed: 4 October 2004].

BBC News. 2001. 'Putting directors in the dock.' 22 January. Available at: http://news.bbc.co.uk/2/hi/uk_news/1130544.stm [accessed: 3 January 2004].

BBC News. 2007. 'Brazil's defence minister fired.' 25 July. Available at: http://news.bbc.co.uk/2/hi/americas/6915977.stm [accessed: 19 January 2010].

BEA. 1990. *Comission d'enquête sur l'accident survenu le 26 juin 1988 à Mulhouse-Habsheim (68) à l'Airbus A 320, immatriculé F-GFKC*. Report f-kc880626. Available at: http://www.bea.aero/docspa/1988/f-kc880626/pdf/f-kc880626.pdf [accessed: 6 March 2005].

BEA. 1992. *Rapport de la commission d'enquête sur l'accident survenu le 20 janvier 1992 près du Mont Sainte-Odile (Bas Rhin) à l'Airbus A 320 immatriculé F-GGED exploité par la compagnie Air Inter.* Final report F-ED920120. Available at: http://www.bea.aero/docspa/1992/f-ed920120/htm/f-ed920120.html [accessed: 14 February 2007].

BEA. 2004. *Accident on 25 July 2000 at La Patte d'Oie in Gonesse (95) to the Concorde Registered F-BTSC Operated by Air France.* Translation f-sc000725a. Comments from the UK Accredited Representative. Available at: http://www.bea-fr.org/docspa/2000/f-sc000725a/pdf/f-sc000725a.pdf [accessed: 28 October 2005].

Benner, L. 1975. 'Accident theory and accident investigation.' Proceedings of the Annual Seminar of the Society of Air Safety Investigators, Ottawa, Canada. October.

Benner, L. Jr. 1992. 'Ranking safety recommendation effectiveness.' Paper presented at the International Society of Air Safety Investigators conference, Dallas, TX, 1992 .

BFU. n.d. *Final Report No. 1793 by the Aircraft Accident Investigation Bureau Concerning the Accident to the Aircraft AVRO 146-RJ100, HB-IXM, Operated by Crossair under Flight Number CRX 3597, on 24 November 2001 near Bassersdorf/ZH.* Available at: http://www.bfu.admin.ch/common/pdf/1793_e.pdf [accessed: 3 August 2009].

Black's Law Dictionary 1990. 6th ed. St Paul, MN: West Publishing Co.

Bleyer, B. 2006. 'Recordings key to fate of LI pilots: Cockpit voices in collision sent to Canada for analysis; Brazil ready to blame fliers.' *Newsday* (Melville, NY). 12 October. Available at: http://www.accessmylibrary.com/coms2/summary_0286-20065366_ITM [accessed: 17 March 2009].

Boughen, D. 1994. 'Air traffic controller liability – the Australian perspective.' Aviation Law Association of Australia and New Zealand Annual Conference, Hamilton Island.

Braithwaite, G. 2002a. 'Air safety investigator training.' Paper presented to the Australian and New Zealand Chapters of the International Society of Air Safety Investigators Investigators Regional Seminar, Auckland.

Braithwaite, G. 2002b. 'Investing in the future – the development of air safety investigator training.' Paper presented to the Australian and New Zealand Chapters of the International Society of Air Safety Investigators Investigators Regional Seminar. Auckland. Available at: http://asasi.org/papers/2002/Air%2 0Safety%20Investigator%20Training.pdf [accessed: 6 December 2009].

Braithwaite, G. 2004. 'Re-inventing (with wheels, wings and sails) a new look at transport accident investigator training.' Paper presented to the International Society of Air Safety Investigators Investigators Regional Seminar, Gold Coast, Australia. Available at: http://asasi.org/papers/2004/Braithwaite_ Investigator%20Training_ISASI04.pdf [accessed: 12 May 2006].

Fox News. 2010. 'Brazilian Court rules 2 US pilots should face negligence charges in deadly crash.' Foxnews.com. 12 January. Available at: http://www.foxnews. com/world/2010/01/12/brazilian-court-rules-pilots-face-negligence-charges-deadly-crash/ [accessed: 20 January 2010] .

Canadian Maritime Law Association. 2008. *Report of the Committee on Official Inquiries into Marine Accidents, June 10, 2008*. Available at: http://www. cmla.org/papers/2008%20AGM%20Reports/Official%20Enquiries%20into% 20Marine%20Accident%20Committee%20Report.pdf [accessed: 19 October 2009].

Capiello, H.C. 2000. 'Culpan al piloto por el accidente.' *La Nacion*, 19 May. Available at: http://www.lanacion.com.ar/nota.asp?nota_id=17330 [accessed: 5 March 2006].

CBC News. 2007. 'Pilot convicted of criminal negligence in fatal Winnipeg crash.' CBC.ca. 2 November. Available at: http://www.cbc.ca/canada/manitoba/story/ 2007/11/02/winnipeg-crash.html [accessed: 17 September 2009].

CENIPA. 2008. Final Report, A-00X/CENIPA/2008. Available at: http://www. ntsb.gov/Aviation/Brazil-CENIPA/Midair_Collision_Final_Report_1907_ English_version.pdf [accessed: 11 June 2009].

CENIPA. 2009. Final Report, A–N°67/CENIPA/2009. Available at: http://www. cenipa.aer.mil.br/cenipa/paginas/relatorios/pdf/3054ing.pdf [accessed: 4 April 2010].

Chuang, C. 2000. 'Critics decide criminal probe of flight SQ006.' *Taipei Times*, 20 November 2000. Available at: www.taipeitimes.com/News/local/archives/ 2000/11/20/62208 [accessed: 28 April 2007].

Chuang, J. 2002. 'Pilot in Singapore Airlines crash gets break on charges.' *Taipei Times*, 15 June 2002. Available at: http://www.taipeitimes.com/News/front/ archives/2002/06/15/140419 [accessed: 26 April 2007].

Clarin. 2000. 'Analizaran Los Legajos de Todos Los Empleandos, Dos allanamientos por el accidente de LAPA.' *La Nacion*, 15 March. Available at: http://www.clarin.com/diario/2000/03/15/e-05101d.htm [accessed: 25 March 2006].

Colmar Court of Appeal. 2008. Chamber of Appeals, 9 April.

Crown Prosecution Service. 2009. 'CPS advises first corporate manslaughter charge under new act.' Available at: http://www/cps.gov.uk/news/press_releases/124_09 [accessed:30 December 2009].

Department of Public Enterprise. 2002. 'Report of non-statutory inquiry into non-fatal air crash at Birmingham on January 1st, 1953.' Available at: http://www.aaiu.ie/upload/general/4736-0.pdf [accessed: 4 April 2003].

Dettling-Ott, R. 1988. 'Criminal liability of airline pilots: Three recent decisions.' *Air Law.* Volume XIII, Number 1, Page 5. Kluwer.

Director of the Tunisian Civil Aviation Authority. 2007. Letter dated 6 December. Appendix 3 to ANSV 2008, *Final Report: Accident Involving ATR-72 Aircraft Registration Marks TS-LBB Ditching Off the Coast of Capo Gallo (Palermo – Sicily), August 6, 2005.* Available at: http://www.ansv.it/cgi-bin/eng/FINAL %20REPORT%20ATR%2072.pdf [accessed: 4 July 2008].

Doe, G. 1997. *Implementation Guide for Use With DOE Order 225.1A. Accident Investigations.* Doe G 225.1A-1 November 26, 1197/Rev.1. Washington, DC: US Department of Energy.

Dondina, P. *Information on the status of the ordinary trial. Judgement of the Court of Cassation, Plaintiffs Expectation.* Available at www.comitato8ottobre. com/./UK-CASSAZIONE%20AGGIORNAMENTI%20AVV.%20DONDIN A.doc [accessed: 7 June 2009].

Downie, A. 2007. 'The chaos in Brazil's blue skies.' *Time,* 3 April. Available at: http://www.time.com/time/world/article/0,8599,1606434,00.html [accessed: 21 January 2010].

Dutch Transport Safety Board. 2001. Final Report 98-85/S-14, N 193 DN, Boeing 76, 10 December 1998. Schiphol: Amsterdam Airport.

Esler, D. 2009. 'Flight risk: the threat of criminalization.' *Aviation Week.* 10 March. Available at: http://www.aviationweek.com/aw/generic/story_generic. jsp?channel=bca&id=news/bca0309p1.xml [accessed: 15 June 2009].

European Council. 1994. *Establishing the Fundamental Principles Governing the Investigation of Civil Aviation accidents and Incidents.* Directive 94/56/EC. *Official Journal,* L 319 of 12.12.1994.

European Council. 2003. Directive 2003/42/EC of the European Parliament and of the Council of 13 June 2003 on Occurrence Reporting in Civil Aviation. Available at: http://eur-lex.europa.eu/LexUriServ/LexUriServ.do?uri=OJ:L: 2003:167:0023:0036:EN:PDF [accessed 27 July 2010].

Evening Post. 2001. 'Cockpit voice recording to be used as evidence in pilot's manslaughter trial in NZ.' 5 April. Available at: http://www.pprune.org/rumours-news/3809-cockpit-voice-recording-used-evidence-pilots-manslaughter-trial-nz.html [accessed: 4 April 2008].

Fenwick, L. 2006. *A World Without Probable Cause, Air Accident Digest.* Beyond Probable Cause, ALPA annual safety forum. Available at: http://www. airaccidentdigest.com/blog/ [accessed: 1 February 2005].

Fenwick, L. and Huhn, M. 2003. 'Criminal liability and aircraft accident investigation.' *Air Line Pilot,* May, p. 17. Available at: http://www.alpa.org/

portals/alpa/magazine/2003/May2003_CriminalLiability.htm [accessed 9 July 2005].

Fetterman, D. M., (1989) *Ethnography: Step by Step*. Applied Social Research Methods Series, Vol. 17. Newbury Park, CA: Sage.

Fitzpatrick, S. 2008. 'Garuda crash pilot facing jail.' *The Australian*. 5 February. Available at: http://www.theaustralian.com.au/news/garuda-crash-pilot-facing-jail/story-e6frg6t6-1111115475725 [accessed: 6 June 2009].

Fitzpatrick, S. 2009. 'Garuda pilot Marwoto Komar to appeal against two-year jail sentence for role in fatal crash.' *The Australian*. 7 April 2009. Available at: http://www.theaustralian.com.au/news/world/pilot-to-appeal-two-year-sentence/story-e6frg6so-1225696957255 [accessed 15 May 2009].

Fleischer, D. 2006. 'Legacy pilots liberated.' *Brazil Focus Weekly*. Section 2.1. Available at: http://www.wilsoncenter.org/news/docs/Fleischer.BFDF12082006.doc [accessed: 27 October 2008].

FlightAware. 2007. 'N168CK Challenger 850 stalled on takeoff Moscow, three injured.' 14 February. Available at: http://discussions.flightaware.com/viewtopic.php?t=2970.

Flightglobal. 2008a. 'Brazil charges over ten TAM Coghonas fatal overrun.' *Flight International*. 21 November. Available at: http://www.flightglobal.com/articles/2008/11/21/319186/brazil-charges-10-over-tam-conghonas-fatal-overrun.html [accessed: 3 May 2009].

Flightglobal. 2008b. 'Engineers face the law over Spanair Madrid crash.' *Flight International*. 17 October. Available at: http://www.flightglobal.com/articles/2008/10/17/317608/engineers-face-the-law-over-spanair-madrid-crash.html [accessed: 7 May 2009].

Flight Safety Foundation. 2001. 'Inadequate response to flight control problems, misuse of autopilot cited in Falcon 900-B.' *Accident Prevention*. Volume 58, No. 2, Page 1. February. Available at: http://flightsafety.org/ap/ap_feb01.pdf [accessed: 7 August 2008].

Flight Safety Foundation. 2002. *Flight Safety Digest*. Special Issue. Volume 21, No 8–9. August – September. Available at: http://www.iaass.org/files/pdf/fsd_aug-sept02.pdf [accessed: 10 June 2003].

Flight Safety Foundation. 2006. *Joint Resolution Regarding Criminalisation of Aviation Accidents*. Flight Safety Foundation. Available at: http://www.isasi.org/docs/Criminalization_FSF_resolution_01-12-10.pdf [accessed: 2 June 2007].

Flight Safety Foundation 2009. 'Investigative co-operative.' *Safety News*. 7 April. Available at: http://flightsafety.org/asw/apr09/asw_apr09_p9-11.pdf [accessed: 6 August 2009].

Flight Safety Foundation. 2010. 'Accident investigator group sign criminalisation resolution.' 13 January. Available at: http://flightsafety.org/media-center/press-releases/accident-investigator-group-sign-criminalization-resolution [accessed 29 January 2010].

Fogarty, D. 2009. 'Auscarts convicted over go-kart death.' news.com.au. 6 May. Available at: http://www.news.com.au/breaking-news/company-convicted-over-go-kart-death/story-e6frfku0-1225710360769 [accessed on: 10 March 2003].

Forbes, M. 2007. 'Pilots "must be prosecuted".' *Sydney Morning Herald*. 24 October. Available at: http://www.smh.com.au/news/general/pilots-must-be-prosecuted/2007/10/23/1192941064519.html [accessed 7 January 2008].

Green, J.T. 2009. 'Aviation law: two commuter airline cases: Comair 5191 and Colgan 3407.' *New York Law Journal*. Online. 30 April. Available at: http://www.kreindler.com/publications/html_pubs/NYLJ-AviationLaw-4-30-09.html citing *In re Air Crash at Lexington, Ky*, Aug. 27, 2006, 2007 WL 4321865 (E.D. Ky. Dec. 6, 2007) [accessed: 5 January 2010].

Haarlem District Prosecutor. 2009. 'OM Haarlem verzoekt Onderzoeksraad om informative.' www.om.nl. 27 February. Available at: http://www.om.nl/actueel/nieuws-_en/@150258/om_haarlem_verzoekt/ [accessed: 2 March 2010].

Hall, J. 2000. *NTSB Symposium*. Available at: http://www.ntsb.gov/speeches/former/hall/jhc000322 [accessed: 5 May 2003].

Hellenic Republic Ministry of Transport and Communications. 1998. Aircraft Accident Report, Aerosweet Airlines, Flight AEW-241, YAK-42, UR-42334.

Hendrick, K. and Benner, L. 1986. 'Investigation concepts.' In Hendrick and Benner. *Investigating Accidents with STEP*. New York: Marcel Dekker.

Hirchman. D. 2008. 'US pilot jailed after accident.' AOPA online. 26 February. Available at: http://www.aopa.org/aircraft/articles/2008/080221pilot.html [accessed: 3 May 2009].

Hopkins, V. 1995. *Human Factors in Air Traffic Control*. London: Taylor and Francis.

Hopkins, A. 2000. *Lessons from Longford: the Esso Gas Plant Explosion*. Sydney: CCH Australia Limited.

Hopkins, A. 2000. *An AcciMap of the Esso Australia Gas Plant Explosion*. Sydney: CCH. Available at: http://www.qrc.org.au/conference/_dbase_upl/03_spk003_Hopkins.pdf [accessed: 15 June 2007].

ICAO. 1987a. *Procedures for Air Navigation Services, Rules of the Air and Air Traffic Services*. 2nd edn. Doc. 4444-RAC/501. Montreal: ICAO.

ICAO. 1987b. *Accident/Incident Reporting Manual*. Doc 9156. Montreal: ICAO.

ICAO. 1993. Human Factors Digest No. 7. Investigation of Human Factors in Accidents and Incidents. Circular 240-AN/44. Reprinted 2004. Montreal: ICAO.

ICAO. 1998a. *Human Factors in the Investigation of Accidents and Incidents*. Montreal: ICAO. Available at: http://www.eurocontrol.int/humanfactors/gallery/content/public/docs/DELIVERABLES/HF11%20(HUM.ET1.ST13.3000-REP-02)%20Released.pdf [accessed: 7 August 2009].

ICAO. 1998b. *Human Factors Training Manual*. 1st edn. Amendment 2 Dated 31 May 2005. Doc 9683. Montreal: ICAO.

ICAO. 1998/2005. *Human Factors Training Manual.* Amendment 2 dated 31 May, 2005. Doc 9683. Montreal: ICAO.

ICAO. 2000. *Manual of Aircraft Accident Investigation.* Doc 9756. Montreal: ICAO.

ICAO. 2001. *Aircraft Accident Investigation: Annex 13 to the Convention of International Civil Aviation.* 9th edn. Montreal: ICAO.

ICAO. 2001. *Supplement to ICAO Annex 13, Aircraft Accident and Incident Investigation.* 9th edn, Montreal: ICAO.

IFALPA. 2008. 'IFALPA concerned by arrest of Captain Marwoto Komar.' Press release. 08PRL18. Available at: http://www.ifalpa.org/downloads/Level1/Press%20&%20Media/2008/08PRL18%20-%20IFALPA%20Concerned%20by%20Komar%20arrest.pdf [accessed: 1 February 2009].

IFALPA. 2009a. 'IFALPA dismayed by Tuninter sentences.' Press release. 10PRL01. Available at: http://www.ifalpa.org/downloads/Level1/Press%20&%20Media/2009/10PRL01%20-%20Tuninter%20Sentancing%20comment.pdf [accessed 1 October 2009].

IFALPA 2009b. 'IFALPA says Jude Mendes' decision to indict Lepore, Paladino and the air traffic controllers is fundamentally flawed and a "crime" against air safety.' Press release. 08PRL09. Available at: http://www.ifalpa.org/downloads/Level1/Press%20&%20Media/2007/08PRL09%20-%20IFALPA%20comment%20on%20Lepore%20&%20Paladino%20indictment.pdf [accessed: 22 June 2009].

IFATCA 2006. Statement: 'Gol Flight 1907.' 24 November. Available at: http://www.ifatca.org/press/251106.pdf [accessed 15 June 2007].

IFATCA 2009. 'Japan's opportunity to improve aviation safety.' Press release. Available at: http://www.ifatca.org/press/300109.pdf [accessed: 15 September 2009].

Infobae.com. 2006. 'Podría prescribir la causa LAPA para ex miembros de la Fuerza Aérea.' 28 February. Available at: http://www.infobae.com/notas/nota.php?Idx=240732&IdxSeccion=0 [accessed: 13 April 2006].

Insurance Journal. 2006. 'French court dismisses suit by 1992 airbus crush victims' families.' InsuranceJournal.com. 10 October. Available at: http://www.insurancejournal.com/news/international/2006/10/10/73091.htm [accessed: 14 March 2007] .

ISASI. 2003. *Positions on Air Safety Investigation Issues.*, 3rd edn August; revised 15 January 2004. Available at: http://www.isasi.org/docs/About_AdoptedPositions.pdf [accessed: 6 June 2005].

ISASI. 2004a. 'Code of conduct.' *ISASI Forum.* January–March. Available at: http://www.isasi.org/docs/FORUM_2004_01-03.pdf [accessed: 22 May 2006].

Jabbra, J.G. and Dwivedi, O.P. 1989. *Public Service Accountability: A Comparative Perspective.* Hartford, CT: Kumarian Press.

Joint Resolution Regarding Criminalisation of Aviation Accidents. *Flight Safety Foundation* [Online]. Available at: http://flightsafety.org/media-center/press-releases/2006-press-releases/joint-resolution-condemning-criminalization-of-accidents [accessed: 2 January 2007].

Kane, R. and Pyne, T. 1995. 'The legal status and liability of the co-pilot.' Part II. *Air & Space Law*. Volume XX. Number 1.

Keane, P. 2002. *Background Information into Report of Non-Statutory Inquiry into Accident involving Aer Lingus DC3 EI-ACF, the St Kieran, near Birmingham on 1 January 1953 conducted by Mr Patrick Keane, SC*. Available at: http://www.aaiu.ie/upload/general/4736-0.pdf [accessed: 2 January 2009.

Kjellen, U. 2000. *Prevention of Accidents Through Experience Feedback*. 1st edn. London: Taylor and Francis.

Kjellen, U. and Larsson, T. J. 1981. 'Investigating accidents and reducing risks – a dynamic approach.' *Journal of Occupational Accidents*. Volume 3. Pages 129–40.

Kletz, T. 2001. *Learning from Accidents*. 3rd edn. Oxford: Gulf Professional Publishing.

Krupka, M. 2009. 'Pilots of Itek Air 737 crash imprisoned.' Airplane Pictures. 28 December. Available at: http://www.airplane-pictures.net/news.php?p=617 [accessed: 9 July 2009].

La Nacion. 2002. 'Seis directivos de LAPA irán a juicio.' 16 July. Available at: http://www.lanacion.com.ar/nota.asp?nota_id=414181 [accessed: 5 March 2006].

La Nacion. 2003. 'Está más cerca el juicio por la tragedia del avión de LAPA.' 2 December. Available at: http://www.lanacion.com.ar/nota.asp?nota_id=550890 [accessed: 12 March 2006].

Langewiesche, W. 1998. 'The lessons of ValuJet 592.' *The Atlantic Monthly*. March. Volume 281. Number 3 Available at: http://www.theatlantic.com/past/docs/issues/98mar/valujet1.htm [accessed 2 May 2006].

LAPA. 2005. *Pagina/12*, 28 July. Available at: http://www.pagina12.com.ar/diario/sociedad/3-54275-2005-07-28.html [accessed: 16 April 2006].

Lederer, Jerome F.J. 1942. Director of the CAA Air Safety Board quoted in Rimson, I.J. 2002. *Investigating Causes*. Available at: http://www.iprr.org/papers/rimsona&mpaper.htm [accessed: 14 May 2005] .

Leplat, J. 1997. 'Event analysis and responsibility in complex systems.' In A. Hale, M. Wilpert and M. Freitag (eds) *After the Event – from Accident to Organisational Learning*. Oxford: Pergamon.

Lewis, C. 2007. 'Russian prosecutors open criminal probe into Moscow jet crash.' Available at: curt.lewis@fsinfo.org [accessed: 5 June 2009].

Lowery, J. and Wilson, P. 2002. 'Case studies: These workers should not have died. Their only mistake was to turn up at work that day.' Victorian Trades Hall Council. Online. Available at: http://www.vthc.org.au/your-rights-at-work/ohs/industrial-manslaughter/case-studies/case-studies/index.cfm [accessed on: 10 March 2003].

Mahaud, P. 2006. 'ATM safety in European press.' Eurocontrol Society and Economic Research Workshop. Available at: http://www.eurocontrol.int/eec/see/gallery/content/public/documents/workshop_2005_Philippe_Mahaud.pdf [accessed: 30 March 2010].

Mateou. A. and Michaelides. S. 2000. 'The Criminal Liability of Pilots and ATC's, Seminar'. Intercollege, Nicosia.

Mateou, A. and Michaelides, S. 2003. *Legal Liability of Controllers & Pilots, IFATSEA. Eurogroup Meeting Report, Zagreb.*

Mateou, A. and Michaelides, S. 2005. 'The intermingling between an aircraft accident investigation, the apportionment of blame and the determination of liability.' Paper presented at the FSF 17th Annual EASS, Safety, A Common Culture, Warsaw, Poland.

May, T. 1993. *Social Research: Issues, Methods and Processes.* Buckingham: Open University Press.

Mayes, P. 'Proactive Air Safety Investigation the Australian Experience.' *Aviation Safety*, H. Soekkha (ed), pp 109–18.

McCartney, P. 2000. Statement of Captain Paul Mccarthy Executive Air Safety Chairman Air Line Pilots Association Before The Committee On Transportation And Infrastructure Aviation Subcommittee U.S. House Of Representatives July 27, 2000 On The Trend Towards Criminalization Of Aircraft Accidents. Available at: http://cf.alpa.org/internet/tm/tm072700.htm [accessed 15 September 2005].

McFadden, R.D. 1989. 'Grand jury inquiry due in USAir crash.' *New York Times.* 26 September. Available at: http://www.nytimes.com/1989/09/26/nyregion/grand-jury-inquiry-due-in-usair-crash.html [accessed: 5 June 2006].

McKellar, G. 2006. 'A world without probable cause.' *Air Accident Digest.* IFALPA Accident Analysis Committee, ALPA annual safety forum. 25 July. Available at: http://www.airaccidentdigest.com/blog/ [accessed: 3 January 2007].

Michaelides, S. 2001. 'The Lockerbie trial: the end of a chapter – not the end of a chapter.' Presented at Cine Studio, University of Nicosia (prior Intercollege).

Michaelides, S. 2004. 'The use of sensitive data in judicial proceeding.' *The Law Journal Coventry University.* Volume 9. Number 1.

Michaelides-Mateou, S. and Mateou, A. 2007. Seeking to understand the effect of the relationship on aviation safety and the criminalisation of pilots and ATCOs. Unpublished doctoral dissertation, University of Middlesex.

Miles, M.B. and Hubermann, A.M. 1984. *Innovation Up Close.* New York: Plenum Press.

Mill, J.S. 1843/1872[1973]. 'A system of logic ratiocinative and inductive: being a connected view of the principles of evidence and the methods of scientific investigation.' In J.M. Robinson, ed., *The Collected Works of John Stuart Mill*, Volume 7, Books I–III. Toronto: University of Toronto Press and London: Routledge and Kegan Paul.

Negroni, C. 1997. 'Six months later, still no answer to TWA Flight 800 mystery.' CNN. 17 January. Available at: http://edition.cnn.com/US/9701/17/twa/index. html [accessed: 16 October 2001].

New York Times. 1994. 'All Safe after Plane Crash.' 10 August. Available at: http://www.nytimes.com/1994/08/10/world/all-safe-after-plane-crash.html [accessed: 4 June 2008].

Nørbjerg, P.M. 2003. 'The creation of an aviation safety reporting culture in Danish air traffic control.' Available at: http://shemesh.larc.nasa.gov/iria03/ p11-norbjerg.pdf [accessed: 12 January 2009].

NTSB. 1990. *Aircraft Accident Report: USAir, Inc., Boeing 737400, LaGuardia Airport, Flushing, New York, September 20, 1989.* NTSB/AAR-90/03. Available at http://www.airdisaster.com/reports/ntsb/AAR90-03.pdf [accessed: 5 June 2006].

NTSB. 1997. *Aircraft Accident Report: In-Flight Fire and Impact with Terrain, ValuJet Airlines Flight 592 DC-9-32, N904VJ, Everglades, Near Miami, Florida May 11, 1996.* Final report. NTSB/AAR-97-06. Washington, DC: National Transportation Safety Board. Available at: http://www.ntsb.gov/ Publictn/1997/aar9706.pdf [accessed: 5 June 2004].

NTSB. 1999a. Preliminary information. Identification: DCA99RA076. Available at: http://www.ntsb.gov/ntsb/brief.asp?ev_id=20001212X19471&key=1 [accessed 29 October 2006].

NTSB. 1999b. 'Study of NTSB aviation accident investigations suggests major changes in how probes are conducted.' RAND news release. 9 December. Available at: http://www.rand.org/news/Press.99/ntsb.12.9.html [accessed: 1 Sept 2009].

NTSB. 2001a. Preliminary information. Identification: DCA01RA002. Available at: http://www.ntsb.gov/ntsb/brief.asp?ev_id=20010330X00677&key=1 [accessed: 5 August 2005].

NTSB 2001b. Aircraft accident report. Number AAR-02/01; NTIS Number PB2002-910402 Available at: http://www.ntsb.gov/publictn/2002/AAR0201. htm [accessed: 30 November 2005].

NTSB. 2003a. Preliminary information. Identification: NYC02LA113. Available at: http://www.ntsb.gov/ntsb/brief.asp?ev_id=20020614X00885&key=1 [accessed: 9 July 2006].

NTSB. 2003b. Summary report. Identification: DCA00MA026. Available at: http:// www.ntsb.gov/ntsb/brief.asp?ev_id=20001212X20472&key=1 [accessed: 2 January 2008].

NTSB. 2003c. *Aircraft Accident Report: In-flight Breakup over the Atlantic Ocean Trans World Airlines Flight 800.* NTSB Number AAR-00/03; NTIS Number PB2000-910403. Available at: http://www.ntsb.gov/Publictn/2000/AAR0003. pdf [accessed 30 August 2000].

NTSB. 2003d. Supplement to Annex 13. *Aircraft Accident and Incident Investigation.* 9th edn. Available at: http://www.ntsb.gov/Events/symp_rec/ proceedings/May_4/SessionIII/Pres_frostell/index.htm.

NTSB. 2003e. Full narrative, Emery Worldwide Airlines Inc. DCA00MA026. Available at: http://www.ntsb.gov/ntsb/brief.asp?ev_id=20001212X20472&k ey=1[accessed: 15 March 2007].

NTSB. 2005. Executive summary, aircraft accident report. NTSB Number AAR-06/04; NTIS Number PB2007-910401. Available at: http://www.ntsb.gov/publictn/2006/AAR0604.htm [accessed 10 October 2009].

NTSB. 2006a. Preliminary information. Identification: DCA06RA076A and DCA06RA076B. Available at: http://www.ntsb.gov/ntsb/brief2.asp?ev_id=20 061002X01435&ntsbno=DCA06RA076A&akey=1 [accessed: 2 May 2008].

NTSB. 2006b. 'US summary comments on the draft final report of the aircraft accident involving PR-GTD and N600XL, 29 September 2006.' Available at: http://www.ntsb.gov/Aviation/Brazil-CENIPA/US_Summary_Comments.pdf [accessed: 10 October 2009].

NTSB. 2007. Probable cause report. Available at: http://www.ntsb.gov/ntsb/brief. asp? ev_id=20068028X01244&key+1 [accessed: 12 July 2009].

NTSC. 2007. Aircraft accident investigation report KNKT /07.06/07.02.35. Available at: http://www.dephub.go.id/knkt/ntsc_home/ntsc.htm [accessed: 4 June 2009].

O'Kelly, B. 2001. 'Inquiry expected into 1953 Aer Lingus crash.' *The Sunday Business Post.* Online. 4 March. Available at: http://archives.tcm.ie/businesspost/2001/03/04/story609247928.asp [accessed: 11 November 2006].

Ortiz, B. 2007. 'Polehinke files suit in crash: REMEMBERING FLIGHT 5191.' *Lexington Herald.* 28 August. Available at: http://www.accessmylibrary.com/article-1G1-168103054/polehinke-files-suit-crash.html [accessed: 5 April 2008].

Ortiz, L.E. and Capaldo, G. 2000. 'Can justice use technical and personal information obtained through accident investigations?' *Air Law & Commerce.* Volume 263. 1999-2000.

Owen D.G. 1997. *Philosophical Foundations of Tort Law.* Oxford: Clarendon Press.

RAE. 1964. *Application of the Results of Slush Drag Tests on the Accident to the Ambassador at Munich.* Farnborough: Royal Aeronautical Establishment.

RAND. 1999. Study of NTSB accident investigations, Chapter 7, Conclusions and Recommendations, (December 1999). Available at: http://www.rand.org /news/Press.99/ntsb.12.9.html[accessed: 20 March 2000].

Pagina/12. 2005. 'LAPA.' 28 July 2005. Available at: http://www.pagina12.com. ar/diario/sociedad/3-54275-2005-07-28.html [accessed: 16 April 2006].

Rasmussen, J. 1977. 'Risk management in a dynamic society: A modelling problem.' *Safety Science.* Volume 27, Issue 2/3, Pages 183–213. As cited by ROSS at NTNU, *Methods for accident Investigation.* Available at: http://www.ntnu.no/ross/reports/accident.pdf [accessed: 22 September 2009].

Reason, J. 1997. *Managing the Risks of Organizational Accidents.* Aldershot: Ashgate.

Reason, J. 2000. 'Human error: models and management.' *British Medical Journal*. Volume 320, Pages 768–70.

Recent Developments in Aviation Law. *Journal of Air Law & Commerce* 295 2009 citing Air Crash at Lexington, Kentucky, August, No. 5:06-cv-316-KSF 2008. Dist at p. 74.

Rediff.com. 2000. 'FIR against Alliance Air pilot, co-pilot withdrawn.' 21 July. Available at: http://www.rediff.com/news/2000/jul/21crash.htm [accessed: 5 June 2005].

Reuters. 2007. 'Brazil's deepening aviation crisis.' Available at: http://www.usatoday.com/travel/flights/2007-07-18-brazil-aviation_N.htm [accessed: 20 January 2009].

Rimson, I.J. 2002. *Investigating Causes*. Available at: http://www.iprr.org/papers/rimsona&mpaper.htm [accessed: 14 May 2005] .

Rodriguez, F. 2002. 'Acusan a militares por el caso LAPA.' *La Nacion*. 17 October. Available at: http://www.lanacion.com.ar/nota.asp?nota_id=441367 [accessed: 5 March 2006].

Rodrigruez, C. 2005. 'La tragedia de LAPA fue elevada a juicio oral con sus nueve acusados.' *Pagina/12*, 6 July. Available at: http://www.pagina12.com.ar/diario/sociedad/3-53334-2005-07-06.html [accessed:5 March 2006].

Rogers, C. 1998. 'The Airbus A320 crash at Habsheim, France, "Why and how the flight tapes were forged".' Available at: http://www.crashdehabsheim.net/CRenglish%20phot.pdf [accessed: 8 June 2004].

Rogers, W.V.H. 2002. *Winfield and Jolowicz on Tort*. 16th edn. London: Sweet & Maxwell.

Rollason, K. 2009a. 'Pilot cleared in 2002 crash death, criminal negligence verdict overturned.' Available at: http://www.winnipegfreepress.com/local/pilot-cleared-in-2002-crash-death-79599732.html [accessed: 26 May 2009].

Rollason, K. 2009b. 'Pilot avoids jail time in crash case.' Available at: http://www.ctv.ca/servlet/ArticleNews/story/CTVNews/20080320/wpg_pilot_tayfel_080320 [accessed: 5 April 2010].

Serrano, A. 2006. 'Comair crash survivor leaves hospital: co-pilot, the lone survivor of Kentucky plane crash, to begin rehabilitation.' CBS News. Online. Available at: http://www.cbsnews.com/stories/2006/10/03/national/main2059120.shtml [accessed: 8 October 2009].

Shawcross and Beaumont Air Law. 2002, 4th edn. Reissue. London: Butterworths.

Sherman, T. 2009. 'Pilot in Teterboro Airport crash indicted on conspiracy charges.' NJ.com. 24 November. Available at: http://www.nj.com/news/index.ssf/2009/11/pilot_in_teterboro_airport_cra.html [accessed: 2 March 2010].

SitiosArgentina.com.ar. n.d. 'Audio de la caja negra del accidente de LAPA.' Available at: http://www.sitiosargentina.com.ar/notas/2009/enero/audio-caja-negra-accidente-lapa.htm [accessed: 24 March 2006].

Skyguide. 2007. 'Skyguide employees decide not to appeal Uberlingen court judgments.' Media release. 20 September. Available at: http://www.skyguide. ch/en/MediaRelations/MediaReleases/ArchivedReleases/20_09_2007_no_ appeal.pdf [accessed: 25 November 2008].

Smith, J.C. and Hogan, B. 2002. *Criminal Law*. 10th revd edn. London: Butterworths.

Stewart, S. 1986. *Air Disaster*. London: Allen.

Stocker, T. 2008. 'Crossair execs found not guilty in homicide trial.' *Aviation International News*, 1 June. Available at: http://www.ainonline.com/news/ single-news-page/article/crossair-execs-found-not-guilty-in-homicide-trial-16143/ [accessed: 23 March 2009].

Swissinfo.ch. 2008. 'Managers acquitted in Crossair trial.' Available at: http://www. swissinfo.ch/eng/Managers_acquitted_in_Crossair_trial.html?cid=6656970 [accessed: 5 November 2009].

Swissinfo.ch. 2009. 'Pilots fined for crashing commercial jet.' Available at: http:// www.swissinfo.ch/eng/news_digest/Pilots_fined_for_crashing_commercial_ jet.html?siteSect=104&sid=10799940&cKey=1244531969000&ty=nd [accessed October 2009].

Taylor, L. 1988. *Air Travel: How Safe is It?* London: BSP Professional Books.

Tench, H.W. 1985. *Safety is No Accident*. London: Collins Professionals and Technical Books.

Thomas, G. 2007. 'A crime against safety.' *Air Transport World*. 1 January. Available at: http://atwonline.com/operations-maintenance/article/crime-against-safety-0309 [accessed: 4 July 2007].

Transportation Safety Board of Canada. 2003. *Aviation Accident Report. Fuel Exhaustion – Collision with Terrain. Keystone Air Services Ltd. Piper PA 31-350 Navajo Chieftain C-GPOW, Winnipeg, Manitoba, 11 June 2002*. A02C0124. Available at: http://www.bst.gc.ca/ENG/rapports-reports/aviation/2002/a02c01 24/a02c0124.pdf [accessed: 5 September 2008].

Tribunal de Grande Instance de Colmar, Département du Haut – Rhin. 14 Mars 1997. *Jugement No 464/97*.

Voss, W. 2009. 'Flight safety foundation criticizes prosecutorial interference with aviation accident investigation.' Press release. Available at: http://flightsafety. org/media-center/press-releases/2009-press-releases/Prosecutorial-Interference-With-Aviation-Accident-Investigation [accessed: 24 February 2010].

Walsh, E. 1999. 'FBI Probe of TWA crash criticized.' *Washington Post*. 11 May. Page A3. Available at: http://www.washingtonpost.com/wp-srv/national/daily/ may99/twa11.htm [accessed: 16 October 2001].

Welham, M.C. 2003. 'Corporate manslaughter: The proposed offence of corporate killing and the potential impact in the EU.' *OSH World*. December. Available at: http://www.sheilapantry.com/oshworld/focus/2003/200312.html#footnotes [accessed:17 February 2005].

Weston, R. and Hurst, R. 1982. *Zagreb One Four Cleared to Collide?* London: Granada Publishing.

White, J. 2000. 'The Alaska Airlines crash: signs point to a wider crisis in air safety.' Available at: http://www.wsws.org/articles/2000/feb2000/alas-f19.shtml [accessed: 12 October 2005].

Winiger, M. 2007. 'You are accused.' Aerocontrol Switzerland. Trans. Sigi Ladenbauer. Available at: http://www.swissatca.org/typo3/fileadmin/content/aerocontrol/ExperienceRep.pdf [accessed: 4 October 2008].

Yang, H. 2003. *Legal Challenges in Patient Legal Challenges in Patient Safety in Taiwan Safety in Taiwan.* Department of Health Care Management, CGU. December. Available at: http://psi.tmu.edu.tw/file/Legal%20Challenges%20in%20Patient%20Safety%20in%20Taiwan-920409%E6%A5%8A%E7%A7%80%E5%84%80.pdf [accessed: 4 March 2008].

Zommer, L. 2000. 'Anularon el embargo que pesaba sobre LAPA.' *La Nacion*, 4 November. Available at: http://www.lanacion.com.ar/nota.asp?nota_id=39526 [accessed: 5 March 2006].

Laws and Regulations

Air Navigation Order (ANO) 2009; came into force 1 January 2010 (UK).

American Air Commerce Act. 1926 (P.L. 69-254, 44 Stat. 568) as later amended by the P.L. 73-418, 48 Stat. 1113–1114.

Canadian Criminal Code (R.S., 1985, c. C-46). 12 March 2010. Available at: http://www.canlii.org/en/ca/laws/stat/rsc-1985-c-c-46/latest/rsc-1985-c-c-46.html [accessed: 20 March 2010].

Canadian Safety Board Act. 1989. Available at: http://www.canlii.org/en/ca/laws/stat/sc-1989-c-3/latest/sc-1989-c-3.html#CANADIAN_TRANSPORTATION_ACCIDENT_INVESTIGATION_AND_SAFETY_BOARD_13522 [accessed: 16 November 2008].

The Chicago Convention – the International Civil Aviation Conference.

The Civil Aeronautics Act (P.L. 75-706, 52 Stat. 973) 1938.

Civil Aviation Act 1982 and the associated secondary legislation. The Civil Aviation (Investigation of Air Accidents and Incidents) Regulations 1996. (SI 1996/2798).

Cyprus Civil Aviation Act 2002, N.123(1) 2002.

French penal code. 12/10/2005 Online. Available at: http://195.83.177.9/upl/pdf/code_33.pdf [1 December 2009].

German Penal Code, Strafgesetzbuch (StGB). 2009. Available at: http://bundesrecht.juris.de/englisch_stgb/englisch_stgb.html#StGB_000G6 [accessed: 22 November 2009].

Italian Penal Code, Codice Penale Available at: http://www.altalex.com/index.php?idnot=36653 [accessed: 24 May 2008].

Transport Safety Investigation Act, 2003 (Australia).

Warsaw Convention 1929 Convention for the Unification of Certain Rules Relating to International Carriage by Air, Signed at Warsaw on 12 October 1929.

Index